658.8

Mastering

Marketing

Macmillan Master Series

Accounting
Advanced English Language
Advanced Pure Mathematics
Arabic
Banking
Basic Management
Biology
British Politics
Business Administration
Business Communication
Business Law
Business Microcomputing
C Programming
Chemistry
COBOL Programming
Commerce
Communication
Computers
Databases
Economic and Social History
Economics
Electrical Engineering
Electronic and Electrical Calculations
Electronics
English as a Foreign Language
English Grammar
English Language
English Literature
English Spelling
French

French 2
German
German 2
Human Biology
Italian
Italian 2
Japanese
Manufacturing
Marketing
Mathematics
Mathematics for Electrical and
    Electronic Engineering
Modern British History
Modern European History
Modern World History
Pascal Programming
Philosophy
Photography
Physics
Psychology
Science
Social Welfare
Sociology
Spanish
Spanish 2
Spreadsheets
Statistics
Study Skills
Word Processing

Mastering

Marketing

Third Edition

DOUGLAS FOSTER

Revised by
JOHN DAVIS

MACMILLAN

To ELIZABETH

without whose love, encouragement and
support this book would not have been
written.

'Devote yourself patiently to the theory
and conscientiously to the practice...'
Confucius (551–479 BC)

Contents

Preface to the First Edition

Marketing is accepted as a major discipline of management. As such it features prominently in most courses on business education and management development. This book defines and explains the basic concepts while avoiding unnecessary jargon. It draws upon the author's experience and practice of marketing and management in Britain, Europe, North America and some developing countries. The book highlights the extent to which successful marketing management must consider other, non-marketing, aspects of management.

The book treats marketing as an activity that can be applied equally successfully to manufacturing industry, services and non-profit-making organisations, whether at home or abroad, for both large and small enterprises. While dealing with the obvious differences encountered in each sector and showing how basic techniques are adapted for them, it avoids the excessive differentiation that has been drawn in earlier books. The cases mentioned will help all readers to appreciate the practical implications of marketing.

The work is aimed primarily at students on BEC National and Higher courses (certificate and diploma) but will also be useful reading for other similar courses. It will be useful too to all executives, being a handy 'refresher course' or reference work on their bookshelves.

Woking, 1982   DOUGLAS FOSTER

Preface to the Second Edition

The contents of the original edition of this book have been thoroughly reviewed and brought up to date. New material has been added to take account of changes in marketing thought since the first manuscript was prepared. This edition brings the subject of marketing in line with present concepts, appropriate for the objectives originally set for this book.

Woking, 1983   DOUGLAS FOSTER

Preface to the Third Edition

Much of the Second Edition has stood the test of time, and is still valid today. However, Marketing is a dynamic area and changes have taken place since 1983 which made a new edition necessary.

In this new edition there is additional coverage of developing areas, and those areas where computers are opening up new developments in old areas. Some of the apparently new areas are simply developments of old ones. Telephone selling and computerised ordering are becoming increasingly common in all areas, but even here the principle is not new. At the consumer level telephone selling is the updated version of door-to-door selling of vacuum cleaners or washing machines of old; or of the representative of the local grocer calling on families for their weekly orders, to be delivered later by bicycle or pony and trap. Equally the perceptions of people change. In the UK we now have a population where no one under 40 has lived in a world without commercial television.

In this new edition a change has been made to the assignments at the end of each chapter. They are now framed so that the reader is led to select a market or an organisation of direct interest within which to apply the topics covered within each chapter. This should ensure more continuity in the practical application of marketing analysis and methods, both for those already in employment and for those free to select their own focus.

On a personal level I hope I have kept faith with the aims and objectives of Douglas Foster, but in ways which match the needs of today's students, managers and teachers.

Henley-on-Thames, 1994   JOHN DAVIS

Acknowledgements

The authors and publishers wish to thank the following for permission to use copyright material: Alec Cairncross for 'Limerick' from *Essays in Economic Management*, Allen & Unwin, 1971; McGraw-Hill Book Company Europe for figures from *Practical Sales Forecasting* by E. J. Davis, Figs 10.1, 10.2 and 10.5, 1988; Times Newspapers Ltd for headlines and extracts from *The Times* – 'CBI Forecast' (8/11/93), 'At last we're set... ' (30/1/94), 'Gloomy forecast' (8/5/93), 'Slow recovery for Forte' (27/1/94), 'Pentos gloom...' (16/12/93), 'Sainsbury indicates...' (20/1/94), 'Building suppliers forecast...' (14/12/93) – and *The Sunday Times* – 'Earthquake forecasts poised' (23/1/94).

Thanks are also due to the following for permission to use copyright illustrations and material: Anglian Group plc p. 272; Barclays Bank Ltd p. 262; Barnaby's Picture Library pp. 8, 9; Cumbria Tourist Board p. 194; Direct Vision Rentals p. 190; Earls Court Information Centre p. 28; Goldlife Magazine (SAI Services UK Ltd) p. 199; Haiwich Ferries/John Carr Industrial Photography p. 259; Lansing Linde p. 207; Little Chef p. 174; Macmillan Distribution Ltd pp. 208, 214; National Meteotological Library p. 231; Norwich Tourist Information Service p. 1; Gordon Roberts pp. 75, 142; Royal Mail p. 91; Sartor Ltd p. 271; Shire Designs p. 181; Stoneway (LCI plc) p. 158; Tesco p. 151; The Butter Council p. 168; The History Guild p. 227; United Distillers p. 117.

Every effort has been made to trace all the copyright holders but if any have been inadvertently overlooked the publishers will be pleased to make the necessary arrangement at the first opportunity.

1 Introduction to marketing

Much has been written about marketing in the past 50 years or so, but stripped of all jargon marketing is simply about gaining and keeping clients or customers. It applies to both trading and non-trading sectors, and to both goods and services. It is concerned with the traditional 'four Ps' of Product, Price, Promotion and Place applied to the marketing of goods, and with the more recent additions of People, Process and Physical evidence to produce the seven Ps applied to the marketing of services.

1.1 The marketing concept

In general terms marketing requires executives to be in a frame of mind that realises if there are no customers there is no business. It does not matter how fancy, complex or academic marketing and other management systems may be, if a company cannot attract customers' business it will eventually be forced into liquidation or merger.

The marketing concept acknowledges that a business geared to serve the needs and requirements of customers will achieve better results over a longer period of time than a company whose executives are not so motivated. The jargon phrase is that the company is *marketing-oriented*. It has placed its customers and their needs or wants at the very centre of its business decisions. The company strives always to identify these needs as accurately as possible so that it can match them more precisely with

Norwich Market: a traditional outdoor market for perishable and other produce, where marketing operates on a person-to-person basis

the products or services it is offering, within its resources and capabilities. It is no longer a case of 'we make only these sizes of pumps (or egg-cups or whatever), take it or leave it', but rather 'what size and type do you require?'

The company will then have ceased to be preoccupied with keeping production facilities loaded in the way *it* wants. Thus it does not produce products which meets *its* own standards but which ignore customers' needs and are not required or cannot be afforded by potential customers. Marketing also involves all the actions necessary to fit a business, its resources, capabilities and experience, to these customer needs. It must therefore identify both potential customers and their needs or wants. It embraces all the commercial activities and these include techniques such as marketing research, statistical methods of forecasting and the application of knowledge of human behaviour drawn from the behavioural sciences.

The main point to be understood here is that 'marketing' seeks to achieve more effective and profitable selling by looking ahead, discovering potential customers or applications and their wants and then devising products or services which match these requirements as closely as possible. Old-style 'selling' was preoccupied with the need to 'make a sale' in the present, without considering the precise nature of customers' needs and longer term developments and changes. The customers a company wishes to serve may also have to be selected from a wide range of possibilities. All these factors, especially the need to consider both the present and the future, make it necessary to formalise marketing as a specific, integrated activity, if sustained success is to be ensured.

Also, Marketing is the name given to the department responsible for carrying out the activities involved in identifying customers and their needs or wants, promoting the products or services offered to them and achieving sales. In more sophisticated companies, it is also responsible for the physical distribution of the products and whatever aftersales services are necessary. However, where physical distribution is a critical activity, or is complex or extensive, it can be assigned to a separate department. In this case there is vital need for close co-operation and communication at all times between Marketing and Physical Distribution management. (In this book 'Marketing' with a capital 'M' will be used to denote the department, rather than the management activity.) Like all other departments of a company, Marketing's responsibilities, powers and authority are delegated to it by the board of directors, or the managing director (or chief executive) acting for the board.

Finally, like politics, business is the art of the possible. A company should produce only what it can sell and it can sell only what it can persuade its customers to buy. Survival is achieved by extracting *profit* from the market, in most instances. Therefore, the process of determining what the company will produce and how this production will be converted into profit must come from the marketing side of the business. It is, usually, the only one able, with some precision, to measure the total demand of each selected market, how this is shared between competitors and different customer categories or regions and how market consumption can be influenced. The marketing function is therefore an important one and must lead the others *in time*.

This does not mean that all future managing directors will be ex-marketing people. It means that until Marketing has studied and analysed its markets, customer needs and total demand for each product or service, confident forecasts cannot be made of the nature and volume of the company's business, i.e. how much of each product can be sold to selected markets or customers. Until this is done, manufacturing, financial and personnel departments cannot know what expectations will be placed on them and thus the contributions they will have to make in achieving the company's business targets. Marketing is thus the lead function but all the major activities of management (marketing, manufacturing, finance, personnel and technical) are of co-equal importance. It is vital, therefore, that there is full and continual co-operation between all these departments.

1.2 The meaning and aims of marketing

Marketing involves the systematic application of entrepreneurship to the almost constantly changing conditions of the present age. It is concerned with the rational and logical use of people, materials, plant, money and other resources to ensure profit, survival and growth over the longest possible period. It is not interested – except in some very rare instances – in a one-year, 'flash-in-the-pan' basis. To achieve this the company must assess objectively every factor important to its business so that decisions are based on judgement, which is in turn based on as much knowledge as it is possible, or practical, to obtain. The application of 'hunchplay' is almost doomed to ultimate failure especially as business becomes more complex and competitive and every business decision becomes more far-reaching in its effect.

(a) Theory and aims

The theory of good marketing is that it should comprehend what is known, make an assessment of what is likely to happen in the future and then evolve a set of guides for action which will lead to improved managerial performance. Marketing is unlikely ever to be able to advance to the stage when it can eliminate all risks and uncertainties. It can reduce the margin of error and the incidence of risk.

The aims of good marketing require the observance of the following five basic rules.

(i)   It must provide a means of classifying, assessing and integrating information relevant to a business. The mere accumulation of facts is not enough.

(ii) It must provide a sound base of thinking about and studying business problems, providing a method of approach which helps to draw correct conclusions which form a basis for action.

(iii) It must be able to explain, predict and control the process it employs and it requires not only an interpretation of facts but an appreciation of their interrelationships.

(iv) It must employ sufficient analytical methods to help solve its problems, existing methods being based on economics, statistics, sociology and psychology.

(v) It should allow the derivation of a number of principles of marketing behaviour which are special to any particular business or technology.

Marketing as a management function aims to give direction and purpose to a company's activities. It does so through the collection and interpretation of information on the company's markets, products and competitors. It uses these facts to indicate what activities should be undertaken or how operations should be modified to meet changing circumstances in the selected product-market activities. Marketing, in conjunction with its sister departments, decides the products to be offered and the total marketing effort that can be placed behind the products. Marketing also aims to monitor the results of the selling and promotional activities to see how they match targeted performance. Adjustments to the operations can be made when results vary too much from plans. In all this Marketing seeks to make the whole company and its management *outward-looking*.

1.3   Some common misconceptions

There have been many misconceptions of what marketing is all about and some of them have survived, surprisingly, into the present day. To many people marketing is still 'market research' or 'advertising'. These two are parts of the total marketing function. Others hold the view that it is 'a rather expensive way of selling' without really knowing how this is so. Marketing improperly applied can lead to greater costs, whereas it is meant to provide improved profit, so in that sense it can be an expensive way of selling. Yet others have a pathetic belief in the cure-all magical powers of this newfangled thing called 'marketing'. Apart from the fact that marketing activities or techniques are not new, this last view may be a result of the still fashionable belief that because a thing is apparently 'new' it must be better than the 'old' one it replaces.

Unfortunately, just changing all titles beginning with 'sales' to those beginning with 'marketing' achieves nothing so long as the mental approach to the business and the methods of doing that business remain unchanged. Just changing titles and hoping all will come right may prove a death-wish for the company. Marketing involves a good deal of hard work, the application of common sense matched to knowledge, the use of certain special skills (explained later in this book) and a constant, total awareness of the market environment in which the company is operating. Improperly applied marketing will just drain off existing profit, not add to it.

There is one further, dangerous misconception arising from the statement that the art of marketing is the art of producing what a market wants. Strict application of this idea can cause trouble. It could lead to additional capital expenditure which the company may not really be able to afford. Or the return obtained may be insufficient to sustain the overall profitability of the company. Worse still, the profitability of these new assets may not compensate for losses arising from some existing assets which may then be under-utilised or made idle. If these idle assets cannot be sold or turned into cash for investment in other profitable operations they will remain as a further drain on the company's profitability.

Since most companies already have substantial investments in plant and facilities, the marketing concept has to be modified. These companies should establish what products they are able to make and, from market research information, they can persuade customers to buy. The cost of this 'persuasion' should not be excessive. In other words, these products must earn the profits targeted for them. Marketing then becomes the art of doing what is possible to obtain optimum profit at minimum cost.

Further, earlier books have tended to over-emphasise the importance of the marketing function. They implied the omnipotence of marketing or that marketing *is* (the whole of) management. Such attitudes are of course far from the truth. Successful management requires the right proportion, mix and balance of all the necessary management activities. No one function is really supreme. Therefore nothing in this book should be read as implying the omnipotence of marketing as a management activity. Inter-departmental co-operation is the key to sustained success in management.

1.4 Why marketing can fail

There are many reasons why marketing can fail to achieve its purpose of improving profitability, sales, market shares and reputation. Bad management can strike here just as in any other area of an enterprise. This may be due to inefficiency, incompetence, sloth or any of the many human failings people are heir to even today. These difficulties may only be remedied by changing the personnel. However, there are other reasons for marketing's failure, and with careful training staff can be shown how not to make these mistakes.

First, there may be total ignorance of what marketing is, what techniques are available and the things they can and *cannot* do or achieve. In this case, the interdependence and interrelationships of the various techniques will not be known either. For example, there is little point in conducting any marketing research (see Table 1.1) if the company is in no position to be able to use the gathered information, or if the cost of the research will be much more than any financial benefit gained through having the research data.

Second, marketing techniques may be used blindly without any thought being given to their relevance to the business in question. For example, a company making construction products all of which are sold against official tenders of one sort or another, announced well in advance of the buying decision, has little need for full-scale marketing research or advertising. Research may be better restricted to analyses of the tenders coming forward so that the company can decide which tenders or products would give its factory the most profitable mix of business. It could then make useful decisions on the prices and deliveries it could offer for the items it wanted. Perhaps the company could load the prices for the unprofitable products or those it would have difficulty in making. This would either help the company to avoid getting orders for the items it did not want, or if it got the orders the profit margins would be big enough to compensate for problems that might be met in manufacture. The advertising might best be limited to corporate advertisements which highlight the name and reputation of the company and the products it made best. Such advertisements would keep the company in the minds of the people who issued the tenders, ensuring that the company received all the tenders it wanted.

Next there is the *ad hoc* use of marketing techniques. The most commonly abused are the marketing research activities. Some companies tend to pursue these occasionally – when they think about them or have some money to spare. The one-off marketing research study can be a waste of time and money, especially as the information obtained can be obsolescent in three months or so. It is better to have a planned programme for marketing research, relevant to the marketing objectives and plans of the company, at various appropriate times of a trading year. These studies should then be continued over subsequent years (how this is done is explained in Chapter 4) to keep the information up to date. However, as mentioned earlier, if the company cannot use the information there is usually little point in doing the research.

Finally there is failure to realise the importance, relevance and cost involved in the use of a technique. For example advertising is a costly venture these days. If it does not help to assist or enhance the selling activities, it could be a waste of resources. There is no point in doing any promotional work (advertising and sales promotions) if the goods are not in stock at depots and points of sale (e.g. shops). Potential customers whose interest is aroused by the promotional campaign will only be frustrated when they find they are unable to obtain the items from the shops. The consumers might even turn against the company and not buy other products it makes.

Nor is there any point in planning to develop new products if the company does not have the plant and skills to make them or if the sales force does not have the knowledge and ability to sell them. Distribution may also be a problem if, for example, the new products have to be distributed in bulk nationally when hitherto only small quantities to a few selected areas had to be handled.

In every example mentioned in this section, failure to achieve satisfactory levels of operation can prove very costly. It could even lead to cash-flow and liquidity problems of such magnitude that the company may be forced to close down! As with everything else in life, the application of sound common sense is needed in the use of marketing techniques. Blindly stumbling along, aping other companies or following fads of the moment, without appreciating what they really have done or why, usually spells disaster, no matter how one looks at it.

1.5   Definitions and practical implications

There have been, and still are, several definitions of marketing. Most of them leave something to be desired, as it is difficult to define succinctly a multi-faceted activity like marketing with its rather complex involvement with both the external and the internal environments of the business in which it is involved. The external aspects cover customers or markets, economic conditions in countries, regions, industries and the trading world at large, competitors and their activities. There are also government controls and regulations of fiscal (especially taxation) matters affecting business and industry and consumer or customer purchasing power, import/export controls and political decisions, e.g. on state ownership of key industries and how mixed (state and privately owned enterprises) a country's economy should be. There are also political decisions which discourage or ban trade with some countries because of disagreement with their political or other systems. Many of these factors are outside the control of the firm. Internal factors cover the resources and capabilities of the company, the degree or nature of innovation required in different technical areas, technological development and trends, the role, nature and extent of sales and promotional activities required, the cost-price relationship and the way price changes and levels affect demand for the enterprise's products or services. As this book will indicate later, the interrelationships between all these are also complex.

(a) Definitions
The definition of the Chartered Institute of Marketing is as follows: 'Marketing is the management process responsible for identifying, anticipating and satisfying customer requirements profitably'.

The American Marketing Association's definition is: 'The performance of business activities that direct the flow of goods and services from producer to customer or user'.

Most definitions encapsulate what is a surprisingly wide range of activities. For example:

(i)   marketing begins *before* the production process when it researches into the design, styling and performance of the product or service that is needed and then on the potential demand that could exist and the market share the company could strive for;

(ii)   then it plays a major role in 'positioning' the product or service against the target segment of the market, deciding whether to aim at the whole market, or whether to aim at the top, bottom or middle of the range, or at some niche market;

(iii) next, because it is not only a question of satisfying demand but also of creating or directing it, a large number of promotional decisions (advertising and sales promotion) have to be made; these cover the selection of media to be used, the size, frequency and content of the advertisements, the nature and duration of the sales promotion activities, not to forget the cost of all these and the actual expenditure budgets that will be possible;

(iv)   then there are the physical distribution aspects of marketing, especially the depot/inventory questions and the transportation of the finished goods not only at the point of manufacture but also throughout the distribution network;

(v)   in addition there are all the selling possibilities to be considered, from the appointment of agents or distributors to any franchising arrangements that may be advisable and any personal selling to be undertaken by the company itself; often dealers and customers alike may have to be educated on the products or services involved, what they can achieve for customers, their sales and profit-earning potentials for distributors and users and for technical products, the various technological factors that should be considered, etc.

(vi)   and finally, how all this will be financed; estimates on the return that would be achieved and the after-sales services needed should be considered before the marketing plans can be agreed and launched.

The Floor of the old Stock Market. Traditional financial markets depended on personal contact, paperwork and 'boards'

(b) Practical implications

The complex practical implications arising from all these considerations are the subject of the chapters that follow. The scope of marketing will become clearer as the reader progresses through this book. It is because of the impossibility of encapsulating all this into a single concise definition that the following description is preferred to any definition. These are the eight key points about marketing.

(i)   Marketing is a philosophy that believes that a business and its decisions should be governed by its markets or customers rather than by its production or technical facilities.

(ii) It is an orderly, systematic process of business planning, execution and control.
(iii) It requires an improved form of commercial organisation.
(iv) It employs improved methods and systems based on economics, statistics, finance and the behavioural sciences.
(v)   It involves a system of commercial intelligence (i.e. relevant information on markets, competitors etc.).
(vi) It places strong emphasis on innovation.
(vii) It is a method for achieving dynamic business strategy and competitive advantage.
(viii) It is a form of management by objectives.

All of these have a common purpose – to serve the customers and meet their needs with products or services designed for that purpose. Points (vi) and (vii) are important at all times but are particularly so in times of static or declining demand, or when competition is intensifying. It is only through striving to be innovative and so having a dynamic marketing strategy that a company can survive in such difficult conditions. Without these, a company can be driven to the wall by more aggressive and innovative competitors. It is also true that many of these points apply to other areas of management, which only helps to prove the integrative nature of management and the need for complete co-operation between the different departments.

A modern dealing room. New financial markets depend on phones, computer networks and screens

(c) Marketing is applicable to all enterprises
The significant point that students of marketing should grasp is that the basic concept of marketing is essential to all types of business. It is not only essential for the manufacture and selling of consumer products but also of industrial products, service industries, state enterprises and even non-profit-making

activities. It is undoubtedly vital for all those involved in international marketing, whether just selling abroad items made in the home country or involving multinational operations through wholly owned subsidiaries, partly owned operations and joint ventures or partnerships. It is even necessary for public utilities. The basic marketing operations have to be modified in various ways to suit them to some of the enterprises mentioned above. The adaptations have to take into account the special characteristics of such operations but the basic tenets of marketing are not really altered. These points will be discussed in subsequent sections and chapters.

1.6   Basic marketing techniques

The techniques normally considered the responsibility of the Marketing Department are listed in Table 1.1. Brief descriptions are given as they are, of course, discussed more fully in the book. However it is worth noting one or two points here.

Many of the terms used have developed through time and may have different meanings in different contexts. For example the phrase 'promotional activity' may be used when only 'advertising' or 'sales promotion' is meant. If 'promotional activity' is mentioned strictly it means all three techniques listed under this heading in Table 1.1. The use of the single word 'promotions' strictly refers only to 'sales promotions'!

There can also be confusion between 'marketing research' and market research. In the past some writers have observed a distinction between the two terms but today they are virtually interchangeable. The more important idea today is that of the Marketing Information System. This is a mix of people, computers and communications methods which ensures that information from both internal and external sources is captured and stored, and is then made readily available for marketing management. Clearly marketing research information will form a major part of the contents of most systems, and this area of marketing information and research will be covered in Chapter 4.

1.7   The marketing mix

Marketing practitioners and academics alike agree that the phrase 'marketing mix' includes all activities involved in moving goods and services from producers to consumers, whether the latter are individuals or corporations. These activities give careful and detailed attention to the 'four Ps'. As Table 1.1 shows, a very large number of such activities exist. However, for most companies, only some of these are relevant and necessary to their business. The art in marketing is to select the most relevant and essential for an operation within the capabilities and cost limitations that apply. The selected items then become the company's marketing mix for their business.

Table 1.1   **Basic marketing techniques**

A   MARKET RESEARCH AND INFORMATION MANAGEMENT: responsible for capturing, storing, retrieving and distributing all information relating to a product or market. This involves liaison with the sales force, accounts, purchasing, production, R&D, to capture any relevant internal information; and liaison with other members of the marketing department to ensure that full use is made of the information available. The marketing research activity, which may be part of the MIS or run as a separate department, may involve any of the following specific areas:

(i)   *Economic research*: study of the economy of a country, region, industry or market – usually concerned with broad studies to establish the basic but key economic and related aspects. The data obtained is, however, quite detailed since these researches are intended to give a good understanding of what is happening in the economy under study.

(ii)   *Market research*: a more detailed study of a market, however defined, to identify total demand or volume of business available in the market – usually for all products or services under consideration – how this is declining, growing or changing, the competitors active in the market and their market shares, ruling market prices, factors affecting the market and trends and developments. Usually a more detailed study of a sector of the economy than (i) above, looking in greater depth at key market factors.

(iii)   *Demand studies*: a very detailed study in depth of the demand for specified products and services to get a clearer or up-to-date picture of what is happening to demand for the products in question. May also be indicated as necessary by the results obtained from (ii) above which may not be detailed enough for definitive marketing planning.

(iv)   *Consumer research*: detailed studies covering the attitudes, opinions and usage made of products among an appropriate sample of people, linked to their personal or occupational characteristics. Such studies provide data on 'images' of products or brands held by those in the market, and 'profiles' of purchasers or users; on attitudes to product characteristics, prices, reliability; on preferences between brands, and so on. May use a range of techniques but essentially involve contact with an appropriate sample of people.

(v)   *Competitor research*: much more detailed study in depth of competitors, what they are doing, what products etc. they are offering, how and why they are successful etc. (i.e. to establish the 'competitor profile'). The information is useful in assessing likely competitor reaction to our own changes or innovations.

(vi)   *Product research*: attempts to discover what products or services are required, or being bought by a market, industry, area or type of customer, the specification and performance expected by customers and the price they indicate they would pay for a stated specification. Tries to establish the technical features required including expected life of the product, after-sales or maintained services expected, etc. Helps to decide what the product range of the company should be.

(vii)   *Sales research*: study of the flow of products or services to the customer. Usually carried out on a continuous basis, and will often include the collection of data on distribution, prices, etc. Will provide information on both the base situation and the effects of any changes in systems, prices, promotional activity and so on.

(viii)   *Distribution research*: helps to identify the physical distribution required to counter competition effectively or to give customers a better service. Also checks if the methods being used are achieving these aims within permitted costs. Also helps to show how distribution may be modified to keep costs under control, where to locate depots, the size of depots, size of inventories, method of transportation to be used, whether to own or lease depots, the type of agents to be used, etc.

(ix)   *Promotional research*: helps to determine the promotional activities required, the nature and timing of them, etc., and the costs involved. Can cover all the promotional activities or just advertising and sales promotions. Also helps to determine how successful current promotional activities are proving and what changes to them are necessary. Helps with decisions on media selection, nature and timing of promotions and all cost and timing aspects.

(x) *Market modelling*: the amount and complexity of data which can be collected mean that some aids to interpretation are often needed. Models, which attempt to provide simplified views of complex situations, are often valuable aids. Some are based on ideas and qualitative factors; some are based on statistical analyses and quantitative relationships. All have the aim of helping in deciding whether recent information is still in line with expectations, and in assessing the likely outcome of future plans. They help to ensure that as much information as possible, for example on the effects of changes, lags between promotions and effects, and so on, is extracted from marketing data and made available to management.

B PROMOTION MANAGEMENT: responsible for all activities in presenting the organisation and its products or services to the world outside. Much of the work is handled through specialist agencies, and much management effort is directed to briefing and controlling those agencies. The main activities fall into three areas:

(i)   *Advertising*: described as 'a paid form of promotional activity by an identified sponsor'. Involves media selection and decisions on the size, type or nature of the advertisement, the copy and number of colours to be used, the frequency of the advertisements, etc. All these influence the 'impact' of an advertising campaign.

(ii) *Sales promotions*: special activities, usually conducted over a limited period of time, to boost sales during peak sales periods, to support ailing products or to help launch new products. Activities include: special price reduction, free offers, banded packs, coupons, free gifts and point-of-sale displays with special posters, banners, show cards, etc. For industrial products: catalogues, technical leaflets, trade-in terms, etc., can be used here. Also exhibitions, seminars and conferences are now seen as part of the work of sales promotion.

(iii) *Public relations*: includes relations with both print and electronic media, and seeks to keep the public or selected target groups correctly informed about the organisation's activities, achievements and future intentions. The role of PR is important in ensuring that what an organisation does well is appreciated outside. But there is also an internal role, in exerting pressure on management and staff generally to rectify those things which may be harming the organisation's standing and reputation. Internal PR, or more widely 'internal marketing', should ensure that all staff are kept well informed about their own organisation – its problems as well as its achievements.

C PRODUCT MANAGEMENT: involves everything to do with the planning and management of the product (or service) side of a company. The work may be divided into:

(i)   *Managing existing products*: maintaining profitability, sales and market shares for successful products; seeking out new customers and applications, especially any markets that may have been overlooked; keeping a watch on prices and costs, etc.

(ii) *Product modification*: when technological or other market conditions change it may be necessary to modify the specification, style or nature of the product or service to prolong its useful, profitable life. In competitive times, modifications may be needed to avoid cost and hence price increases or to reduce them. May be necessary also if the original concept or specification for the product or service proves to be wrong or is not being accepted by customers.

(iii) *Product rationalisation*: technical and market changes may be such as to make it impossible to modify a product, or the cost of modification may be too high in relation to the benefits (profit) which would be obtained. Competitors' new products will also make the company's products obsolete and all products and services eventually reach the end of their profitable life. In these instances, the products concerned have to be removed from the company's product range.

(iv) *New product development*: this is necessary if the company's long-term survival is to be assured and to take over from rationalised products. Also needed when major technological changes have taken place or are forecast and when a company wishes to expand its activities into other areas (technical or market) Involves the search for, assessment, planning and launching of new product/service ideas. When a company intends to move into an entirely new activity involving new technology it is often called *diversification*.

(v) *Product presentation*: involves development of packaging, promotional and advertising material as appropriate, and in conjunction with procurement and production departments, designers, printers, advertising agencies, etc.

(vi) *Pricing and profit management*: involves decisions on the pricing strategy, policy and plans to be followed and monitoring sales and profit results obtained with recommendations on any changes that are necessary. In profit planning, Marketing works with Manufacturing and Finance in agreeing what the company's profit targets should be and any subsequent changes dependent on results obtained.

D   MARKET MANAGEMENT: concerned with everything to do with the planning and management of the market side of a company's business activities. Again, this can be divided as follows.

(i) *Managing existing, successful markets*: making sure that operations continue successfully in the selected markets (or market segments) in which the company operates; keeping track of developments concerning customer needs, the effect of changing technology and competition, etc.; ensuring that the marketing activities are achieving optimal results etc.

(ii) *Modifying markets*: the original selection of markets, or more correctly market segments, may not have proved successful; may be necessary to change the market mix by selecting a different category of customer in any given area or segment; or as the company develops, other categories of customer within a market segment can be added to the operations.

(iii) *Market rationalisation*: like products, markets have a finite life; they cease to be profitable or the company cannot exploit them profitably any more. Other factors may make it advisable for the company to withdraw from certain market segments and, usually, put the resources to more profitable use. Market rationalisation is then necessary.

(iv) *New market development:* again, if a company wishes to survive and develop in the long term, new market development is necessary, especially if market rationalisation has been essential. Involves the search for and assessment of possible new markets and the planning and launching of marketing operations into them. (Note also *diversification* in C (iv) above.)

E   SALES MANAGEMENT: responsible for all aspects of the sales activities of the company. Work involves:

(i) Planning the size, nature and extent of the personal selling operation, whether involving face-to-face or telephone selling, and the size, location, training and qualifications of the sales force.

(ii) Selecting the administrative and other methods to be used and the size and nature (also the qualifications) of the sales office staff.

(iii) Recruitment, remuneration and training of the members of the sales department, especially the sales force.

(iv) Devising a suitable monitoring service and information system to keep track of results v. plans and so recommending any alterations that may be necessary.

F   PHYSICAL DISTRIBUTION MANAGEMENT: responsible for all activities to do with physical distribution. This includes:

(i) *Depots*: number, size, location, whether owned or leased.

(ii) *Inventories and inventory control*: size, maximum and minimum levels, reordering levels, cost of, etc.

(iii) *Channels of distribution to be used*: agents, distributors, franchises, etc., and terms of agreements.

(iv) *Transportation*: whether to use own fleet, have annual contracts with suitable transport organisation, or use casual hiring as needed; whether to use road, rail, sea or air transport, etc.

(v) *Administration*: all administrative matters concerned with above; cost and cost control, insurance, control paperwork, etc.

All the functions in the total marketing mix are variable so that the emphasis that management places on any element it is using will change according to circumstances in the company and its markets. For example in difficult trading times the company may find it necessary to conduct more market, demand or consumer research since it needs accurate information on these matters to counter competition more effectively. It cannot afford to make mistakes. In boom times, when companies can sell all they can make, such precision in information gathering may not be necessary and may represent unnecessary expenditure on research. If the company is selling all it can make, knowing that it could sell more may not be immediately important though it could point the way to long-term development.

Or should the company need more extensive or intensive advertising it may have to raise prices or reduce costs to make the additional funds for this available. If a new technological development makes a substantial or critical portion of its products obsolescent, the company may have to intensify its work in product modification and new product development. Where competition is intense it may be necessary to step up the personal selling activity. In the two last examples mentioned, it may be necessary to cut back on some other marketing activity in order to make available the additional funds needed.

In the case of marketing intangibles such as services (e.g. banking, investment services, tourism or travel facilities) some of the traditional four Ps of Product, Price, Place and Promotion may need modification, and there is increasing emphasis on the Personnel involved, the Physical evidence linked to the service, and the Process through which the service is provided. More will be said about these factors later, but a simple example in the holiday market will illustrate these additional aspects. Prospective travellers will begin to form views of a travel company from the moment of first contact. They will judge sales or booking staff, whether they meet them face-to-face, by phone or letter. Hence the need for thorough training to give a good impression. They will judge whatever physical evidence is available, such as brochures, the time taken to answer queries or answer the phone, the cleanliness of branches or agents and so forth. They will judge the process of booking, whether forms are easy to complete, whether what is being bought is well set out, whether it is quite clear what payments are to be made and for what, and so on.

In the end a company must thoroughly analyse its own business (markets, products, competition, customers etc.), get to know what is important for success and then select its own 'mix' of marketing activities. By trial and error and careful monitoring of results it will learn, eventually, which 'marketing mix' produces the best, or optimal, results for it, in the long term as well as the short term (see also Section 11.1).

(a) Marketing Strategy And Planning

The terms used to describe the processes of setting organisational goals and achieving them have changed considerably in recent years, with inevitable differences in the terms used in older texts. For our purposes we can define two terms of immediate importance:

Strategy is concerned with meeting the objectives of an organisation, or of some part of it. Thus we have Corporate Strategy concerned with the overall aims and objectives, but we have Marketing Strategy concerned with the more specific objectives of the marketing department. At the corporate level the objective may be to secure a return on capital employed of x per cent, and the strategy chosen to meet this objective may be to concentrate activity on the organisation's core activities. The marketing strategy following from this may then be to expand use of existing products in existing markets. In all these cases there is a definition of the broad approach at each level, but no detail of *how* the objectives are to be achieved.

Planning is concerned with the detail of implementing the agreed strategy. At each level a plan will cover the resources needed and the means to be used to implement strategy. The plan should include forecasts of the expected results, and where these do not fit the objectives, either the objectives, the strategy or the plan will need to be changed.

Corporate objectives and strategy will be determined at board level. Departmental objectives and strategy will be determined at director level. Planning will be at senior or middle management levels, under the overall control of the director. Detailed marketing plans for products or services will then be developed by those responsible for day-to-day marketing of each product or brand, whatever their specific titles may be.

Strategy establishes the long-term intentions (objectives and targets) while planning specifies the short-term action programmes that will be followed to achieve the strategy. Plans will be altered to counter changes in market factors (economic, competitive, technological, political and such-like) but strategy is usually only altered when some major change has occurred in the business environment or the company is changing course (i.e. moving into a new technology and thus markets and diversifying strongly to ensure the company's survival). *Marketing strategy* is primarily concerned with optimising profit and return on investment, not maximising sales. If there is any conflict between the first two objectives and the third, the first two should normally take precedence. In so doing the critical factor of market shares will come right, as will sales volume. In practice the *marketing plans* followed and hence the marketing mix selected will be a compromise between what is ideal and what is practical. The latter is determined by the constraints of minimum costs and the talents and assets available to the company, of which the most critical is usually money (funds).

In arriving at the best strategy and plans possible, executives must use thorough, scientifically based assessments and judgements of their present and forecasted future. The planning is research based, not the consequence solely of intuition or hunchplay, though these two should not be spurned completely. When information and data are scarce or non-existent, intelligent use of intuition and hunches based on experience, knowledge and past performance in related areas may be the only methods available. In all cases, however, executives must not be too introspective. They must think through their own situations to those of customer and competitor. They must appreciate the marketing strategies and mixes of their major competitors and the managerial concepts and criteria which motivate customers and competitors.

As readers will appreciate now – or later – many variables influence the decisions taken on marketing strategy and planning. They may, however, be classified under five headings or groupings.

(i)   *Product strategy and planning*: involve decisions on product range and mix, rationalisation, modification and new product development; these in turn require consideration of product life-cycles, warranties and guarantees and, especially for consumer goods, packaging design, branding and trademarks. The work entails not only consideration of the physical product but also the satisfaction of customer needs.

(ii) *Market strategy and planning*: involves decisions on all aspects of the market mix, market segmentation, new market development and the relationship of these points with the product strategy and policy.

(iii) *Pricing strategy and planning*: involves one of the most difficult decision areas for executives and covers the prices and discounts to be operated, trade terms etc. These are themselves conditioned by cost aspects, the prices that are justified for the specification, performance and other properties of the products or services and selling methods that will be used. The overall aim here is to ensure that the company achieves its *profit targets* and objectives.

(iv) *Promotional strategy and planning*: involves decisions on the personal selling, advertising, sales promotions and PR activities to be followed. While these must be so co-ordinated as to optimise the company's communication with the selected markets and customers, they must also be integrated with all the other marketing activities and hence strategies and policies.

(v)   *Physical distribution strategy and planning*: involves all decisions to do with the distribution of the product or service, especially the selection of the marketing channels and methods of distribution to be used.

All five of the above form another way of referring to the marketing mix.

(b) Product–market strategy and positioning

As mentioned above, decisions on product and market strategy and planning are closely interrelated. Without a strategy it is difficult to plan on any consistent basis. Without plans the strategy will not become effective. With a proper combination of strategy based on the talents and strengths of the organisation, and marketing appreciation of potential customers and their needs, products or services can be correctly *positioned* in the selected markets.

By 'positioning' we mean the strategic placing of a product in its market. A product may be positioned at the 'top' end of a market, where good design, high quality of production, reliability and so forth, should attract buyers seeking those properties. There may not be many, but they may be prepared to pay a high price. At lower levels there may be good value-for-money products attracting larger numbers of buyers at moderate prices; and below them products designed to sell largely on a low price. With some products emphasis may be on their technical qualities, while others may emphasise aesthetic or emotive properties. Given the range of positions which can be adopted in many markets an early decision is needed about the position a product is intended to occupy, to guide all subsequent development.

Correct positioning ensures that greater profits should accrue if the needs of market segments are correctly assessed and products are developed or adapted so that they have a competitive edge within that segment. It follows that all the marketing factors described above must be planned to ensure a consistent and favourable presentation or image to the chosen target group. Hence product positioning follows from strategy, and provides the basis for marketing planning.

All the points above will be discussed in more detail in the chapters that follow. In conclusion it is worth stating that marketing decisions cannot be made in a vacuum or in isolation from each other. It is dangerous to experiment with single variables while assuming that everything else is constant. While the mechanics of writing a book and the limitations of the human brain make it necessary for the subjects of markets and products to be considered in turn, it must be realised that decisions based on these studies must be made in the integrated or interrelated manner that has been stated above.

(c) Development of marketing philosophies

It is worth making a brief sketch here of how and why business and economic developments since the Industrial Revolution in the late 1700s made it necessary for company executives to consider the use of marketing in all businesses. In very early times everyone existed in a subsistence economy. The individual family units grew sufficient crops for their own needs. They were, in today's terms, very small smallholders, cultivating meagre plots of land. If they grew more than they needed they would barter the surplus, before the general advent or acceptance of money, for the things they could not grow or make themselves. When money began to be used they would sell their surplus, negotiating prices individually, and use the cash to buy whatever else they needed. As the feudal system developed in Europe, the greater part of the land was owned by the barons and the sovereign. The ordinary people, serfs, worked the land for their masters. Either they were permitted to work small plots in return for military service with their baron, or the bulk of the crop went to the owner of the estate and the peasants were permitted to keep a small amount for their own existence, or they worked just for their keep. The wealth of the country resided with the barons, and the ordinary population, much smaller than in modern times, had no wealth and no real purchasing power.

With the advent of the Industrial Revolution the old system changed, gradually at first and then ever more rapidly as industrialisation progressed. Many more goods, in ever-increasing variety, were produced. People who worked in the factories were paid for their labour and this gave them some purchasing power. As their wages increased so did their ability to purchase an ever-widening choice of goods. As mass production developed and as the population increased, the purchasing power of consumers and the ever-widening choice open to them increased. Demand for all products and the competition between them intensified. As production techniques improved, especially in more recent decades as automation increased, the direct labour content in manufacturing was reduced and the cost savings this achieved was passed on in the form of lower prices. This trend was intensified as automation and other improved techniques led to greater output. The increased earnings of the work-force allowed more people to afford the necessities of life and eventually a life-style in which the psychological needs (e.g. travel, leisure activities, entertainment and numerous services) gained in importance. The need for the more efficient distribution of this ever-widening range of goods and services became apparent.

However, in the earlier days when markets were many and mainly unsatisfied (i.e. demand exceeded supply), products and services enjoyed a seller's market. Businesses were production-orientated. Markets were many, goods were scarce and quite often made to order. The need to 'sell' anything was minimal. As industrial activity intensified throughout the world, markets became less plentiful and goods less scarce. They were made more and more for stock to gain the benefits of large batch or continuous mass production. These stocks had to be sold and the emphasis changed to a 'sales orientation'. As competition increased the need to improve distribution and to use advertising, sales promotion and more effective personal selling led to the need to identify markets, potential customers and their needs, the price they would pay and so on. Thus evolved what we know today as 'marketing'.

It was the consumer goods area that first identified the need for marketing. However, by the 1950s in most developed countries and some developing ones, unexploited markets for industrial products were less numerous and goods were usually in plentiful supply. The basic problem was to find customers for a company's products. Further, consumers, whether domestic or industrial, became more discriminating and demanding in what they were prepared to buy. In a buyer's market the customer is a force to be reckoned with and has to be prompted, either as an individual consumer or as an institutional or professional buyer in industry, to become a purchaser of any item, whether consumer goods or industrial products.

Today there is generally more capacity to provide both goods and services than there is demand. In times of boom there may be temporary shortages in some sectors; in times of recession there will be a wider range of excess resources, leading to unemployment leading to even further reductions in demand and so forth. While governments and international bodies may try to restrain excess demand or to stimulate demand in recession the success of individual organisations will depend on good management generally, but in particular to an ability to move with markets. Sound marketing strategies and plans should enable an organisation to use its resources to anticipate and meet market needs, and to survive by developing a sustainable competitive edge over its rivals.

1.8 Marketing and the smaller company

Executives in smaller companies may understandably wonder how the concepts of marketing can be applied in their case without incurring heavy costs. They may be influenced in their thoughts by knowledge of the substantial marketing operations, large expenditure budgets and marketing departments of major industrial or service groups such as those in the oil, vehicle, chemical or food industries, or banks, building societies, airlines and so forth. They may feel that the marketing approach is beyond their means.

In reality, while the marketing activities of such companies are substantial, measured in terms of their total business or turnover, marketing operations are not excessive and costs represent a small percentage of total operating costs and are held within these reasonable bounds. Their marketing departments, while seemingly large to most people in terms of the number of people working in them are only as large as their very complex activities (many products involving several technologies and markets or user industries) require. A large marketing department is only required by a large business.

For smaller companies, the size of the marketing operation must be scaled down to match the needs of the business. A small company, especially if it is not trying to sell goods to the mass or national consumer market, will have no need for extensive and costly market or consumer research or demand studies. Its advertising activities can be very limited and selective. It may not need to use sales promotions at all, except to produce catalogues or leaflets on its products and if a special, small new product is in hand, send a few free samples to important customers to try out and report back on their usefulness and so on. The sales force too could be small and carefully selected and dispersed throughout its limited markets. As mentioned in Section 1.7 the art of successful marketing lies in the ability to identify and select only those techniques which are relevant and essential to a business. That is, a company should use only those techniques which improve the profitability of its business and help it to survive and develop over the long term as well as the short term.

The more specialised services could be bought, as needed, from the many sound organisations that now exist to provide these services. This avoids the need to add to overhead costs by trying to have appropriate specialists on the staff. It allows companies to select the specialists who have a good reputation for doing the work needed and who therefore have the experience, skills and knowledge to do it well. (In fact many large companies are now using such outside experts and saving on their own marketing overhead costs.) For example, market research facilities can be bought from appropriate market research consultants. The cost of the work can be charged to pre-taxed income. Even a £50 million group with six companies avoided heavy fixed costs by using research consultants and having just one person at head office to control and supervise all marketing research work.

To apply marketing successfully to a small company, the executives must first develop the frame of mind mentioned earlier in this chapter. This leads them to identify customers and their needs – including potential customers – so that the opportunities open to the company in their selected markets can be perceived. The potential and capabilities of the company can then be matched more precisely to these opportunities.

The executives must recognise that it is of little avail to hanker after a particular market or group of customers if the company's facilities just do not allow it to operate profitably in that area. Nor should they make a superb product for which there is little or no demand. With objective assessments of the markets they could tackle and the total demand involved, they could make appropriate sales plans to capture the market shares they require. They will of course have assessed the strength and skills of the competition they would face. Their marketing and sales plans should of course match their production capacity and cost capabilities. They will then be able to properly position their products in the selected market segments and sell them at prices which will provide the best profit possible.

In estimating market demand the executives may have called in marketing research consultants to help them. If the company is very small, they might also have used other management consultants to set up the necessary organisation, information and control systems, especially accounting systems, records and methods. Once all donkey work has been done, even the smallest company should be able to keep things running well. Advantages which large organisations once had in using computers for accounting, for management or marketing information systems, and so forth no longer apply. These and other benefits are now widely and cheaply available to small companies through PCs and their related software.

Marketing techniques are as relevant to small operations as to large ones. Failure to recognise this will hinder the growth and continued well-being of the small company and may lead to liquidation. The application of these techniques does not necessarily require a major change of staff or organisation. It requires, principally, a change of mind leading to a more objective review of the company, its products, markets and customers. This is particularly important for large and small companies in difficult trading times.

1.9 Marketing industrial products

Marketing techniques were originally developed for use with consumer goods sold to consumer markets. Probably because of this there was considerable resistance to the use of marketing for industrial products. Even now, several decades later, resistance to the use of marketing techniques in some companies manufacturing industrial products can be encountered. In these cases they hold to the belief that their products or technology or their customers' technical requirements make their business 'unique' in some way and this uniqueness 'saves' them from having to be involved in marketing. The implication is that there is something 'not quite gentlemanly' in the activities normally ascribed to marketing. 'What the consumer goods boys get up to does not concern those of us in the manufacture of industrial products and plant.' All the words in quotes above have featured frequently in arguments against the use of marketing. How wrong the last quote is, in more ways than one, will become clear in the text of this book.

At first glance, there would seem to be many differences involved in the marketing of industrial products, that is, marketing goods and services to industrial users rather than the individual consumer or the consumer markets. However, the marketing principles involved remain the same and so do the basic techniques. The observable difference lies in the blend of marketing mix used. For example, with consumer goods, greater emphasis has to be placed on the persuasion of the individual consumer to buy the goods. That is, greater use is made of advertising, sales promotion, merchandising, distribution and personal selling.

With industrial products and especially technical plant and equipment, emphasis is placed on the technical aspects and performance of the products, the economic contribution they make to the business of the companies buying them and in direct selling. The last usually involves sales people with the appropriate technical training and experience, negotiating contracts, often of substantial value, with other highly skilled professionals who make the buying decisions in the client companies. Whereas a 'consumer sale' to an individual may be small in volume (one or two items) and value, 'industrial sales' are of substantial volume or quantities and are of much greater value. (However, where consumer goods are sold to supermarkets and major chains of stores or shops, sales may involve large contracts of considerable value. In these cases the marketing and selling operations resemble those for industrial goods.) None the less there are some special differences or characteristics of industrial products markets which need to be taken into account and which call for some modification of basic marketing techniques. These are discussed in the sections that follow.

First, though, there is need for a clear statement of what is meant by consumer goods and industrial products marketing. Consumer goods are all those items sold to the ultimate user for personal or household use, usually without further processing (other than the cooking of foodstuffs). Excluding the wholesaling function (where items are bought in quantity) purchases are made in small quantities, sometimes on impulse or by force of habit. The exceptions are consumer durables (cars, washing machines, cookers and other household appliances, television sets and so on) where careful thought is given to cost or price and the suitability of the item for the purpose in mind. This is particularly so during hard economic times. As almost everyone in a country requires consumer goods, nationwide distribution and sales are involved though the use of 'market segmentation' (see Section 6.3) helps to limit the problems encountered here. Generally the distribution and stockholding arrangements are substantial and complex. Channels of distribution (see Chapter 9) are long. Personal tastes and preferences dominate and there are a large number of potential customers.

Industrial products and services are sold to business and institutional buyers including agriculture, central and local government bodies, state or nationalised industries and public utilities for use in some form, in the conduct of their business. In this category are included raw materials, fabricated materials, components, other semi-manufactures, capital goods, machinery, building supplies, consumables (items used in manufacturing processes such as greases, oils, cleaning materials etc.) and industrial services (e.g. repair, maintenance etc.). However some goods, such as cars, furniture, computers and many others, may be bought both by individuals or by industry. One lesson which established computer companies such as IBM or ICL had to learn was that the marketing of PCs to industrial users was very different from marketing mainframes, and was much closer to consumer marketing. It involved channels of distribution rather than direct negotiating; keeping in touch with mass markets rather than a few major users of mainframes; selling on standard specifications rather than specially designed systems. This eventually led to selling on price in markets with little product differentiation. Hence in many cases it is the method of purchase (individual, small-volume sales v. large-volume contract sales) which determines the method of marketing used. Now let us consider the special characteristics of industrial markets.

(a) Derived demand

The demand for industrial products is said to be derived in nature since it depends on the demand for the end-product or service to which it makes some contribution. Because one product may be sold to different industries this derived demand will have many facets. Further, while most manufacturing companies buy a product for the economic contribution it makes to their business (e.g. saves them from having to invest capital and labour in making the product themselves, enhances the saleability of their own end-product, etc.) others may buy for social or political reasons. For example a local authority may build a new school and 'buy' all the items needed for this and to equip it. It is however primarily concerned with the social aspect of enhancing the educational facilities in its area. The central government may build a new motorway. In this case it is concerned with economic, social and political considerations. The first should help to improve the infrastructure of the economy by contributing better communications and hence distribution facilities. The social aspects may lie in the removal of traffic congestion from the area. The political aspects include the enhancement of the reputation and so on of the ruling party in the eyes of the electorate.

Consider also the case of the manufacturer of a plasticiser needed for the manufacture of some plastics. The plastics may be used by many users. One may use it in the manufacture of a circuit unit that fits into a computer or television set. The ultimate users of the computer or television set may have no idea what plasticiser has been used in the plastic making up the components of the finished article – and they may not care! Yet on the success of the plasticiser in use may depend the correct functioning of the plastic on which the circuit is mounted and hence the circuit itself and the computer or television set using the latter. It could be helpful for the plasticiser manufacturer to be able to discuss matters with the ultimate users. However, it can be appreciated that this is not possible, the lines of communication are too long and anyway the final user is not very aware about the plasticiser, its properties and performance.

In addition a high stable demand for the end-product, in this case the computer or television set, does not necessarily mean there will be a corresponding demand for the plasticiser. The plastics manufacturer may decide, for technical reasons, to use something else or the manufacturing process may change. In other cases, if government policies restrict consumer or user demand (accidentally or deliberately!), manufacturers of these goods may reduce the size and frequency of their orders for the raw materials, components or capital equipment they need for their business. In some instances, replacement or renewal of capital equipment may be deferred. Thus, if the plant was due for replacement say every seven years, but orders were deferred for say three years, the replacement period or life of the plant would be extended by nearly fifty per cent. This would have a serious effect on total demand for the equipment, reducing it substantially. Thus demand for any individual item may become unstable or at least difficult to predict.

(b) Value and frequency of orders
The purchasing officers with manufacturing companies are highly trained professionals, often with degrees in economics and other appropriate subjects. They are aware that buying items at the most advantageous terms requires them to place substantial orders at the right times. The size of the order depends on the economic situation at the time but it means, almost invariably, that individual orders are of substantial quantity and value. Further they know they must keep the inventory (stocks) of bought-in items to certain specified levels. To exceed them is costly for the company. Falling below minimum levels might disrupt production. So they have to match the timing of their orders with their company's production plans and level of inventories at the time. This means that orders will be carefully timed and with the need to buy as economically as possible will occur less frequently than impulse buying by individual consumers.

In some industries, and in some areas of retail trading, the search for economies in stock-holding has led to 'just-in-time' deliveries. Here deliveries are made to a tight schedule, virtually onto the production line, or to individual supermarkets, so that stock-holdings are reduced to only a few hours or days. Close co-operation is then required between the two parties, with the emphasis on regularity of supply. Such operations have become possible through improved communications based on computers holding current information on stocks, vehicle movements and forecasts of demand. But while deliveries may now be in smaller quantities, ordering will still be on a contract basis, often covering supplies for many months ahead.

The sum total of these and other factors means not only that orders for industrial products, and especially capital equipment, are of greater value and occur at less frequent times than orders for consumer goods but also that forecasting demand and the pattern of sales (how sales will occur during a year) can be more difficult. The first point also makes each order for industrial products more important to the sellers. Miss an order and there may be a long wait for the next. In bad economic times this can adversely affect the cash flow and liquidity of the selling organisation. It is this fear of losing an order that may be one of the main reasons why prices for industrial products tend to approach the lowest possible level. (Intensifying competition is another. Pricing aspects are discussed more fully in Chapter 7.)

(c) Market definition
Theoretically it is easier to define markets for industrial products than consumer goods. In the latter case, everyone in a country is a potential customer

and finding who are the real customers can be a major market research and
statistical exercise. In the former case, industrial customers for any given
product are much more limited in number. Further, as industries tend to group
themselves in fairly easily identified geographical areas, usually near the
major sources of supply for their essential materials, it is not too difficult to
decide the geographical location of potential markets. (In recent decades in
Britain the movement of companies to development areas and so on has led to
industries being more widely spread than before but it is still easy to identify
their general geographical locations.)

However, most industrial products are sold to users in several industries.
Deciding which industries are potential users of a product or how and why
some are using the product calls for considerable knowledge of a wide range
of technologies. Market research and demand forecasting, if they are to be
well done, call for considerable knowledge on the part of marketing executives and their manufacturing department colleagues. In addition, since a
larger proportion of total demand resides in the hands of a limited number of
firms, one wrong answer (deliberate or accidental) in the course of a demand
study can produce disproportionately misleading or incorrect results. So
defining a market may seem easy but in fact there are many pitfalls for the
inexperienced and unwary.

(d) Technical factors

Obviously technical factors predominate in the marketing of industrial products.
Potential users require considerable and detailed information on the specification,
performance, expected life, quality and reliability of the product. They will also
need information on maintenance needs and especially the assurance that
between maintenance times the product will function properly. Also maintenance
should not be too frequently needed. Thus while price is still an important consideration, it concedes precedence to technical factors.

Since the technical aspects and performance of an industrial product are of
chief importance, potential customers will not normally respond to the type of
advertising and selling used for consumer goods. They are not persuaded by general blandishments containing vague statements and claims which cannot be
proved or disproved conclusively. They are interested in hard facts. Direct personal selling, involving detailed discussion of important technical aspects, is
required instead. The more technical the product, the longer will the negotiations
take. Where the new equipment has to be tested and approved (as with oil refining plant) the negotiations may take years.

(e) Buying motives

Buying decisions for industrial products fall into two broad types. On one hand
are the decisions concerned with items which have been bought before, often
many times, and where the specification is unchanged since last time. This is
known as a 're-buy' situation, common with routine supplies and unchanged
components. Here as long as the last delivery was satisfactory and price differen-

tials are unchanged, a straight repurchase decision is quickly taken, and may even be initiated by computer.

The second category concerns items not previously ordered, or ordered at such long intervals that much time and effort may be required in finding sources of supply. Lengthy processes of comparing specifications and prices, checking on reliability of goods and of deliveries and so forth may follow, involving many people in the customer organisation. In some cases of new developments, the new component or plant may need to be developed jointly by a supplier and the customer. These are known as 'new-buy' decisions.

In between these two extremes of straight re-buy and new-buy decisions, there are many which involve re-buying but with a modified specification. These, not unnaturally known as 'modified re-buys', take up a great deal of time in purchasing departments as specifications change.

Generally industrial marketing and purchasing are based on hard facts such as specification, delivery, price, adherence to quality standards (e.g. BS 5750 and related international equivalents aimed at ensuring high and consistent standards of supply). It may then appear that less tangible factors are of little importance, but in fact when there is more than one product available, all of which could do the job in mind equally well and at competitive costs, the final buying decisions as to which product to buy could be based on irrational considerations. The group, or purchasing officer, making the final decisions may prefer one supplier over another. This may be because years previously the preferred company had helped out the buying organisation, when the latter was in difficulties. The fact that the supplier may not be in a position to do so again may not be realised. A buying decision exercising this preference is irrational. Or the purchasing officer may prefer one salesman to another for no real reason. Then if the former decides to place the order with the person he prefers that decision is also irrational. (If the two or more products under study are *not* equal as regards key economic, cost, technical and performance details, a decision not to take the best available product could be judged to be irrational.)

Buying motives can be classified under two headings.

(i)   *Company patronage motives*: these vary for different categories of products but all are the result of cost-benefit considerations in relation to the efficiency and profitability of the buyer's own operations.
(ii) *Product patronage motives*: these vary with the class or type of buyer, but again cost-benefit considerations feature.

Figure 1.1 lists the principal motives involved under these headings for different categories of industrial products.

Awareness of what are the primary motives and the order of priority assigned to them by major customers helps executives marketing industrial products to plan their operations with greater precision. Note that price often has a low priority. In the case of high technology products, technical factors, especially performance, reliability and output (where relevant) will usually be judged by potential buyers as being of supreme importance.

PRODUCT GP MOTIVE GP	CAPITAL EQUIPMENT	RAW MATERIALS COMPONENTS & SUPPLIES
COMPANY PATRONAGE MOTIVES	performance after-sales service past experience of sellers general reliability of sellers credit facilities price	quality delivery reliability ease of access to supplier (communications & physical distribution), price & terms ability of seller to meet any emergency performance
PRODUCT PATRONAGE MOTIVES	economy of operation and productivity reliability – related to eqpt, the company and its services durability and labour-saving aspects of the equipment credit terms and facilities price	suitability reliability and uniformity of quality reliability of supplier, especially delivery degree to which the purchased item enhances the saleability of the end product R&D record of supplier price

Fig. 1.1   **Buying motives for industrial products**

(f) Buying decisions

With consumer goods the buying decision is often taken by the individual consumer. Where goods are bought in bulk on contract by wholesalers, supermarkets and other chains, the buying decision may be taken by a professional 'buyer' or a group of executives responsible for the purchasing decisions. With low-cost, non-technical industrial products used widely, the same may apply. However with technical products the buying decisions will depend on a group of executives as well as the purchasing officer. The greater the cost of the product, the greater its importance to the potential buyer's business, and the more technical the product is, the larger will be the number of executives involved in the purchasing decision. The technical departments as well as manufacturing, perhaps even at director level, will want a say in the decision. So will the financial director. For decisions concerning vital or substantial plant the chief executive might also be involved. The purchasing officer may then be primarily concerned with carrying out the decision of the group.

The greater the technical content of a product the longer will be the time required to arrive at a buying decision. The development of a new product from its original idea will also take longer, the more so if there are several tricky technological points to be handled. Finally, the replacement of a technical product may not depend solely or entirely on the life of the product. All the associated economic factors will have effects, either in hastening or retarding the replacement of the original item. It should be clear that there are obvious dangers for suppliers who do not maintain close contact with their customers.

Today there is an increasing tendency for industrial companies to work more closely with their suppliers, rather than treating them at arms length almost on an adversarial basis. In some cases there are mutual benefits in the joint development of new components, using the knowledge and expertise of the suppliers' R&D department allied to the purchasers' own technical expertise. Keeping suppliers informed of production schedules, model changes and so forth helps them to produce appropriate supplies on time for the benefit of both parties. Joint examination of current components and processes may well lead to simplifications or improvements which neither party alone might manage. Hence supplier and buyer now increasingly see their roles as a partnership for their mutual benefit, rather than as antagonists competing for marginal benefits in costs, delivery schedules, and so forth.

1.10   Marketing services

The original four Ps of the marketing mix, Product, Price, Promotion and Place or Physical Distribution, need extending when we are dealing with services. These four factors have traditionally been enough for manufacturers to take into account when planning their marketing, although even here their limitations are being realised. For service marketing three more Ps covering People, Process and Physical evidence are important.

People are important. They are needed to deliver an efficient and pleasant service. A major element in service marketing is the contact between staff and customers, whether in a supermarket, a bank, a plane, a hospital or whatever, and whether in face-to-face contact, by phone, letter or fax. It is then vital that staff are not only courteous and considerate, but are well trained, well informed and consistent in their contacts with customers.

The *Process* by which customers are served is important. Customers should be able to find what they want easily, and to have choices plainly set out. They need to know what they have to pay, and to have all the processes from initial enquiry to settlement made as straightforward as possible. Where forms have to be filled in these should be designed to be user-friendly, even if this may make entry into computers at a later stage slightly more difficult for staff. Training of staff is therefore of great importance.

The *Physical evidence* of clean and well-lit premises may be taken for granted by most customers, but care is needed at all stages. The design of reception areas, privacy in making one's requests or needs known, clear direction signs, air conditioning and so on, are all important. However the physical side must not be overdone. Too much emphasis on decor may be taken as a sign of excessive profits, or a waste of resources. As in all areas of marketing, a balance is needed, and the impact of the surroundings must be assessed or researched from the standpoint of the customer.

These three additional factors apply across the whole range of services, whether trading or non-trading. They apply to banks, airlines, schools, hospitals, and wherever there is a direct interface between customer/user and supplier. The way the service is provided, the way the tangible aspects associated with it are maintained, the ease of completing the paper-work or the transaction are all important. They all add to, or detract from, the image of a service or an organisation, with effects on user satisfaction and ultimately on usage or sales.

The World Travel Exhibition brings together suppliers and distributors in a major service industry

The need for the additional dimensions in service areas applies in both consumer and industrial markets. A firm of management consultants based in a scruffy or dirty building, employing rude or unhelpful receptionists or telephonists, and making life difficult for clients would probably not prosper. An airline may lose customers through poor check-in facilities, dirty planes or sub-standard cabin services. A bank may lose private or commercial customers because staff fail to handle requests efficiently, letters are poorly composed or typed, the process of opening an account, obtaining an overdraft, or withdrawing money is too complex.

Today most banks, retailers, airlines and other service organisations realise that attention must be paid to People, Processes and the Physical evidence, as well as to the basic four Ps. Staff are being trained so that they can be more helpful and efficient. Forms and processes are being redesigned to be more user-friendly. Premises are made more welcoming. Progress is being made.

Given the greater realisation for a marketing approach to service areas, a number of factors which make service marketing different can be seen. These are discussed below, but first it is useful to explore further the service area itself. Many physical products, from consumer durables like TV sets or cars, through to industrial equipment such as mainframe computers or power stations, require servicing by the original suppliers or their agents. Equally many services depend on some physical factors in order to operate – check-out tills, cash dispensers, computer terminals, aircraft, waiting areas, and so on. Hence the boundary between product markets and service markets is not clear-cut. Many markets involve some elements of both product and service marketing, and the additional three Ps are becoming more important in nearly all areas.

In many industrial markets, (and a few consumer markets) staff from the producing company may be involved with the buyer or user from the initial development stage through to long-term maintenance. The term 'Boundary Crossing Personnel' (or BCP) is used to cover such people, and effort spent in training them to recognise their vital role in marketing their product and their company has been well repaid.

Some factors which do differentiate service marketing from product marketing deserve mention, and are outlined below.

(a) Perishability
Services cannot normally be stored on any significant scale for future use or sale, leading to needs to meet peak demand as it arises. The effects can clearly be seen in any supermarket, as the flow of customers through the checkouts varies from day to day and hour to hour. Similar fluctuations on different time-scales occur in air transport, electricity generation, hospital, hotel and cinema occupancy, schools and colleges, and so on. This may cause severe problems of matching supply to demand, and of making best use of resources.

(b) Inseparability
Services are generated and consumed at one time, with the supplier and the user being involved together. Often the span of time is short. A customer in a bank or supermarket may only be involved for a few minutes. A flight may last for several hours, or a holiday for several days or weeks, but still the provider and the user are together. Servicing of products may be less continuous, as with cars, but still the machine and the mechanics need to be together for a few hours, even if it is only once a year.

(c) Intangibility

The core element in any service is intangible. Advice from a doctor, a solicitor, a travel agent is intangible, even though it may be written down, and even though following the advice may involve tangible factors such as medicines or buying a house or a holiday. Because of the difficulties of forming opinions in advance of the likely value of the advice, we tend to take note of the surroundings, the appearance, the manner of the people, and so forth.

(d) Variability

The nature of services, the personal elements involved on both sides, and the other factors listed above, combine to cause variability in quality. Producers of mass services, retailers, banks and so forth, will try to minimise costs by segmenting their markets and providing a uniform service to all customers in a segment. Since the service is being provided by staff in many different places and to many individual customers there may be problems of ensuring consistency. This can be helped by the proper design of the service and all the factors associated with it, and by the proper training of staff. Well designed forms, covering all likely situations, clearly set out, will reduce the risk of hesitation or confusion in handling customers. Good training will ensure competent handling of all types of enquiry and all types of customer.

Within many services however there may be a need to vary the offering to meet specific needs of some customers. Airlines and supermarkets provide extra help for mothers with small children or for the disabled. These variations arise within the envelope of the standard service. However there are often opportunities for providing a range of services at different price levels. Airlines offer First and Business or Club classes as well as Tourist. Supermarkets offer a range of brands of a product to cater for different taste or budgets. But the basic service of transport or buying goods is there for all.

At the other end of the scale the services provided by consultants, whether medical, financial, legal, management or whatever, will be geared more closely to individual needs. But the services supplied by any one consultant or company will be within some specialism, and to a prescribed standard.

It follows that the form of the service, the degree of uniformity or variation, the levels of service to be offered, and so forth demand at least as much study, market research and planning as the marketing of more tangible consumer products.

Assignments

At the end of each chapter assignments will be suggested helping you to see the application of the subjects covered to real situations. It is suggested that you should take one or two specific markets as themes running through all your assignments. If you are already in work, then you should look closely at the products or services your organisation is providing, bearing in mind that most marketing theory and concepts can be applied not only to trading companies but also to not-for-profit organisations, such as the NHS or charities.

If you are not yet working then select areas where you have experience as a consumer, or where family or friends can offer insights or information.

For this first chapter you should consider how far the ideas discussed could apply in your chosen field. How far does your chosen organisation appear to be market orientated, as opposed to being sales or product orientated? Does it have a marketing department? If not is this because everyone is involved in marketing, or because no-one is? Is there any research into customers' needs or wants? Who determines prices? Who plans and designs new ventures? What market(s) is the organisation in?

The firm and its markets

The marketing concept discussed in the last chapter emphasises the close, but often changing, relationship between the firm and the markets it seeks to serve. This applies to both the private and public sectors. The nature of the relationship depends on various market (or environmental) factors. Consideration must be given to the market economy, the society comprising the markets, the laws and ethics of society, the competitive situation, the social responsibilities of the business, human resources available, inflation and unemployment. The rates of change occurring in all these affect the volatile nature of the relationship. Further, when economic times are hard, attitudes change often unpredictably. Political factors accentuate the change in these relationships. The effects may range from local changes due perhaps to new buildings or motorway construction to changes taking place on international scales. Developments in the EEC, in Russia and Eastern Europe, and the North American and Latin American Free Trade Areas will all have international effects. The key aspects are discussed in this chapter.

2.1 Business and society

From the Industrial Revolution to the end of the Second World War developments in industry, science, technology, transport and communications all appeared to support each other. They added to the general wealth of the world, or at least of the industralised nations. The net result also appeared to be beneficial to society at large. Even if the increased wealth was unevenly distributed and a minority remained at subsistence level, the majority, to differing degrees in different countries, achieved improving levels of wealth often undreamed of by earlier generations. The optimistic view was held that the intelligent application of human endeavour, knowledge and skills would maintain this growth in wealth and happiness. It seemed that all problems could be overcome. The expectations and quality of life seemed to improve in every decade, helped along by technological and other developments and discoveries. There was no reason why growth, in all its meanings, should not continue indefinitely.

The social developments stemming from the above demanded that growth and innovation should be continued. There was hope, if not belief, that continued progress would eventually eliminate the poverty and squalor that still remained. These views rested on the belief that business could provide a never-ending stream of goods and services. Improving educational standards would create new wealth through the creation of greater knowledge. This would solve economic and social problems and would lead to a better understanding of the human environment. Greater knowledge of human behaviour would extend these benefits to an ever-increasing number of the world's population. Competition would not only help to create this new wealth but would also direct it in the right direction and distribute it in a just pattern.

Since the Second World War this optimism has been somewhat blunted. Economic and technical growth and developments seem to have been more successful in putting man on the moon than in increasing the wealth and well-being of people in less economically developed areas of the world. Claims of 'national interest' have been used to support uneconomic or ailing industries in some areas, to the detriment of otherwise viable activities in others. Purchasing power of some industrial countries or organisations has been used to the detriment of less powerful agricultural societies. Rounds of GATT negotiations (General Agreement on Tariffs and Trade) aimed at reducing inefficiencies in international trade drag on for years as countries fight over details.

On the positive side there is increasing awareness about the effects of pollution, the need for conservation of natural resources and the dangers in the destruction of the environment. Many of these influences have been recognised in the marketing area, with greater emphasis now being placed on socially acceptable marketing objectives and strategies. Hence the increasing emphasis on products which are environmentally friendly, can be recycled, are green, and are produced using fewer natural resources. On the positive side too there is the realisation that big is not necessarily beautiful nor inevitable. Many organisations have been able to challenge the giants in their markets through concentration on 'niches', some eventually becoming leaders in their fields. While economic factors still lie behind marketing decisions, wider groups of influences are being brought into consideration.

(a) Economic systems

Economics may be described, simply, as the social mechanism concerned with the many aspects associated with production and distribution. It is an important area for study since all societies, whether in developed, developing or less developed regions of the world, face a scarcity of important resources (money, skilled labour, raw materials, land, food). There are insufficient resources to satisfy all needs. The resources are finite while wants are infinite. This then is the basic economic problem facing all societies.

The executives in all enterprises have the task of making optimal use of scarce resources to satisfy the maximum number of consumer needs. Marketing is concerned with linking consumers to producers so that the latter can make correct decisions about the goods and services to be produced to satisfy customer needs, or wants. The organisation as a whole has to decide what products or services should be produced, the quantities that should be made available, how they should be provided to maximise profitability and consumer satisfaction and how the output should be channelled to the markets (customers) that desire them.

Economics is also described as a 'social science'. The use of the word 'science' indicates that economists try to identify and measure scientifically the important relationships between the many factors at play in the economic system. These relationships are so complex that their exact nature cannot always be identified, although modern Information Systems and analytical techniques have enabled some progress to be made. Models of the economy of a country can be developed, but for forecasting purposes these still need to be fed with assumptions – and making the correct assumptions is still an inexact process.

Controlled experiments are not always possible as in the physical sciences since economics involves people acting individually or in groups. While human behaviour can be generalised into various categories according to the backgrounds, expectations and status of different groups of people, such behaviour even within a group can vary considerably. The *science* of economics is, in many cases, the *art* of estimating correctly variable behaviour patterns. Further, these patterns have the habit of changing, sometimes for understandable reasons (e.g. inflation or deflation) but often for reasons more associated with changes of personal values or aspirations. The failure of some forecasters to predict the course of events in the UK during the early 1990s was largely due to a failure to appreciate a change in consumers' patterns of saving or spending, known as their 'propensity' to save or spend.

In practice, therefore, economic decisions cannot be free of subjective judgements and cannot depend only on objective appraisal of relevant facts. Often these 'facts' are unknown and their interrelationships still subject to much conjecture and argument. They rely quite often on personal views of intervening factors. An example of the last point is the size the public sector of an economy should be. Another is the degree of government intervention (or interference, depending on personal political outlook) there should be in a nation's business activity. In Britain there have been changes in the balance between the private and the state sectors since the Second World War, with first a swing to nationalisation of many industries and services, and in the 1980s a swing back to the private sector. Other countries seek different levels of balance between the two sectors, from the USA and Japan at one end of the spectrum to the extreme levels of central control reached by communist countries until many of them collapsed around 1990. The problems of the Eastern European countries are now having serious effects on economic conditions in the rest of Europe.

However, economists try to establish as objectively as possible the principles which under given conditions show how an economy should work. From this they try to predict the likely outcomes of specified policies. The inexactitude of the art is indicated, however, by the many instances when the outcomes do not match the predictions too closely. Decision-makers can thus be understood for brushing aside such theories, especially if the predictions are based too much on assumptions rather than accepted facts. They may also place different weights (importance) on the assumptions depending on the type and nature of their businesses and customers.

(i) *Free enterprise (private sector) economies*
This is where economic decisions are taken through the mechanism of the market-place, through the free operation of the forces of supply and demand. Two examples are the United States of America and Japan. Such economies may be more accurately described as 'capitalist' rather than 'free enterprise' when they are dominated by monopolistic organisations.

(ii) *Collectivist (public sector) economies*
Here all business activity is state owned or controlled. Decisions are taken collectively by the central government or its appointed agencies such as state planning committees. These were seen at their fullest extent in Communist countries such as the USSR, China and Cuba. Some developing countries with authoritarian, but not necessarily communist, governments may tend to follow policies of state control because of shortages of resources of all kinds, as well as for reasons of political power.

(iii) *The mixed economy*
This is the system commonly found in many countries. While government involvement may be unavoidable in some key sectors, such as defence, activity is divided between the public and private enterprises. In the UK public protection is provided in most areas by regulation, and some part of the movement towards European economic union is concerned with the unification of standards across the countries in the union. Where services are necessarily provided by the state problems may arise between central bureaucratic control, and the freedom to best meet local conditions. Citizens' charters attack the problem from one direction, while 'opting-out' of hospitals, schools and so forth is aimed at putting more decisions into the hands of local people aware of local needs and opportunities.

The above is a thumbnail sketch of a very big and complex subject. Like all such it is imperfect and subject to argument. Readers wishing to study this subject in greater depth should turn to a companion volume in this series, *Mastering Economics* by J. Harvey (Macmillan, 1989). Chapters 1 and 2 are of particular interest to marketing students.

(b) Business, society and the economy
The meaning of the term 'business enterprise' changes as the character and structure of the economy, its markets and the social expectations of the role of business change. The practical relationship between firms and their markets will then be modified. This fact must be appreciated by executives since changes in corporate plans and operations will be necessary if the sustained success and survival of the company is to be ensured.

Society itself is an economic organisation. Firms play active roles in society by reacting to the opportunities and constraints facing them. Executives controlling successful enterprises see these as being determined by the character of the society in which they operate. Governments also respond to this character by their policies and actions. If they sense that society wants more government involvement in constraining business activity (often claimed to be 'for the common good') they will initiate suitable policies. If they think the majority require more free enterprise they will change their policies, if sometimes reluctantly. If business flags for any reason and this is seen as a threat to national prosperity, governments are compelled to remove or alleviate the obstacles facing the business community. In the past actions taken by one government to protect or promote its own economy may have had adverse effects on other countries. Hence the move to supra-national organisations such as the EEC, North American

Free Trade Area or Latin American Free Trade Area, seeking overall strategies 'for the common good'. How far such developments will generate more healthy business environments remains to be seen.

Executives must formulate their company's policies bearing these points in mind. All have bearing on the correct business strategies that should be applied. They must be aware of the role their business plays in society. This seems obvious in cold print. In practice it is much more difficult to implement because of imperfect knowledge of all these factors. The assumptions that may then be necessary are difficult to perceive accurately.

(c) Social responsibilities of business

In the last decade or so there has been growing awareness that businesses of all sorts have various social responsibilities they cannot ignore. These range from codes of conduct to the ethics of what they do, efficient utilisation of scarce resources, pollution and destruction of the environment and fair trading. While many organisations may continue to ignore these issues, more and more are taking a responsible attitude towards them. In some cases this is in response to direct activities by 'single issue pressure groups', but more generally it is a reflection of broader changes in attitudes and opinions among consumers.

Increasingly there is evidence of effects on policy formulation. Many organisations take their own impact on the environment and on society very seriously, sometimes at considerable cost to themselves, but sometimes because they can see a marketing opportunity. Hence the proliferation of 'green' products, of organically grown foods, of 'ozone friendly' packaging and so forth. In marketing writings the term 'Societal marketing' is becoming more common, reflecting policies which take account of the environmental and social factors as well as the more traditional factors.

There are still problems in deciding where the community's interests lie. How far will consumers accept higher costs and thus higher prices of environmentally friendly processes and products? What should be done about cheaper imports from areas less responsible about the environment, and still using processes causing pollution? Who is to decide between alternatives – say between nuclear power plants which avoid carbon dioxide and other emissions and fossil fuel plants which produce these emissions but avoid potential nuclear dangers? Can the ideas of societal marketing have sufficient impact to overcome the more traditional ideas of profit maximisation, expansion and growth? Will co-operation between governments and producers be enough? Will legislation and its rigid enforcement be needed?

2.2   Business and competition

Executives cannot ignore the competitive situation. They risk running into increasing difficulties and court disaster if they do. Yet many executives tend to pursue their own personal goals and these seldom coincide with profit optimisation. Competition occurs at all operational levels of business and in all functional areas. Two companies manufacturing the same type of product will compete in terms of design or formulation or specification, quality, sales, advertising, delivery, merchandising, packaging and price. However, while price is too often considered the prime competitive weapon, non-price competition can be more important. This is very true for products where quality, appearance and taste are considered important criteria by customers. Note from Figure 1.1 the low rating of price for industrial products where the dominant criteria are usually technical points.

Competition is both *intra-industry* (i.e. between firms in the same industry) and *inter-industry* (between companies in different industries). In present-day conditions, as competition increased nationally and internationally, labour and raw material costs rose steeply and companies diversified into new activities and technologies prompted by major technological advances, inter-industry competition has intensified. As standards of living and consumers' ideas on the quality of life improved so both forms of competition increased.

Competition is not now restricted to similar or near-substitute products. For example exotic holidays in distant lands now compete with other household purchases. The purchase of a better house competes, for a time, with the purchase of household appliances or a new car. Providing the children with a better education, which usually means expensive, private schooling, may compete with all other purchases if it takes all the family's discretionary income. These are just a few examples but they suffice to stress that business survival and profits in a free market or capitalist economy are not guaranteed by an economic system based on the survival of the fittest.

(a) Competition and marketing

To people not in business competition may be just a word. To those in marketing it represents a matter of business life or death. It is a basic life-style of free market economies and has many dimensions (economic, legal, ethical, psychological and political (see Sections 2.9(a) and 6.7). It is more intense in a consumer-based economy than in the planned and controlled environment of the former communist countries. Even here however there could be intense competition among managers to secure the resources needed to run their own empires.

Competition emphasises changing profit opportunities and stresses the need for greater innovation, especially in relation to the differential advantages in a firm's markets. It enhances the primacy of objectives, planning and innovation on a continuous basis so that a firm's offerings to its markets can be adjusted to match the changing competitive situation. It should stimulate the development of new products and services, new applications and markets and technological advances. In these situations promotional activities, personal selling, merchandising, packaging and price are all competitive weapons to be used by any firm.

In thinking of competition, executives often think only of the past and their thinking is often limited to their own experience. Insufficient attention may be paid to developments and trends in the environment, in technology, in materials or in the needs and tastes of potential customers. Hence new models are designed which would have been successful in the markets of the past, but which will not match the conditions which will prevail when they are due to be launched.

Attempting to remain competitive by replacing existing products with new versions will not help an organisation whose products are already obsolete, and this raises a vital problem for management. This is to distinguish between a weakening of a competitive position within a market and a structural change in the market itself. In the first place ground lost to competitors may often be regained simply by appropriate repositioning or refurbishing of the product range. In the second, where vital factors have changed to alter the whole structure of a market, it may merely be throwing good money after bad. Even worse, this action may well foster the mistaken belief that with the redesigned products, 'once things return to normal' sales will return. Remaining competitive within a product field requires vigilance within the market. Remaining in business requires vigilance on a wider basis, watching the behaviour of the market itself.

2.3   Theory of business strategy and policy

Deciding what business strategy and policy to follow involves executives in a detailed study of all the above points. Unfortunately while senior management does this, middle and junior executives are usually preoccupied with their own tiny bit of the operation. They fail to view the activities of their firm as a corporate whole. They tend not to give any thought either to the wider implications for society of what they do. While the development of *corporate planning* (see Chapter 3) has helped to overcome this, it is still not being used as widely as it should be. Further, business strategy and policy formulation is no longer the preserve of economists. Sociologists and social psychologists have positive contributions to make to this work.

(a) Human aspects
It has been fashionable for a long time, and continues to be so today, to believe that the main concern of executives is to balance the divergent interests of the different groups comprising the firm. They seek to balance the competitive claims of shareholders, financiers, customers and employees. Because resources are scarce the solution appears to lie in increasing the size of the firm's business as quickly as possible. They believe that this leads to unity of purpose (to grow and prosper as quickly as possible) and that it is in the self-interest of all groups to assist the board to achieve the objectives of growth and higher profits.

Unfortunately employees frequently behave in ways which indicate they have only qualified acceptance of this simple concept. They resist managerial control, withdraw their labour, disrupt output, indulge in absenteeism, give less than a fair return for their earnings and impose their own protective devices such as demarcations and restrictive practices. The affluent society, rather than healing these conflicts, has heightened them, especially when labour seeks to maintain wage differentials.

It is only in recent years that the importance of human aspects of firms has been realised. Various attempts have been made to lessen conflict, reduce absenteeism and improve labour productivity. The significance of good human relations and better management of human resources is better appreciated even if the early attempts have been frustrated by the intransigence of workers, management and governments.

(b) Conflict

Conflict seems to be an integral feature of business organisations. The search for improved harmony has advanced various theories on human motivation and how these can be used for the general good and that of the firm. They include 'job enrichment', 'job satisfaction' and better 'job design'. In recent years attempts have been made to promote 'industrial democracy' and 'worker participation' without an equally full exploration of their implications.

Participation can mean anything from autonomy on the job for individual workers to joint decision-making on an equal basis by work groups and management. Democracy can range from a vague consensus of opinion to the exercise of countervailing power against the unilateral authority of management. Difficulties arise because all these concepts underestimate the pluralistic nature of industrial organisations.

(c) Labour and manpower policies

It is obvious from the above that labour policies must acknowledge the varying personalities of the different groups of workers. Also redundancies cannot be considered as impersonally as the disposal of unwanted equipment. Unemployment creates social, political and psychological problems which increase the incidence of conflict in firms and society.

Labour policies are also conditioned by the *quality* of the labour available. How well trained and educated are the people? How suitable are they for the tasks in hand? How healthy and industrious are they? What is the mobility of labour? This last question covers both occupational mobility (the ability to move from job to job, e.g. an engineer becomes a college lecturer) and geographical mobility (willingness to move from one area to another). It is therefore not just the question of hiring anyone for a job but engaging the right person with the right skills and appropriate experience. These thoughts apply to all areas of management including marketing and especially the sales force, when labour policy has to be decided.

2.4 Public control

The significant development in Western economies in the latter half of the twentieth century has been the increasing involvement of governments in business activity. Public control, overt and covert, has increased. This is not only in terms of the proportion of GDP devoted to public sector activities but also in the additional responsibilities assumed by governments to regulate and influence businesses and consumers in the private sector. Such involvement extends to regulations and laws controlling working conditions, inter-firm competition, disclosure of corporate information and consumer protection. Executives appear to tolerate these restrictions but do not deny that they are extensive limitations of their activities.

Executives are faced with the need to be prepared to change traditional business policies to match current circumstances. This is akin to Marketing having to change objectives, strategies, policies and operations to match changes in customer needs and wants. They have to identify and adopt new performance criteria and roles for their firm and themselves. They have to consider the appropriateness of their existing and possible new concepts to present and future problems and needs.

2.5   Objectives of the firm

A firm is not an isolated economic unit. It must survive and thrive in the general economic system of the countries in which it operates. Therefore it must take note too of the objectives of government economic policies. In most countries this policy is dictated by the following objectives.

(i)   Improve or at least maintain the standard of living, though hard economic conditions may demand a departure from this for the short term. For example, in trying to reduce inflation some deterioration in the standard of living is unavoidable. As soon as inflation is controlled reversion to this objective should have priority.

(ii)   Maintain a sound balance of payments position, though again in inflationary times this may be difficult to do.

(iii)   Maintain reasonably full employment so that all who wish to work may do so. Again with inflation this may not be possible. Some economists believe that in order to control modern inflation, the ideal of (over-?) full employment may have to be modified.

(iv)   Achieve reasonable price stability. For an exporting country like Britain, too violent and frequent price fluctuations can be destructive to the economic well-being of the nation, especially the balance of payments position. Price increases linked to wage increases can produce 'cost-push' inflation (see Section 2.6).

These objectives permit a government three basic strategies although they tend to use a mixture of two or all of them!

(i)   Follow policies designed to maximise the country's productive capacity.

(ii)   Implement policies that change (increase or decrease) the degree of utilisation of existing capacity – for several reasons – by changing levels of demand and expenditure by industry and the individual consumer.

(iii)   Devaluation.

The problems of balancing objectives and of developing and changing strategies to meet rapidly changing conditions have been all too evident recently, not only in the UK but on a European and world scale. Changes in interest rates, government spending and borrowing, exchange rates and so forth show how different factors may be moving in opposing directions at the same time. Unfortunately the uncertainty generated is not good for business, either within or between countries.

(a) Company objectives

Decisions on corporate objectives and policies must take into account the points mentioned in the preceding sections. The nature of the business and how this is likely to change, or must change to take account of forecasts on the future of the business environment, must also be considered. It will be appreciated that most firms will have a diversity of objectives. While the planning process should strive for compatibility between these objectives, circumstances may place the emphasis on one objective at a given point in time and another objective at another period. Flexibility in decision-making is necessary. There must be willingness to switch priorities as economic and market factors dictate.

The aim should be to limit the number of objectives to those that are important and relevant to the long-term survival and prosperity of the firm. In general terms, these objectives are as follows.

(i)   Survival for as long as possible.
(ii)   Maintenance and increase of profits.
(iii) Improvement of market shares, provided this does not reach the 'point of diminishing return' (see Figure 2.1).
(iv)   Achieve long-term growth and other developments.

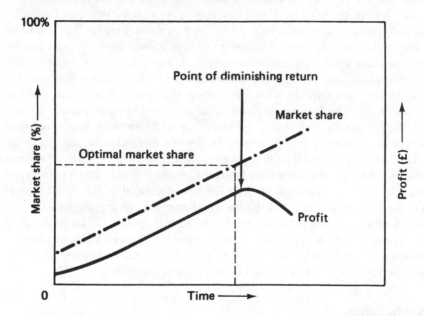

Fig. 2.1   Point of diminishing return and optimal market share

Survival is usually considered the most important, the ultimate objective. It can have different implications. For some companies standing still is not possible for various market and technological reasons. They must grow or die. For others, growth except at moderate rates may be too risky or overstretch their limited resources.

Growth is highly necessary in competitive economies. If a competitor is allowed to grow too big it will have increased its power and may be able to eliminate the static firm. Growth properly planned and controlled leads to stability of profits and sales volume. It can take many forms. It can mean expansion of the geographical market coverage and thus sales volume. Or it can be in improvement in excellence (quality, technical aspects and so on). Growth can also be achieved by company acquisition or merger. The main danger is that growth can be pushed too far and cause the firm's resources to be over-stretched, often to breaking point.

Profitability is important. Without profits to cover contributions to future development and satisfy the needs of workers, shareholders and financiers, a company will die. Increasing profitability is thus a major aim of any business policy. Without it the other objectives cannot be achieved. Consideration must also be given to the *margin* by which revenue must exceed costs to allow for corporate taxes, current interest rates on borrowed capital and so on.

Increasing market shares and sales volume are also necessary. These ensure survival, growth and profitability. However, increased market shares and sales do not necessarily increase profitability. If the effort is pushed too far, each incremental increase in profit or sales may mean that the corresponding incremental increase in costs becomes too high, or more than the increase in profit. This is the 'point of diminishing return'. Total profit can be eroded. Further, if a firm has a large market share it becomes vulnerable to competition, especially from smaller companies. The latter with their lower overheads and other costs have little difficulty in nibbling away the odd percentage point or two from the big firm's market share. The big company can soon find that the total result of all these 'nibbles' can be critical loss of market share, thus business and competitiveness. This is most likely when the smaller firm can identify a 'niche' or small market segment where it can profitably offer a product or service more closely tailored to the needs of those customers than the major company can supply. Finally, if a given market is not expected to offer long-term profitability it may be better to carry out a phased withdrawal from that market. The assets released by this could then be put to the development of a new market with better long-term prospects.

It will be appreciated that determination of business policy cannot be divorced from the many variables in the business environment. Nor can Marketing leave it to experts elsewhere in the firm. Marketing executives have an important role to play here. How they do it is detailed in the chapters that follow.

2.6 Inflation

Inflation may be defined as a sustained upward pressure on prices resulting in a general rise in the level of prices and thus in the cost of living. The rate of inflation is the percentage increase in the general price level for a given period (year, month etc.). It is usual to differentiate between demand-pull (or 'demand') inflation and cost push ('cost') inflation.

Demand inflation is the upward pressure on prices that results when aggregate demand is in excess of aggregate supply of goods and services and supply is inelastic. Suppliers in a free economy will then charge the highest prices they can for goods in short supply. This type of inflation can be caused by a consumption boom with a decreased willingness to save by consumers and a corresponding fall in investment demand. Or it can be due to increased government expenditure without restriction of consumer demand or by an export boom without curtailment of home demand.

Cost inflation occurs when pressure on prices is caused by increases in costs without corresponding growth in output. This can be due to lack of productive resources, (capital, plant and labour), excessive wage increases or unwillingness of the productive workers to work harder or longer hours. Increased wages is not the major culprit, however. Rises in prices of imported raw materials (as at the end of the 1970s with oil), increased cost of capital due to high interest rates and excessive drive for higher profits are other substantial contributory factors.

In fact in all cases of inflation both demand and cost elements are present. Like unemployment, inflation tends to feed on itself. If the community expects inflation to continue they will make allowances for it in their economic bargains. Individuals will strive for higher earnings. Firms will seek higher profit margins. This can be aggravated by incautious government actions ranging from increases in direct and indirect taxes to maintenance of artificially high exchange rates to bolster the currency. Hyperinflation is said to exist when inflation rates reach very high figures.

The bad effects of inflation are insidious. Even when the rate is low at only 2 or 3 per cent it leads to a redistribution of wealth and income with no regard to social justice. High rates disrupt economic life leading to more bankruptcies and higher unemployment. If it gets out of hand (hyperinflation) there can be a breakdown of the whole economic system and it can even undermine a country's political system.

Marketing executives have a very real interest in what happens to inflation. The end result for them can be intensified competition as firms fight to maintain their sales volume from a smaller cake of total demand. Inflation can also put up their operating costs until it becomes doubtful if the firm can continue with some or all of their operations. Customers' willingness to buy can decline rapidly. Marketing executives, with their colleagues in other departments, must study the whole complex problem and deduce the implications for their firm's business.

2.7 Unemployment

Unemployment may arise from general variations in economic activity, as recession follows periods of expansion, or it can arise from structural changes in demand. In the early 1990s the UK, and most of Europe, were suffering from both effects at the same time. Firstly there was recession with reductions in demand from consumers who had borrowed heavily towards the end of the 1980s, and who were cutting back on purchases to service and repay the debts they had incurred. Secondly there were marked structural changes as the demand for armaments was reduced following the ending of the Cold War. Both effects simultaneously raised unemployment levels in the UK to over 10 per cent of the work force.

Whatever the cause, unemployment leading to a drop in income of the unemployed will accentuate the drop in demand. More will become unemployed and so income, expenditure (or demand) and output will fall further. The thing tends to snowball. Whatever form it takes, unemployment wastes resources and, if it is sustained over the long term, leads to considerable human misery and suffering. Again, in their planning and actions, Marketing cannot ignore the subject of unemployment and its effects on the business environment.

2.8   Demand

Demand refers to the willingness *and ability* of consumers to buy products and services. Marketing executives are responsible for forecasting the demand for their goods and services under varying market and economic conditions. As stated, the multiple variables involved make this a difficult task. The size and nature of demand is affected by general economic conditions including inflation and unemployment, promotional activities and personal selling, product range and development, and technological and other environmental factors. Demand does not have an unalterable character and individual firms are not faced by an inflexible situation.

Indeed for most countries, the demand picture for many products and services had become very complex and potentially unstable. While most of the items above are generally controllable by the firm, there are others which are not. These include government and political actions, regulations and controls by foreign countries and major technological breakthroughs. There are also various situations that affect demand. These are as shown below.

(i) *Buyer rejection*
This occurs when buyers do not want the product regardless of the marketing strategy followed. Products and services must therefore be designed to match customer wants more precisely.

(ii) *Buyer dynamics*
This refers to the time when customers' needs and preferences change requiring the seller to modify or change its product range. This situation does offer new opportunities and sellers must perceive the shifts in customer wants.

(iii) *Buyer autonomy*
Especially in free market economies customers have reasonable freedom of choice. They are not so easy to manipulate as some executives believe, witness the many new products that have failed. Unless a product or service offers an advantage (real, or as imagined by customers) the potential buyer will not be sold. Again, a good understanding of product–market situations and customer attitudes is required.

(iv) *Buyer motives*

Many motives are at play and those relevant to industrial products have been listed in Figure 1.1. Those for consumer goods will be discussed later (Chapters 4 and 6). Identifying the motives that are paramount in any sales situation is not easy. Product-market strategy and policy must lead to the appropriate positioning of a product or service in the chosen market segment(s) if it is to be successful.

(v) *Buyers and demand*

Whilst most buyers, especially the individual consumer, enjoy purchasing a good, particularly one that is new to them, demand does not exist automatically. It is not 'something' that is there and sellers just go along and take their share. In modern competitive economies, demand has to be created, potential customers have to be made aware that they have an unsatisfied need. Once it has been created, demand has to be nurtured so that there is reasonable, profitable life for the products or services involved. The correct use of marketing techniques is necessary. Marketing executives are concerned to create and develop demand that is of real importance to potential customers, i.e. not pure 'gimmicks'. Other executives must also appreciate what Marketing is doing in this respect.

(a) Elastic and inelastic demand

The basic principles discussed here generally apply to all products and services. Perhaps only the specially produced, one-off product appears not to, but in fact the underlying principles still apply. However, demand for some products and services is more flexible than that for others. This fact must be taken into account in the pricing process (Chapter 7). Two basic situations are, however, possible, that of *inelastic* and *elastic demand*.

Demand is said to be *inelastic* when it is comparatively insensitive to price changes. For example, if the price of a product is reduced by *x* per cent and demand does not change, or increases by less than *x* per cent, then it is said to be inelastic. Similarly if prices are raised by *y* per cent and demand remains the same or falls by less than *y* per cent, it is also said to be inelastic. On the other hand, if demand changes substantially as prices change then the demand is said to be *elastic*. In academic terms, these two descriptions refer to the incremental change in demand that takes place with proportionate incremental changes in price. Little or no change in the former indicates an inelastic market while big changes show that demand is elastic. There are several reasons why these conditions arise and these are covered in the later chapters.

In most practical situations both elements are usually present. Total demand for any product group can be elastic over some part of the price range and inelastic over others. There are many reasons ranging from the simple fact that some products may be more essential to customer needs than others, some may be used widely and thus required in bulk so that price reductions prompt buyers to take advantage and build reasonable stocks of them, to those where technological or other factors are of greater importance than price. Also there are products and services (e.g. electricity and water, petroleum products etc.) which customers cannot do without, so they just have to buy them even when prices rise. In these cases total usage over a year may be static anyway, so purchases may not increase even if prices are reduced. Storage may not be possible, or prove expensive, as with electricity and water, or it may be dangerous, as with petroleum products which are potential fire and explosion hazards. So in studying the nature of demand, executives should think in terms of *relevant portions* of total demand and not just total demand itself.

There is a further aspect of elasticity which is important at the level of the organisation or the brand. While demand for a product may be inelastic, or only slightly elastic, demand for a brand may be highly elastic. Hence changes in the price of petrol may have little effect on demand, and demand is largely inelastic. However for the individual brand demand may be highly elastic if its price is moved out of line with the general market level. In such markets, when prices move all brands tend to move together. Within segmented markets overall elasticity of demand may differ between segments. Hence demand for basic foods may be largely inelastic while demand for convenience foods may be highly elastic. In each market or segment, analysis of the basic patterns is needed as a guide to pricing decisions.

2.9   The economic environment and marketing

It is worth summarising why marketing executives must understand the effect the economic environment and its many variables have on a business operating in it. First, marketing executives are responsible for the successful conduct of their activities within the business system of the firm and its markets. This involves analyses and decisions that establish the strategy, policies and goals (or targets) for their operations. This affects also the development of a suitable organisation and its associated methods of operation, the attainment of the necessary resources to allow them to create successful marketing offerings (products and services) and effective control of the entire activity.

Second, in the analyses and identification of product-market opportunities they must take account of the interactions between the business system (firm) and the economic and other variables at play. These considerations must therefore also cover technological, social, political and legal factors. These economic aspects cannot be ignored, especially as the economic cycle is itself dynamic and can move from a state of recession or slump, through that of depression, recovery and boom. The economic variables change as the economy moves through this cycle. How they change will affect customers' willingness to buy products and services and thus the marketing operations needed to sustain business success.

(a) Market factors, demand, market mix and shares and product-market strategy

To end this chapter a few words on the relationships between market factors, total demand, market mix, market shares and product–market strategy would be useful.

The *economic* aspects of importance to marketing considerations include the general state of the economy and relevant industries, income levels (especially

personal disposable incomes – or pdi – for consumer markets), the income structure of the different customer categories (e.g. age groups etc.) and the turnover of
firms. As these improve or grow, so normally should total demand for products
and services. Indeed, once essential expenditures have been met, the increased
balance of pdi remaining may be spent on greater purchases of non-essentials and
luxuries (e.g. expensive holidays, the second car, other durables etc.) or may be
saved or invested. In the last two cases, demand for banking, investment and
insurance services would be increased. When they decline (e.g. price increases
exceed growth in earnings and pdi is squeezed; unemployment increased and so
on) total demand will fall as everyone is forced to buy less of all products and
services. Or, as the earnings of one customer group rise so should their pdi and
their ability or willingness to spend more on essentials and non-essentials. However psychological factors also come into play, and in times of rising incomes
consumers tend to borrow and spend in anticipation of continuing prosperity,
thus aiding growth. In times of recession, with actual or feared unemployment,
consumers will cut back on non-essential spending thus further reducing market
activity and prolonging the recession.

The *legal* aspect covers all the laws and regulations that control people's lives
and the actions of business organisations. These can inhibit or enhance demand
for products and services. They also can restrict or assist business activities, the
products that can be sold, how they may be and so on, thus contributing to
demand growth or decline. For example in 1992 in Britain, regulations were
enacted that made it an offence to drive a vehicle whose tyres had a depth of
thead of less than 1.6 millimetres. These controls produced a boom in sales
almost immediately and have had some effect on the volume of replacement
sales. On the other hand, banning the use of cyclamate artificial sweeteners in
edible products and drinks has seen demand for these almost wiped out. Demand
for products using alternatives (e.g. Sorbitol) has increased.

On the *social* side attitudes of both consumers and businesses towards the
quality of life, standards of living and to wider issues, such as the environment,
can change. Wider car ownership plus hypermarkets have changed shopping
habits for many. Home ownership has expanded at the expense of renting, fostering the growth of DiY. Changes in outlook, often instigated by pressure groups,
have caused furs to disappear from clothing, and are causing lead to disappear
from petrol. On a *socio-economic* level most homes now possess the main
labour-saving devices as well as TVs and other electronic devices, so that the
growth experienced in these sectors while ownership was increasing has now
fallen away. After the initial stocking-up of homes demand in these markets has
declined, and now depends mainly on new home formation and the replacement
of failed items.

Technological developments, including new raw materials or new ways of
using established ones, also influence the level of demand for the end-products. If
a new machine tool is produced that provides more efficient, better production or
quality at no extra cost, or allows costs to be reduced leading to lower prices
without loss of profit, the better quality and lower prices could increase sales and
demand for the product. New ideas such as xerography can alter the entire pattern

of needs and purchases by all who have reprographic requirements. The computer has led to many developments that stimulated demand not only for its own products (hardware and software) but for many other items also. The development of reinforced glass fibre material has pushed out many traditional ones (e.g. wood and mild steel) for many products. Because products in the new material were so much better, had low maintenance needs, better eye appeal perhaps and initially were cheaper and lighter, so easier to handle, demand for them grew. However as the price of the new material rose rapidly in recent years, demand has fallen off. The effects of inflation have taken their toll here too.

These are just a few examples to show how changes in market factors affect the level and nature of demand. The nature and intensity of *competition* also has effect. If competition is fierce, total demand may not be affected but the fight for market shares will be more intense. While competition is limited, the firms already in the business can strive for substantial market shares, and in the process could stimulate interest from customers and so the demand for the products involved. When total demand increases, firms may decide not to increase their market shares, being content with the extra volume the increase in total demand should bring them. If they have spare capacity, they could decide to step up their marketing to gain a larger market share. If the economy is depressed and total demand falls they may choose between fighting harder to maintain their share or accepting a smaller market share, thus contracting their business. In the latter case they may feel that they could defend their business more effectively against intensifying competition.

All this will require firms to rethink their decisions on their market mix (which markets should they exploit or leave?) and the products or services they will offer to them. Thus they will have to review their product-market strategies and policies. The existing ones may no longer be tenable or advisable. Review of their pricing policies would also be needed. These are just some of the inter-actions at play between the five subjects that form the heading of this subsection. There are others, but these are sufficient to show readers that in marketing a thorough examination of the implications of all major changes and their effects on interrelated aspects is vital for success and dynamic management.

For readers wishing to study the economic aspects in greater depth, recourse to Jack Harvey's book, *Mastering Economics* (Macmillan, 1989), is recommended. For marketing students particular attention is drawn to Chapters 1 to 6.

2.10   The future

In the past many companies could work on five-year rolling forecasts, with the details filled in for one or two years ahead, and the rest in outline. Today with many changes taking place, from the establishment of common markets to changes in local industries, and from the severe cut-backs in some industries such as coal or steel to the rapid growth (and in some cases early decline) in new industries and processes, forecasting in any detail more than a few months ahead is hazardous.

Some signs are clear for those who can read them. First, increasing use of technology in industry is leading to more demand for highly skilled people and to reduced demand for those who are less skilled. Overall there will be less demand for labour in industry, more time outside work (whether as leisure for those employed or through unemployment) and more demand for services. However overall demand for labour, whether in production or in service industries, will fall. The ability of any government to provide jobs by specific spending on infrastructure or more general attempts to stimulate the economy will therefore be limited.

Second, international competition will increase in intensity. The revolution in global transportation and the fact that the new technologies will allow, say, Asian labour to assemble and export high technology products, will increase competition in developed countries. The need for Western economies to export more will increase pressures for protectionism in trade. All these factors will provide new challenges to marketing and management. They must seek higher *added value*, rather than increased volume, by optimising price and reducing costs and go for specialised world markets. They must seek out micro-economic opportunities and there may be many of them in future years.

Assignments

Describe the markets in which your chosen organisation is involved. Are they industrial or consumer markets, for goods or services? Are they mass markets or niche markets? Are the markets segmented?

How competitive are the markets? Is competition based on price, design, reliability, or what? Who are the main competitors?

What (do you think) are the marketing objectives of the organisation?

Marketing's role in management

Sustained success in management demands continuous co-operation, of a high order, between all the departments of a firm, acknowledging the inter- and intra-dependence of all managerial decisions and action. No one management discipline is omnipotent. All are co-equals though sometimes, according to the nature and needs of a business, one activity might have to be the leader. The discontinuities of modern business environment have forced many executives to acknowledge these realities. It has also been necessary to abandon the previous concept that each discipline of management should be contained – or cocooned? – in its own watertight compartment, into which others trespass at their peril. It is appreciated now that every discipline must be totally involved in, and committed to, corporate activity.

Figure 3.1 outlines the principal disciplines and departments in manufacturing enterprises. For service industries, some departments are not required (for example, possibly engineering and research and development departments) and others (for example, manufacturing or production divisions) may appear in a different guise. In the latter case, if the firm were a tour operator, providing packaged tours of various kinds, the people responsible for making advance selection and booking of accommodation, transportation and other services, would be the equivalent of manufacturing industry's production department. They 'produce' the 'goods' (packaged holidays) offered to the consumer.

It will be useful to outline briefly in this chapter where Marketing fits into, or co-operates with, all the other activities of the firm as outlined in Figure 3.1. It is not an isolated activity that can stand aloof from the other departments of the firm.

Some responsibilities are shared between all departments. For example the image of an organisation, the way it is thought about by people, is a responsibility shared by all. While the main burden of developing and maintaining a positive image for an organisation and its products may fall to the marketing department, this must be based on satisfactory design, production, delivery and so forth. While the image can easily be damaged by direct factors such as poor quality product or slack delivery, it can also be harmed by factors not directly relating to products or customers – such as dirty vehicles, scruffy buildings, accidental pollution of the surroundings and so on. Every organisation has an image, by design or default, and all activities and all departments contribute towards it for better or worse.

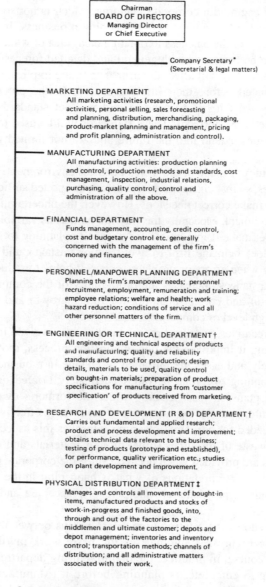

```
                    ┌─────────────────┐
                    │    Chairman     │
                    │ BOARD OF DIRECTORS │
                    │ Managing Director │
                    │ or Chief Executive │
                    └─────────────────┘
                             │
                             │── Company Secretary*
                             │   (Secretarial & legal matters)
                             │
      ──── MARKETING DEPARTMENT
              All marketing activities (research, promotional
              activities, personal selling, sales forecasting
              and planning, distribution, merchandising, packaging,
              product-market planning and management, pricing
              and profit planning, administration and control).

      ──── MANUFACTURING DEPARTMENT
              All manufacturing activities: production planning
              and control, production methods and standards, cost
              management, inspection, industrial relations,
              purchasing, quality control, control and
              administration of all the above.

      ──── FINANCIAL DEPARTMENT
              Funds management, accounting, credit control,
              cost and budgetary control etc. generally
              concerned with the management of the firm's
              money and finances.

      ──── PERSONNEL/MANPOWER PLANNING DEPARTMENT
              Planning the firm's manpower needs; personnel
              recruitment, employment, remuneration and training;
              employee relations; welfare and health; work
              hazard reduction; conditions of service and all
              other personnel matters of the firm.

      ──── ENGINEERING OR TECHNICAL DEPARTMENT†
              All engineering and technical aspects of products
              and manufacturing; quality and reliability
              standards and control for production; design
              details, materials to be used, quality control
              on bought-in materials; preparation of product
              specifications for manufacturing from 'customer
              specification' of products received from marketing.

      ──── RESEARCH AND DEVELOPMENT (R & D) DEPARTMENT†
              Carries out fundamental and applied research;
              product and process development and improvement;
              obtains technical data relevant to the business;
              testing of products (prototype and established),
              for performance, quality verification etc.; studies
              on plant development and improvement.

      ──── PHYSICAL DISTRIBUTION DEPARTMENT‡
              Manages and controls all movement of bought-in
              items, manufactured products and stocks of
              work-in-progress and finished goods, into,
              through and out of the factories to the
              middlemen and ultimate customer; depots and
              depot management; inventories and inventory
              control; transportation methods; channels of
              distribution; and all administrative matters
              associated with their work.
```

* Sometimes one of the top executives in
  Financial Department; deals with Company
  Secretarial and Legal matters.

† If not a department of MANUFACTURING

‡ If not a department of MARKETING

Fig. 3.1   The major functional divisions of management

3.1   Marketing and corporate planning

It is logical to begin with corporate planning, which is not so much a management technique but a complete way of running a business. It involves detailed study of all facets of the business to obtain a clear idea of what is being achieved so that this can be compared with general and detailed forecasts of future developments and how they will affect the firm. The future implications of every decision are evaluated before their implementation. In the process the company defines clearly what it has to achieve and will set standards of performance against specified time horizons. These standards will be used to measure results. The time horizons extend into the future and are not limited just to the annual budget period.

Continual study is made of the firm's business environment, current and possible future ones, so that changes and trends can be spotted sufficiently in advance for the firm to make correct decisions. However, the uncertainties existing in any business environment, especially the way the numerous variables involved interact and change, make it impossible for corporate planning to *guarantee* results. However, it does help the firm to avoid major mistakes and to take remedial action quickly when errors or problems occur. It helps to reduce the risks taken and, in most instances, increases the profitability of the company. It aids in the more purposeful and correct planning for future growth and development and maintains a high level of competitiveness.

Since all executives, at some time or another, are involved in the work of corporate planning, it improves the communication process, motivates executives more effectively and eases the initiation of change in a business system. In the process of planning everyone becomes adequately briefed on everyone else's activities and plans, at least as they affect the former's own responsibilities. Being better informed, the executive team works more effectively. Also the control system needed for corporate planning improves this aspect of management, reducing the waste of resources (time, money, materials and effort) and makes sure resources are provided when needed. Since the corporate planning model is based on realistic interpretations of what is happening in the business environment, the resultant proposals are more readily accepted and implemented by executives.

Figure 3.2 shows the relative time relationships between management disciplines while Figure 3.3 summarises the basic work involved in corporate planning. Of course, in practice, the manufacturing department does not wait for Marketing to complete its planning before it (Manufacturing) begins its work and so on. The planning goes on concurrently with executives of all departments in regular consultation with each other. For example, product managers will have discussions with production and quality controllers and appropriate financial colleagues to arrive at consensus decisions. However, Manufacturing, Finance and Personnel cannot finalise their own ideas until Marketing has nominated what it proposes to do regarding the product-market mix and associated activities in the period covered by the corporate plan under formulation.

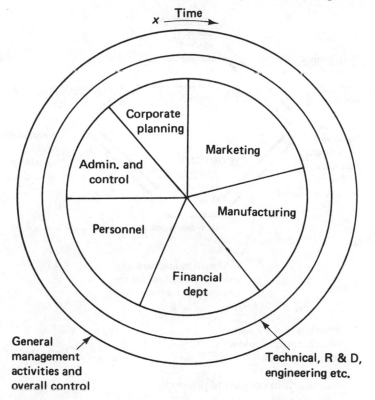

Fig. 3.2   **Relative time relationship during the planning period**

Further, if *X* represents the time when the new plan must start, so the corporate planning work must start some few months before *X*. This explains the position of Corporate Planning in Figure 3.2. This figure illustrates only the time relativity between the different management disciplines and stresses that every facet is involved at some time or other. Engineering, R and D, technical and general management activities are shown as concentric rings around the major disciplines to emphasise that the latters' decisions and operations are also affected by the former (four) activities.

(a) The corporate plan and planner

Initially, company planning was concerned with problems associated with the determination of the facilities and financial resources that a firm needed. Now, with intensive competition and especially in tough economic conditions, attention must also be given to the markets which should be served and the products offered to them. This means that consideration must also be give to associated areas of marketing such as prices, product quality, market and consumer profiles, distribution, merchandising, packaging and promotions; in fact the entire marketing operation. Thus Marketing is very much involved in the planning and decision-making work of the corporate plan. All the other disciplines of the firm

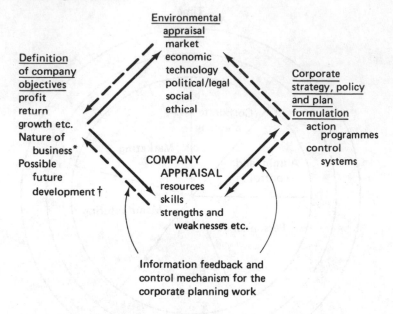

* 'What business are we in?'
† 'What business should we
  be in for the future?'

Fig. 3.3   Basic work in corporate planning

are similarly involved in this exercise. The corporate plan is made up of different elements based on contributions from all the department and may be represented by the simple illustration shown in Figure 3.4. The important thing to remember is that these contributions and decisions are reached through mutual inter-departmental agreement.

The company executive responsible for corporate planning decisions is the managing director or chief executive. This responsibility cannot be abrogated. However, it is usual for the considerable work involved to be delegated to another senior member of the organisation, the *corporate planner*, who is respons-ible for the work to the chief executive. The planner is not a line executive in that he or she does not make decisions, give orders to lay down or determine objec-tives. The executive studies the wider economic environment, paying particular attention to changes or anticipated developments in areas of importance to the firm. These include ones relevant to the company's present and future interest. The latter will include consideration of possible long-term developments and growth planned for the firm. From the results of this work the corporate planner can advise, indicate and recommend courses of action to the line executives, from the different operating divisions or departments, forming the planning group. This allows the executives to arrive at more correct decisions than other-wise. However, the decisions and the implementation of the agreed plans remain the responsibility of the line executives or functional managers.

MARKETING ELEMENT	MANUFACTURING ELEMENT
FINANCIAL ELEMENT	PERSONNEL/MANPOWER ELEMENT
ADMINISTRATION ELEMENT	CONTROL METHODS ETC.
Board requirements	Corporate Planners' forecasts

Note: The layout should not be read to mean that any one 'element' is more important than the others. The 'Board requirements' and 'Corporate Planners' forecasts' are shown since the first set the initial, preliminary targets for the planning work. The second makes vital contributions to the forecastng work on which the decisions are based (see also text, Section 3.1(b)).

Fig. 3.4   Simple illustration of the elements of a corporate plan

The corporate planner is responsible for indicating when plans are not being properly implemented or are going off course. This advice will usually be supported by further recommendations on the corrective action needed. Quite often the planner will also act as an arbitrator when executives from different departments are in some conflict and cannot reach agreement on decisions or actions. Besides having the appropriate training and experience, the planner must be an imaginative, creative person able to grasp quickly the meaning of business trends and understand how all changes in the business environment are likely to affect the firm's business. He or she must obviously possess tact and have rapport with the chief executive and colleagues from all the other departments of the company, for without these qualities success in the corporate planning work will not be easily achieved.

(b) The corporate planning process
Figure 3.5 outlines this process and Figure 3.6 summarises Marketing's involvement. The work usually begins with the board reviewing the firm's progress, the future needs of the company, its shareholders and other interested groups and what is believed to be happening in the business environment. From this they will be able to indicate the provisional objectives and targets for the forthcoming planning period. Line executives in the meantime have been conducting a detailed analysis of their departments' activities, the successes and failures. Guided by the board's indicated requirements, line departments, collectively and individually, study the situation to determine what each of them can do in the future, given the *status quo*. They will also indicate what could be done if more resources are made available.

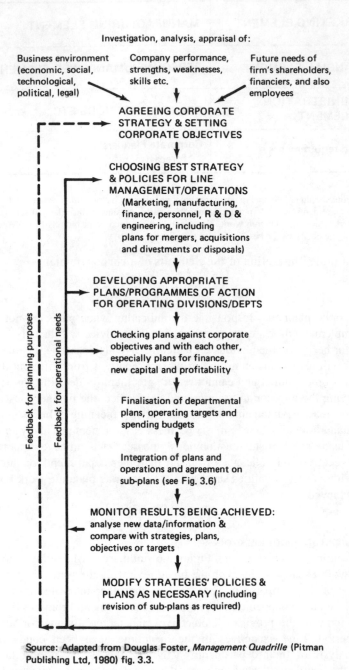

Investigation, analysis, appraisal of:

Business environment   Company performance,   Future needs of
(economic, social,   strengths, weaknesses,   firm's shareholders,
technological,   skills etc.   financiers, and also
political, legal)   employees

AGREEING CORPORATE
STRATEGY & SETTING
CORPORATE OBJECTIVES

CHOOSING BEST STRATEGY
& POLICIES FOR LINE
MANAGEMENT/OPERATIONS
(Marketing, manufacturing,
finance, personnel, R & D &
engineering, including
plans for mergers, acquisitions
and divestments or disposals)

DEVELOPING APPROPRIATE
PLANS/PROGRAMMES OF ACTION
FOR OPERATING DIVISIONS/DEPTS

Checking plans against corporate
objectives and with each other,
especially plans for finance,
new capital and profitability

Finalisation of departmental
plans, operating targets and
spending budgets

Integration of plans and
operations and agreement on
sub-plans (see Fig. 3.6)

MONITOR RESULTS BEING ACHIEVED:
analyse new data/information &
compare with strategies, plans,
objectives or targets

MODIFY STRATEGIES' POLICIES &
PLANS AS NECESSARY (including
revision of sub-plans as required)

Feedback for planning purposes

Feedback for operational needs

Source: Adapted from Douglas Foster, *Management Quadrille* (Pitman
Publishing Ltd, 1980) fig. 3.3.

Fig. 3.5   The corporate planning process

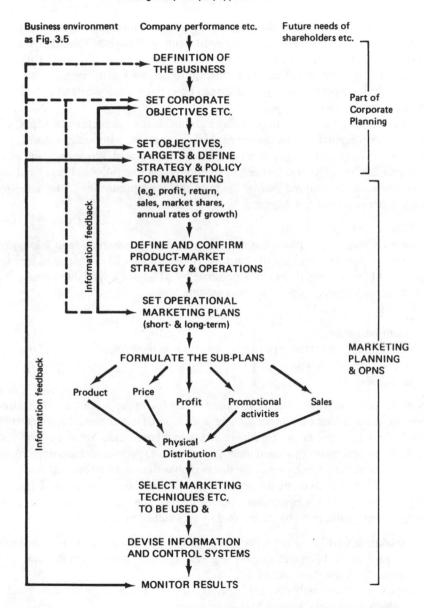

Investigation, analysis, appraisal of:

Business environment as Fig. 3.5

Company performance etc.

Future needs of shareholders etc.

DEFINITION OF THE BUSINESS

SET CORPORATE OBJECTIVES ETC.

Part of Corporate Planning

SET OBJECTIVES, TARGETS & DEFINE STRATEGY & POLICY FOR MARKETING (e.g. profit, return, sales, market shares, annual rates of growth)

DEFINE AND CONFIRM PRODUCT-MARKET STRATEGY & OPERATIONS

SET OPERATIONAL MARKETING PLANS (short- & long-term)

FORMULATE THE SUB-PLANS

Product   Price   Profit   Promotional activities   Sales

Physical Distribution

SELECT MARKETING TECHNIQUES ETC. TO BE USED &

DEVISE INFORMATION AND CONTROL SYSTEMS

MONITOR RESULTS

Information feedback

Information feedback

MARKETING PLANNING & OPNS

Source: Adapted from Douglas Foster, *Planning for Products and Markets* (Longman, 1972).

Fig. 3.6   The marketing process and corporate planning

The aim is to identify the range of strategies, policies and objectives that would be possible. In practice the board indications, the forecasts and suggestions of the corporate planner and the initial forecasts of the line departments agreed between themselves are not likely to be an exact match. This is illustrated simply in Figure 3.7. Thus there has to be some compromise. Either the board will have to lower its sights, or line departments will have to raise theirs or the corporate planner will have to rethink the long-term forecasts. In general all three groups will have to do some 'horse-trading' to narrow the differences that exist so that ultimately they can arrive at agreed objectives, strategies and policies for the company.

Then line management can go ahead and finalise their departmental plans, still maintaining regular communications and agreement with each other's programmes. When all has been finally agreed and integrated, the operational plans can be launched. The results need to be monitored carefully and regulated and any amendments required can be made at the appropriate time. The stage-by-stage process is shown in Figure 3.5.

(i) *Objectives*

Corporate planning requires the definition of both *quantitative* and *qualitative* objectives. The first provide the hard targets executives have agreed to aim for, while the latter remind them of the rationale by which they agreed to operate. For example, quantitative objectives must include:

> profit
> return on assets
> sales volume and turnover   } targets specified for every year of the plan
> annual rates of growth
> for the above

Note that profit and return are given priority over sales. In the past managements have been too preoccupied with 'making a sale' and assumed that acceptable profits would result. This need not be so, especially in modern conditions. Yet if the firm concentrates on optimising profit and return, sales volume, prices and thus sales turnover resulting from the achievement of the first two objectives must be correct.

Qualitative objectives are descriptive and can range over many possibilities. It depends on the firm's operations and resources. The following are just a few examples of qualitative objectives used by this author in past years:

> the company will only enter operations to which it can make positive and vital contributions to ensure success (e.g. management skills, technical and other essential know-how etc.);
> the company will only consider a project it can enter at the right scale* and in which it can obtain the right market share;*
> the company will achieve growth* also by acquiring companies whose failure can be traced to lack of managerial skills which the first company has in suitable amounts;
> the company must be capable and willing to mount the right scale* of marketing and other activities to achieve the right level* of performance.

(a) initially

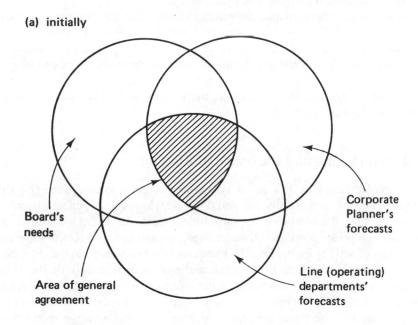

Board's needs

Corporate Planner's forecasts

Area of general agreement

Line (operating) departments' forecasts

(b) compromise position

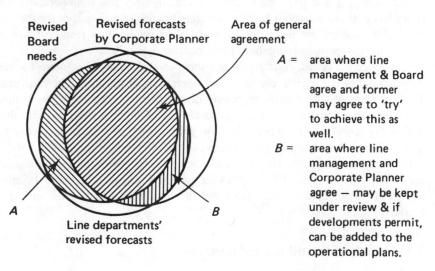

Revised Board needs

Revised forecasts by Corporate Planner

Area of general agreement

A

B

Line departments' revised forecasts

A = area where line management & Board agree and former may agree to 'try' to achieve this as well.

B = area where line management and Corporate Planner agree — may be kept under review & if developments permit, can be added to the operational plans.

Fig. 3.7 Corporate planning: conflict of views

The items marked * had of course to be quantified and be in accord with the corporate quantitative targets which had been set.

In deciding on the corporate objectives to be adopted, the firm must obviously take account of the company's strengths and weaknesses. It should seek to exploit its strengths to the full and avoid getting too involved in its weak areas. Obviously attempts should also be made to rectify the weaknesses and increase the company's strengths, especially when diversification into totally new business ventures is planned. To conclude, the various 'audits' needed are listed in summary form in Figure 3.8.

3.2   Marketing and the board of directors

The detailed activities of a board vary from company to company. The legal requirements of each country are also different. However, in general, boards of directors have the following responsibilities. First, the board establishes and approves corporate plans and all major strategies and policies, selecting the general areas of activity for the firm. This responsibility is invested in the chief executive, who is answerable to the chairman and other members of the board. Decisions taken here are dependent on the information provided by the operating divisions, including Marketing. This should happen not only in the annual planning period but also throughout the year when the reports on the results being obtained are issued.

Second, the board approves and maintains overall control of annual operating plans and budgets. Third, it approves and controls capital expenditure and the use of all assets entrusted to the firm by its investors. Fourth, it selects the most senior managers and fixes their terms of employment and remuneration. The board has collective responsibility to its shareholders and investors for the efficient utilisation of the assets in its care. It discharges this responsibility by making the company as profitable and successful as possible.

In practice the board, collectively and individually, must show interest in and commitment to the objectives, plans and operations of the firm. The individual directors charged with specific responsibilities must involve themselves in them and advise and assist their executives to the full without interfering with their day-to-day actions, except when things are going wrong or seem to be outside the responsibility and capability of executives. The directors must seek a balance between control and supervision of and interest in the work, providing encouragement to the firm's employees. Thus there must be close and continual contact and co-operation between the board and the operating departments, including Marketing.

3.3   Marketing and manufacturing

If a firm is to be successful and is to remain so for as long as possible, close, continual co-operation and communication is needed between Marketing and Manufacturing departments. The degree of success will depend on the degree of co-

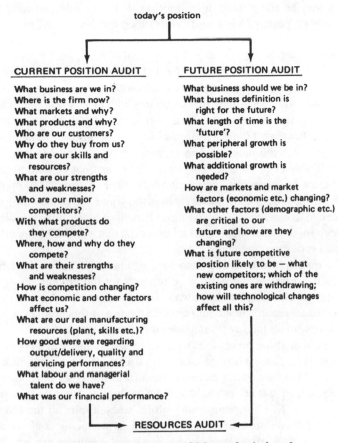

today's position

CURRENT POSITION AUDIT

What business are we in?
Where is the firm now?
What markets and why?
What products and why?
Who are our customers?
Why do they buy from us?
What are our skills and
   resources?
What are our strengths
   and weaknesses?
Who are our major
   competitors?
With what products do
   they compete?
Where, how and why do they
   compete?
What are their strengths
   and weaknesses?
How is competition changing?
What economic and other factors
   affect us?
What are our real manufacturing
   resources (plant, skills etc.)?
How good were we regarding
   output/delivery, quality and
   servicing performances?
What labour and managerial
   talent do we have?
What was our financial performance?

FUTURE POSITION AUDIT

What business should we be in?
What business definition is
   right for the future?
What length of time is the
   'future'?
What peripheral growth is
   possible?
What additional growth is
   needed?
How are markets and market
   factors (economic etc.) changing?
What other factors (demographic etc.)
   are critical to our
   future and how are they
   changing?
What is future competitive
   position likely to be — what
   new competitors; which of the
   existing ones are withdrawing;
   how will technological changes
   affect all this?

RESOURCES AUDIT

What are our financial resources? Adequate for the future?
What additional finance will be needed for the future?
What will be its cost? Thus what return has to be achieved?
How will our present plant & skills meet future needs?
What additional plant and skills of all kinds will be needed?
How can these be developed? How much must be obtained
   from outside the firm? What is the likely cost?
How good has the firm been in utilising all resources?
What improvements in utilisation are needed/or possible?
What manpower training and management development needed?
How good have been the firm's cost and credit control systems?
What improvements needed?
What cost reduction programmes would be advisable?
What is our present labour/management needs? What increase
   will be necessary for the future?

FUTURE CORPORATE ACTIVITIES & OBJECTIVES

Fig. 3.8   'Audits' for planning purposes

operation achieved. At its worst, if the executive are not really talking to each other (they may be going through the motions but in practice refusing to understand the other's point of view and needs) then the firm could be heading for disaster. Unfortunately the seeds of conflict lie in their opposing responsibilities to the firm.

Manufacturing must keep its plant loaded to satisfactory levels to meet cost and productivity targets. Marketing is responsible for earning the company's profit, obtaining and maintaining market shares with products of the right quality. This also means that the volume of sales should be right for the attainment of these targets. However, Manufacturing, in its overenthusiasm to keep unit costs low, could produce too much of one or more products and Marketing may be unable to sell this extra volume. The market may just not be able to absorb the extra quantities for economic, competitive or other reasons. Marketing is then stuck with unsold stocks and considerable effort (time and money too) may have to be expended to clear them. Any nominal benefit of lower unit production costs will be lost in the additional marketing costs that would be incurred. This problem still arises too frequently.

Then the quality standards expected by customers can lead to further conflict with the cost constraints and profit requirements for the product. For example a manufacturer of electric blankets, aware of the hesitancy, if not fear of many users of the latent hazards that could arise in the use of this product, will want to offer blankets with all the latest safety devices. It will also have to achieve a certain percentage mark-up on ex-works prices to satisfy the firm's profit or return targets. Manufacturing, having certain unit cost targets to meet, will argue that fitting all these devices would increase manufacturing costs beyond acceptable limits. The resultant sale prices could then be too high to compete with prices ruling in the market. This last point could inhibit sales despite all the safety attractions. The need for all these devices might hold up production and increase costs further because of the extra development work that would be needed. The availability of the product would also be delayed and could let competitors establish a strong position in the market. Some compromise is needed, and this cannot be reached unless there is total co-operation and communication between the two departments involved.

Thus it will be appreciated that co-operation is needed on the product range to be produced (quantities, timing of the output), inventory levels and the modification, rationalisation and new product development that will be required over specified periods of time. Then there are the questions of quality standards, performance, reliability and the maintenance or service that customers expect. Further, there are the subjects of unit sale prices and costs that have to be agreed. Thus marketing executives, especially marketing, sales, physical distribution and product managers, will have to maintain close liaison with production planners and controllers, quality controllers, R and D experts, technical and engineering executives. As the material content of the products can also be important, purchasing executives will be involved in discussions from time to time. Marketing executives responsible for the promotional activities will also be included in appropriate discussions. Without all this, the manufacturing programme cannot be matched to the marketing operations and successful marketing cannot be assured.

In some markets it is important to design up to a standard e.g. aero engines, and prices will be secondary. In other markets, e.g. fast moving consumer goods (fmcgs), it is vital to design down to a price if the product is to succeed. In either case if after all the efforts by all parties, costs do not permit the company to offer its products at prices the market will pay, the product must be rethought or abandoned.

Recently further areas needing close co-operation between marketing and manufacturing have become apparent. Many consumers have become concerned with the processes used to develop and provide what they buy. On one hand they are demanding cosmetics which have not involved testing on animals, eggs from free-range hens and packaging made from recycled waste and which is itself bio-degradable. On the other they are demanding products which do not contain additives, do not involve chemicals such as CFCs which are detrimental to the environment, or timber from rain forests and so forth. Hence the production processes themselves become a matter for discussion between manufacturing and marketing if products are to gain consumer acceptance.

A sound basis for co-operation will be established if both departments appreciate the other's tasks, objectives and problems and work closely to find mutually acceptable solutions. Compromise on both sides is necessary. For example, Marketing should not demand unreasonable delivery times, nor the achievement of specifications and quality outside the possibilities imposed by plant limitations and cost constraints. Nor should Manufacturing insist on plant locations and sizes which may suit its needs but impose unreasonable problems on Marketing. Strictly, plants or factories should be located close to major markets. However, if the road and other transportation facilities pose problems, for example the road network may be inadequate so that traffic bottlenecks occur, other locations may prove to be better. On the other hand if production requires easy access to large sources of power supply (e.g. large amounts of cheap electricity are needed for aluminium production, so ideally access to hydroelectricity is required) the factories may have to be some distance from the major markets.

Then the size of the plants must be considered by both departments. If a very large factory is needed to keep unit costs down but this creates delivery and sales problems which Marketing cannot resolve except at high costs, further compromise is needed. Further, the technical excellence or standards need to be agreed. There is little point in Manufacturing producing superb products which nevertheless are too expensive for customers or are not required. Applying the engineering standards of the aircraft industry to kitchen appliances may produce products with great reliability and extended lives. But the cost of building in that reliability may price the goods out of the market, and the extended life may be unused if the product has become obsolete. Increasing emphasis on Total Quality Management should ensure that products are designed from the start which can be produced efficiently and will meet market needs at acceptable costs and prices, but the whole process depends on close and continuing co-operation from all departments.

3.4   Marketing and the financial department

Financial executives have interests also in the points discussed in the preceding section and so close co-operation between Finance, Marketing and Manufacturing departments is needed. The executives in the Finance Department (or whatever name used) are accountable for the efficient management of the company's money. This responsibility covers not just money but all investments in plant, equipment, buildings and other facilities. For example, financial executives will wish to verify that the decisions reached on costs and prices will in fact lead to the attainment of the firm's plans regarding profits. They will play a strong role in profit planning (see Chapter 5) and in monitoring the results achieved by Marketing.

Then there are the questions of cost control, cost reduction programmes (to improve funds utilisation), credit control, the settlement of the company's invoices and payment of its bills. While Marketing should not be used as the firm's debt collectors, it must ensure that the company does not become heavily involved in too many bad debts, or the risk of them. Marketing's involvement here must not be such as to endanger its long-term prospects. Similarly, while the credit control system is a necessary safeguard and Marketing must see that it adheres to it, credit controls should not be so severe as to inhibit business, especially future prospects. For example, it might be academically correct to limit credit given to small, relevantly insignificant customers. Yet small customers can develop, sometimes unexpectedly and quickly, into major customers. Often they will not forget the tight constraints placed on them and may then favour competitors who were more liberal with their credit in earlier years. Nor should financial control systems be imposed on the firm so rigidly that they hinder the operations and development of Marketing and Manufacturing, especially long-term possibilities and the growth of the company as a whole.

(a) Budgetary control

The nature of control in business is often misunderstood. It is frequently associated with restrictions or restraints. Yet control systems are intended to guide the business activities of a firm to correct judgement, decisions and actions in the attainment of agreed corporate and associated departmental objectives and targets. In every area involving expense of any kind, control of expenditure is needed if things are not to get out of hand. However, these budgetary controls should be realistic and be arrived at through discussions between Finance, Marketing and other operating departments. The systems agreed should also indicate when remedial action is required, when operations are veering off course.

Properly done, budgetary control systems, linked with close co-operation between all departments, will allow the Finance Department to achieve its three basic aims without unduly restricting the activities of colleagues. These aims may be summarised as:

(i)   keep the business solvent with sufficient liquidity for the firm's needs and purpose;

(ii)   provide the firm with the finance necessary to sustain operations and achieve the developments that have been planned;

(iii) provide the means whereby the firm can satisfy, at optimum levels, the economic and other needs of customers and all those who work for or are associated with the company.

These aims cannot be achieved if there is little or no co-operation between Finance, Marketing, Manufacturing and the other departments. In fact financial strategy formulation plays a vital role in the shaping of the firm's other strategies and policies. Financial executives cannot arrive at a sound financial strategy in isolation from other colleagues.

(b) Project appraisal

Capital investment decisions are amongst the most difficult to make for any firm. When capital is scarce and has been made expensive by rising interest rates and thus costs, the difficulties are increased. Further, investments may often be difficult to alter when once made and are sometimes irreversible. For example a hotel group's decision to invest in a new hotel requires considerable capital, and once built the hotel is not easy to change to other usage. Sound investment decisions and project appraisal can only be achieved through detailed consideration by all operating departments, especially Marketing.

The process is very similar to that followed for all planning decisions. All relevant facts have to be gathered and studied in depth. The consequences of the alternative decisions possible must also be considered both for the short and long term. The market situation, including all the market and other factors that might affect it, must be studied. The commercial risks involved cannot be ignored also. So here too close co-operation is needed between all the firm's departments, especially those that will be affected by the final decision. The four major departments, Marketing, Manufacturing, Finance and Personnel, will therefore contribute to this task of project appraisal.

3.5 Marketing and the personnel department

All firms are social organisations comprised of individuals striving, hopefully, to help the company realise its plans and achieve agreed targets. The prosperity of a firm depends on the efforts of the human beings it employs. Without the right amounts of shop-floor and managerial personnel, with the requisite skills and capabilities, a firm cannot hope to perform satisfactorily, especially over the long term. Personnel executives in Britain were, for far too long, subjected to too low a status in a firm. They have now achieved their rightful place in the management process, as the experts on all aspects of personnel matters including manpower planning for the future. Colleagues in the other departments cannot ignore them with impunity when decisions on personnel matters have to be made. Marketing, particularly dependent on getting the right personalities in jobs requiring persuasive abilities (i.e. sales, distribution, promotions and marketing research) have special need for their help. A high degree of co-operation between Marketing and Personnel is necessary.

The work of this department may be summarised briefly as follows:

(i)   *Employment*: selection, recruitment, remuneration and terms of employment of shop-floor and managerial labour (though senior executives are the responsibility of the board - see Section 3.2).
(ii)   *Training and education*: training and development of all employees to keep them abreast of developments in their specialisms and to prepare them for promotion; selection of colleges and courses for the general education and development of key employees; etc.
(iii) *Labour relations*: including joint negotiations with trade unions and management; labour utilisation and improvement of this; job evaluations; wage rates; etc.
(iv)   *Health and safety*: the health and safety of the employees; reduction of hazards involved in the firms activities and associated social aspects (social club, canteen, nursery centres, etc.).
(v)   *Research*: to ensure that personnel activities are in accord with advancing knowledge on selection, training, remuneration and manpower planning.

In carrying out its responsibilities, Personnel implements the agreed personnel policies of the firm and makes recommendations when these should be changed. It also operates as the company's experts in the behavioural sciences, interpreting the behaviour of individuals and groups within the organisation. The department advises colleagues on the implications of such behaviour for the achievement of departmental and company goals. Thus again, close and regular consultation with colleagues from other departments, including Marketing, is essential for more effective management.

3.6   Communications

Given the need for extensive co-operation between all departments, it is worth considering briefly the subject of communications within a firm. Good communication systems are vital if co-operation is to be successful. This is considered to be particularly vital when Personnel are devising job descriptions and specifications for other departments. Misunderstanding here can lead to mistakes in recruitment with very unfortunate results for the employees recruited and the firm as a whole.

Too often a firm's failure can be traced to bad communications and the resultant misunderstandings. Effective communications is not a propaganda exercise but the art of correctly informing and persuading others. It is not a flood of directives from seniors to juniors that inundate, irritate and frustrate the recipients. It should be a multi-channel flow of ideas between all levels of the enterprise, as necessary. Also executives should not only talk or write; they should be prepared to read and listen to the other's point view. Listening to the other fellow, rather than just pretending to listen, is essential to good, effective communications.

The communications system must also be selective. Information sent to an executive should be relevant to that executive's task and responsibilities. At some time or other, in an imperfect world, this can mean that someone will not get the information needed. The answer is not to create a complex system but to build an atmosphere of co-operation that allows the executive to retrieve quickly the missing piece of information.

The other basic ground rules for good communications can be summarised as follows. First, the purpose of the communication should be clear and the message itself should possess clarity and not be open to misunderstanding. Next, the background of the recipient should be appreciated so that the form of the message is correct. People, according to their education, experience and training, use words differently. Key words should therefore be used in the context the recipient will use. Checking the proposed message with a colleague, especially one with a similar background to the recipient, can help to avoid misinterpretations. Finally, a follow-up to check that the communication has been understood correctly and the right action has been taken helps to overcome communication problems.

(a) Barriers to communication

The nature of the human animal must also be remembered. Each one can be egotistical, self-centred and selfish, interested only in its own well-being and progress. There may be also an inflated opinion of its own abilities and powers. No one is entirely free of these traits. Thus from time to time the executive can be secretive or uncommunicative. These failings may also be due to lack of intelligence, simple ignorance of the subject discussed, overwork or some other character defect. All these have to be taken into account.

People's individual nature, character and behaviour patterns vary widely. A few will receive a message as it was intended. Some, probably a greater number, will resist or resent the import of the communication, resulting in total misunderstanding. This may be due to some remote but deep-seated prejudice. Then there are others who because of some deep prejudice just will not accept any message however it is put. Further, the size of the firm can increase the distortion factor. The greater the number of layers of supervision or management, or its geographical or physical spread, the longer will be the lines of communication. This will increase the possibilities for misunderstanding. The inter-staff relationships are also more complex and, given the greater time lag involved, communication problems can increase. Finally, the difference in corporate and social status will also determine the variance between points of view on the subject being communicated.

(b) Resistance to change

Communication problems can increase when a firm plans any change in either its organisation and methods or in its business strategies because some executives will resist such change to varying degrees. This is regardless of the essentiality of the need to make changes. This resistance to anything new is a natural phenomenon of the human being. All are guilty of it at some time or another. Humans cling desperately to the known or familiar and are apprehensive of anything new.

In business, change can have three effects. The first is the behavioural aspect of change in that it causes employees to change their method of work in some way. Second is what is called the social effect. The established relationships between individuals alter as their method of work changes. Finally, there is the psychological effect; the reactions of each individual to the relevance of the changes in work, personal prospects and the assumed needs of the company. How bad the third effect is depends on the scale of the other two effects.

Resistance to change may not be due so much to the change itself being opposed but rather the way the change is brought about and what the individuals imagine the real effects will be, especially for themselves. The change may be just a signal for resistance which, in the absence of a common cause, may have been smouldering just below the surface for some time. Therefore executives have to anticipate resistance to any change and estimate its possibility intensity. They must try to avoid the building up of dissatisfaction on other fronts which may well up when any change, even those irrelevant to the cause of the dissatisfaction, is introduced.

The factors affecting an individual's reaction to change are usually as shown below. They have complex interactions with each other. As listed they are not necessarily in the right order for everyone.

(i)   the extent of feelings of insecurity;
(ii)   the extent of trust in the management, unions and work groups;
(iii) the manner in which the change is introduced and implemented;
(iv)   the predisposed feelings about change of any kind;
(v)   the view of immediate historical events relevant to the change and some-
       times, those not relevant;
(vi)   specific apprehensions (or expectations) about each particular change;
(vii) the prevailing cultural beliefs and norms which might be in conflict with
       the change and which may, in part, be a result of background, education,
       upbringing and experience.

Resistance to change may be reduced or overcome if the following principles are kept in mind.

(i)   change is more acceptable to people who have participated in planning for
       it rather than to those who have had it imposed on them;
(ii)   change is more acceptable when it is not seen as a threat but rather as an
       opportunity for greater endeavour and advancement;
(iii) change is more acceptable to those who are not affected by it than those who
       are; the latter will attempt to defend the system apparently under attack;
(iv)   change is acceptable to those who are new on the job;
(v)   change is more acceptable when an organisation has been trained to accept
       change as a normal development and a continuing necessity in present-day
       circumstances;
(vi)   finally, changes are more readily accepted after partial changes have been
       successfully implemented, i.e. change should be planned to take place in
       steps which are easily understood and accepted by those involved.

In other words, change is accepted when it is understood and when the executives involved have played a part in planning and implementing it.

All this must also be taken into account when planning a sound, effective communication system.

3.7   Future management

Management procedures and methods are dynamic and subject to change. Methods applicable in the middle of this century have long disappeared, and other will have evolved by the beginning of the next. The development of computers and telephone networks linking them throughout the world is leading to more people doing at least some of their work at home rather than travelling to an office. People such as representatives or long-distance truck drivers, used to working away from a base, can now be kept more closely in touch through lap-top computers and modems, or through mobile phones. Data capture, through such means as 'electronic point of sale' or EPOS equipment, can now provide up-to-the-minute information on rates of sale or stock positions. Central computers fed with this data can compare stocks and projections of demand and initiate orders from warehouses or suppliers. Beyond that automation has taken much of the drudgery out of many jobs, raising the status of the remaining operators, and providing cleaner and more comfortable conditions of work. However it is worth remembering that the dire warning of the 1960s of massive decline in the demand for labour as a result of these trends has not materialised. There has been some structural unemployment as some jobs have become obsolete, but most unemployment still seems to be cyclical, linked to slumps in demand rather than changes in technology. In many areas it is management which has been most affected, and the traditional pyramids of layers of managers have been much reduced. Flatter management structures are now more common, with fewer levels and far more information leading to more rapid decision-making processes.

Assignments

Do you think your chosen organisation is market led or production led? Is it producing what it can sell, or selling what it can make? Are the products or services keeping up with market requirements?

How far do you think concern for the consumer features in the organisation's thinking? Does there seem to be any link between marketing and corporate planning? Is anyone marketing marketing – or does it need marketing?

Does your organisation appear to welcome or to resist change?

4 Marketing information

The considerable amount of data and information that flows from marketing research (see Table 1.1) allows executives to identify product–market opportunities. It leads also to a better understanding of the marketing processes that are used and permits more efficient and effective control of the marketing operations. The work involved provides the basis for strategy and policy planning and formulation and for decision-making purposes. The 'flow' itself should be two-way between the firm and its markets or customers. Otherwise the many questions that have to be answered in the planning process cannot be dealt with satisfactorily. The key questions were indicated under 'Marketing Research' in Table 1.1.

However, it is worth repeating that what actually takes place in a market is conditioned by many factors or variables, internal and external to the firm, which are notoriously unstable in themselves and their inter-relationships with one another. This is particularly so where human behaviour aspects, responses to product or service offerings and marketing activities, are concerned. Thus while this data and information flow helps to reduce uncertainty and risk, it cannot be precise in all details.

Since they are used indiscriminately, it may help the reader to define what should be meant when the words 'data', 'information' and 'intelligence' are used in this context. In its most correct sense, 'data' comprise statistical facts presented in some specific format.

'Information' is descriptive and explains the rationale of what is happening and gives direction to, or indicates the purpose of, the associated data. Without it, the marketing problem that has to be solved cannot be fully understood and the associated data may be of little value. Thus 'data' is said to be 'passive' while 'information' is 'active' in that it allows correct decisions and actions to be taken. The collection, interpretation or analysis and utilisation of data and information provide a firm with the marketing 'intelligence' service it needs.

Marketing research itself can be defined as 'the systematic and objective search for and analysis of (data and) information relevant to the identification and solution of any problem in the field of marketing'. Note the use of the word 'systematic', which stresses the need for careful planning of the research in all its stages. This requires a clear and concise statement of the objective of the exercise, the techniques to be used, the information that is required and the analytical techniques that will be employed. The word 'objective' stresses the need for impartiality, that is, seeking the facts without colouring due to already held views and opinions. Many practitioners hold that research intended to prove a prior opinion may be wasteful, though there will be occasions when research may be used to test whether a belief, long held, is true or imaginary.

4.1 Marketing intelligence systems

A marketing intelligence system is concerned with the analysis and interpretation of data and information, not mere data collection. It is concerned with problem prevention as well as problem-solving tasks. It must indicate what changes in present circumstances mean for the future and how a firm may influence its product–market destiny. It should induce innovative and risk-acceptance possibilities. Through anticipation of future possibilities, it guides present actions which in turn shape the firm's future. It is concerned not only with the immediate or short-term aspects but also with intermediate and long-term possibilities.

The ideal marketing intelligence system has thus to perform four inter-related functions. First, it should pinpoint marketing problems. Second, it should collect all available data and information relevant to these problems. Third, through the analysis of the intelligence, it should determine what changes may be necessary to overcome the anticipated problems. Fourth, it must suggest ways in which these changes can be implemented. However, it is unreasonable to assume that any system can obtain all the information it needs. Time and budgetary limitations are the main constraints but some information or data may just not be available. Nor does everyone have perfect analytical ability. The real significance of some intelligence may be overlooked or misinterpreted.

These disadvantages are ever-present and arrangements should be made that allow the system to react quickly when such 'errors' are discovered. The system should also be designed to keep out the irrelevant intelligence even though this may not be easily perceived. It should act as the nerve centre of the firm, providing information and intelligence for each level of management as quickly as is relevant to executives' needs and their ability to use the information effectively. By continually monitoring a firm's markets and its own progress, the system can indicate when operations are deviating from plans and recommend corrective action. For example, if increased competition is making the company miss its sales, profit and return on assets targets, the system should indicate how competition is proving more effective and thus the alterations the firm should make to its own activities.

4.2 Types of marketing information and intelligence

Marketing information and intelligence have to suggest possible answers to a number of questions. Some important ones are listed in Table 4.1 for easy reference. In trying to cover such a wide spectrum of study, it helps to recognise the five natures or sources of information and intelligence. These are described briefly below.

(a) Internal information
This is obtained from all the firm's own records of its activities, past results and forecasts. Every department has a useful contribution to make here. Given a good reporting system, information is easily available on sales, sales costs and profits; production capacity, volumes; inventories; distribution and delivery; pricing;

Table 4.1   **Key questions to be resolved by marketing information**

Markets

What is the total market potential?
How is this changing? What factors causing change?
How is the market segmented?
What segments are we in? Should we be in?
What market shares are possible?
Who are the competitors? How, where, why, when do they compete?
What can be done to counter this competition?
What distribution should be used? What channels?
What inventory levels are needed? Where and when?

Products

What products do customers want?
Are there any unsatisfied needs?
How do our products compare with competitors re quality, performance, reliability,
    maintenance etc.?
How relevant is our product mix for the future?
What changes in the product mix are indicated? When?
How are technological, economic and other market factors affecting this?
How relevant are our after-sales services of all kinds?
What changes in services are indicated?
How do our costs and prices compare with competitors?
Is there price elasticity or price sensitivity?
How should we alter our costs and prices?

Other

How effective are our marketing operations?
In particular, how effective are the promotional and personal selling activities?
How effective and accurate are the marketing research and intelligence systems?
What modifications are indicated for the future?
How effective are our reporting and control systems?
What changes are necessary for future developments?
etc., etc.

In reality these questions should be answered for all markets, home and overseas!

promotional expenditure; cash flows and other financial matters (e.g. cost control exercises, credit control); manpower and personnel matters including labour availability, turnover and utilisation. Often internal records provide the best and only sources of such vital data. With the general availability of computers there should be no barrier to the effective use of this information. It provides not only the historical base information for forecasting but is useful in achieving more effective control of ongoing operations. For example airlines are able to discover what the seat availability is for specific flights at any time. Manufacturers can get instant status reports on sales to date, prices operating, inventory positions, current market shares and even estimates on the profit being earned. Banks can get instant printouts on the status of deposits and withdrawals at each branch, the amount and type of loans made and so on.

(b) External information
This is collected from a wide variety of sources, and can range from hard facts to rumours. It allows a company to analyse and assess the competition it is facing, and changes in the technological and economic conditions affecting its business situation. Social, environmental, legal and political information is increasingly important as wider issues may affect the firm. Any of this information may show where there are either opportunities or threats in a market. Because of the wide range of data potentially available it is useful to have some formal structure within which to collect and analyse information. One format, known as PEST analysis, covers Political, Economic, Social and Technological factors, and is particularly valuable when considering entering an export market. Some of the main factors under the four headings are these:

Political   – stability
                  complexion
                  attitudes to business
                  constraints on investment/funding
Economic   – state of the nation
                  GDP/GNP gross and per head
                  cost structure, taxation, grants etc
                  infrastructure
Social   – life styles
                  demographics
                  religion/ethics
                  pressure groups
Technology – research and development
                  developments in materials or processes
                  energy resources
                  skills of labour force
                  environmental impact

An alternative format has been provided by the five forces suggested by Michael E. Porter. These forces acting on an organisation are due to:

the power of competitors,
the power of buyers in the market,
the power of suppliers to the organisation,
the threats posed by potential entrants
the threats posed by substitute products.

The overriding factor is that there is so much external information which might be collected that some discipline must be established on what is to be held, for how long, in what form, and so forth if an efficient system is to be developed. Then regular audits should be conducted to ensure that the system evolves with the needs of the organisation, and that deadwood is cut out to make room for new growth.

(c) Position intelligence

This indicates the firm's current position in its industry and is evolved from (a) and (b) above. Opinions can be formulated about the effectiveness of the selling activity, advertising, marketing costs, the relative profitability of product lines and estimated return on assets.

(d) Projective intelligence

A company can use the three sources listed above to develop forecasts of sales and revenues. These help first at the planning stage, by evaluating the probable effects of alternative plans. They help afterwards by providing a base for judging progress.

(e) Decision intelligence

Records the firm's decisions on present and future strategies, policies, plans and control methods. It establishes the pattern for future marketing commitments and records the rationale for the decisions taken. Thus at any future date executives can refer back to this intelligence to remind themselves how and why these decisions were taken. Then it forms the springboard for further future planning and decisions.

4.3   Types of data

Data (and information) is also sub-classified into two groups.

(a) Primary data

This is generated by original research designed to answer specific questions. It covers facts which are not known and have not previously been published. For example an hotel group may wish to know the nationalities of its guests and the purpose of their stay (business, holiday, other personal reasons). Or a manufacturer may wish to establish if there is any pending change in customers' requirements (e.g. in the formulation of the products bought, its quality or life, price and so on). For firms using marketing research regularly, the primary data from one study may become the secondary data for another.

The research for primary data should be tailored to the needs of the firm commissioning the study. Thus it has the advantage of *specificity*, being tailored to situations currently confronting the firm. Another advantage is that of *practicality* in that this data deals with real situations, to a greater or lesser degree. The disadvantage is that its collection is often costly in time and money. It may take some time to construct the frame-work of the research as well as to carry it out and this time may not be available, especially if the research is badly timed (left too late for example). Then the firm may not have made sufficient allowance in the budget for all the work to be done. Hence the need for careful forward planning of marketing research.

Observational methods can also be used when studies of customer responses, customer movements and sales techniques are required. They should give a more objective picture of behaviour than reliance on respondents' accounts of how they behave, thus reducing response bias. However, this assumes that researchers

Personal interviews are still a major form of data collection, whether at home for consumer products, at work for industrial research, or elsewhere. Pictures or other 'prompts' can be used, as here, to help communication with the respondents.

are accurate and diligent observers and that the act of observing does not alter the behaviour of those being observed. Further, the method reveals little about respondents' state of mind or their buying motives. Thus motivational research may be needed (see Section 4.4(b)).

Most methods of data collection can be used in either of two situations. We can observe or measure events, attitudes, and so forth either within the normal environment, or in an *experimental situation*. When measuring in the normal environment we simply collect the data we need while taking care not to influence the results in any way. Thus we may measure sales of goods, whether people remember our advertising, or customers' opinions about a product, while being careful not to expose our contacts to any special factors.

In an experimental situation we not only measure, but we *change* the conditions in some way. We may change the content or the weight of advertising, alter prices, modify a product or introduce a new one, to find out how people react to the change. This normally means that at least two sets of measurements are needed, one taken before the change and one or more afterwards, so that effects can be assessed.

For some purposes we take a series of measurements, such as monthly sales, or awareness of a brand name among potential customers, in order to track our progress. The results may show trends or changes which may be correlated with events such as price changes or bursts of advertising. However such correlations need careful interpretation and will not normally provide conclusive proof that a cause-and-effect relationship exists. Many other – perhaps hidden – factors may also be at work, such as seasonality. If a true relationship is suspected, then we may be able to design an experiment to test specifically whether it is real or not.

The experimental method is generally more powerful as a means of testing cause-and-effect relationships than simple tracking of measures through time. The scale of an experiment can range from a simple test of, say, the acceptance of a new pack for an existing product, through to a complete experimental launch of a new product in a limited test market area.

(b) Secondary data

Secondary data is information that is already available from official statistics and other government publications, research organisations, university and major banking reports, competitors' and customers' publications, trade associations and the firm's own records (see Section 4.2(a)). A firm's primary data from a previous study can become the secondary data for a future research programme. The stock of secondary data available has increased over the years but, like experts' views, is only as good as the compilers. Further, the method of compilation varies from country to country. This applies particularly to official statistics so it is advisable to leave their interpretation to executives experienced in deciphering national statistics, usually nationals of the countries concerned. Care is also needed to note that the extent and value of official statistics vary from nation to nation. For example the United States of America, through its Department of Commerce and the libraries of its embassies, can provide comprehensive information if the enquirer's needs are clearly defined in the former's terms. In many developing countries, understandably, official statistics may be unavailable or valueless. Again, the researcher should check the veracity of the sources used.

Secondary data has the advantage over primary data that it is less costly to obtain. It is cheaper to visit a library, embassy or government department to study relevant documents than to mount a full-scale field research. Executives tend, therefore, to consider what published data is available before they design the research project. Care is needed, however, to ensure that cost saving does not overrule the need for objectivity nor forget the objective of the research. Over-emphasis on keeping costs low can inject bias into the results if the research is not as detailed or selective as is dictated by the problem being investigated. In addition, secondary data is anyway easier to obtain, in most cases, than primary data and some information may only be obtainable from secondary sources.

Besides the danger of injecting *cost-bias*, mentioned above, there is the disadvantage that much secondary data is of *limited applicability*. Rarely does this data fit the firm's exact intelligence requirements. By its nature also, it is *obsolescent* if not *obsolete*. Once gathered, data and information have short relevance since market and other factors are in states of continuous change. This is particularly true in times of great innovation or economic recession. Customers' incomes, attitudes, circumstances and requirements are not static but alter in various ways. Incomes and profit increase and decrease. Technical requirements are overtaken by technological change. Permitted activities are altered by political, legal and social changes. There is also the question of *limited credibility* in that doubts may exist about the validity of this data. There is thus need to consider many points before placing too much reliance on secondary data. For example, studies of an industry's expenditure on promotional activities would not be homogeneous if the number and nature (size etc.) of the firms studied varied in every study or if, for example, the definition of promotional costs was also changed frequently.

(c) Sources of information

The range of sources available varies from country to country, and for different industries. Some of the more general sources are listed in Table 4.2.

Table 4.2 **Some major sources of data and information**

Customers	current; potential; in present markets and ones to be developed in short and long term.
Distributors	including agents, franchisees where used, i.e. all in the firm's distribution network (present and potential future), at home and overseas.
Competitors	home and overseas; from the latter will come greater co-operation and could lead to licensing, with mutual benefits.
Research organisation	in firm's own industry and those of current and potential customers; especially 'experts' in subject under study.
Trade associations	in firm's own industry and those of current and potential customers; especially 'experts' in subject under study.
Government departments	including quasi-governmental bodies (e.g. various commodities marketing boards, British Standards Institution, British Tourist Authority, Monopolies and Mergers Commission); embassies (libraries and commercial attaches at home and abroad); State (nationalised) industries boards.
Publications	trade, government, corporations and major banks, company reports; specialist magazines; newspapers; technical and scientific papers.
Official statistics	
Others	e.g. directories, stock exchange reports, universities, professional and learned societies, chambers of commerce, international bodies (e.g. United Nations, International Labour Office); registers such as Kompass.
The firm	all internal departments and divisions.

The UK is fairly well served with statistics from government and other sources. Researchers in every company should be aware of the summary publications such as *The Monthly Digest of Statistics* and the *Annual Abstract of Statistics*. There are also more specific government publications such as the *Business Monitor*s relating to particular industries or service sectors. The *Family Expenditure Survey* and the *National Food Survey* are examples of government reports showing how consumers spend their money. In many industries trade associations collect data from individual members and collate it in ways which provide useful industry trends and comparisons, but without revealing details about individual companies.

(d) Value of information
While the value of any piece of information will vary from company to company and the situation to be resolved, the value of information, in general terms, depends also on the following:

> the degree of uncertainty prevailing about the possible outcomes of the alternative courses of action open to the firm;
> the size of any losses which could result from a wrong decision, in turnover, profit, or whatever, using only existing information;
> the extent to which additional information might reduce the uncertainty or risk, or the amount of money at stake.

The greater the initial uncertainty, the larger are the consequences of making a wrong decision. Further, the greater the amount by which the information is expected to reduce uncertainty the more valuable the information appears to become to executives.

Thus, if the cost of obtaining the information is greater than the value of it, consideration should be given to whether its collection would be worthwhile. Generally the answer may be not to gather such information but there are many instances when it may be advisable to go ahead. For example the value may not be totally quantifiable in money terms; the information may not eliminate uncertainty or guarantee increased earnings or profit but it could provide knowledge that at a future date may be useful or needed. This consideration helps when a choice has to be made between the packages of information that should be gathered and there is a limited budget making the collection of all of them impossible.

How the value of information is estimated is a complex subject embracing Bayesian Theory, decision trees and other classical approaches of marketing research statisticians. They are outside the scope of this book and those wishing to go into this subject in more detail should turn to the many specialist books on it. However, the marketing and research strategies selected should specify the information that should be obtained. This should be consistent with the research budget provided. The budget in turn should be consistent with the objectives and targets that have been agreed for the entire marketing operation.

(e) Data collection
Some information is collected continuously, some is collected through specific *ad hoc* research. Continuous data collection may be from internal sources, or

from external sources such as government departments or commercial research organisations. Internal figures will include orders, shipments, invoiced values and so on. External figures may range from general economic data through to the sales of goods through shops, awareness of advertising and so forth.

Ad hoc data is normally problem specific and is collected through panels or surveys set up to answer particular marketing questions. These may range from the acceptability of a new product, reactions to a proposed advertisement, the current image of a company or brand, or whatever areas marketing management may need to investigate.

The division is not absolute, and some information relating to specific problems may be available from continuous sources. Some information initially collected through an *ad hoc* project may subsequently be collected from a continuous source, to track the effects of any action taken. So the whole data collection process needs to be reviewed and revised regularly to keep it up-to-date. If the system is not kept in line with marketing needs resources will be wasted on information no longer needed, while more important information is ignored. A balance however needs to be struck between being up-to-date and retaining potentially useful historic information on trends, major events and so forth.

4.4   Types of studies

(a) Market research
Table 1.1 listed some of the purposes for which market research is used, and in this section some research methods will be described. First however it is useful to review briefly a number of types of research which will be described in greater detail later.

Desk research is conducted by assembling and analysing existing secondary data on a market or topic. It may be carried out as a continuous activity within the Market Intelligence function, often linked to weekly or monthly market reports. It is the starting point for research into specific problems, to gain as much benefit as possible from existing information before engaging in the more costly processes of collecting new material. In either case this may involve many of the types of information already mentioned, such as internal sales data, external data from government or trade associations, or reports, articles or any other available information. Very often desk research using secondary data will provide sufficient information to complete a specific research enquiry, but in many cases it will be necessary to go further. This will mean collecting new information specifically to solve the research problem. Such new data is the Primary data described in Section 4.3(a). As costs tend to increase rapidly once new primary data has to be collected, we should be sure that the new data is necessary, and that our secondary sources have been exhausted.

Primary data can be collected in a single operation, such as testing consumer reactions to a proposed new product, and this is called *ad hoc* research. Alternatively it may be collected through *Continuous research*, as when tracking the rate of sale of a product to consumers, or the audience for television, and so forth. In most continuous research a *panel* is set up using a representative sample of the target population, and successive sets of new data are collected at regular intervals. In other cases, where asking questions may influence the contacts, research is based on a series of separate but similar samples.

There is a further division between *Qualitative research* and *Quantitative research*. In some cases it is necessary to have firm figures on which to base decisions, such as the proportion of the target group in different age-groups or in different parts of the country holding particular opinions or using a product or brand. Quantitative research is then needed, based on large samples from the appropriate population, with comparable information being collected from each unit in the sample. In other cases it may only be necessary to have a broad view of the ideas, opinions, images and so forth held by people in a group of the population, and here assessments based on discussions with only a few people may be enough. In general:

> Qualitative research will produce information of greater 'richness' but which may not be fully representative of the population of people being researched.

> Quantitative research properly conducted will produce information on a more narrow and pre-determined basis, but which, within the limits of sampling error (see page 96) will reflect the situation among the population.

These types of research can be applied over a wide range of topics and among a wide range of groups of people. Most market research tends to be among private individuals as buyers or consumers, but an increasing amount is being done among industrial concerns or institutions. Given a planned and unbiased approach there is no reason why valid and useful results cannot be obtained covering a wide range of goods and services, from both consumer and industrial markets, and in both the public and private sectors of activity. Some of the areas of application are described below.

(b) Consumer studies

Research among buyers or users of products and services provides a basis for describing their general characteristics or 'profile'. The factors which are commonly involved are listed below, and these profiles form the basis for market segmentation.

In many markets a simple description of consumers is only the starting point, and more detailed research may be needed into the behaviour and motivation of people in different segments as they make their decisions to buy or use. In some markets it is important to consider the profiles and the motives of both the buyers of a product and the users. Housewives may buy breakfast cereals for reasons of nutrition and price, while children eating them judge on taste or the gifts in the pack. People giving presents may view products or brands very differently from those receiving them. Production managers using machines or components on the shop-floor may look hard at reliability and quality, while people in the Purchasing and Accounts departments may be more concerned with prices and discounts. For simplicity in the following sections the term 'buyer behaviour' will be used to cover all aspects of behaviour by those who influence purchase and use, as well as those making the decision to buy.

(i) *Consumer profiles*

Before we can usefully start talking to people or asking questions, we need to decide on the types of people to contact. We may have firm ideas from desk research or from previous projects, or we may have to make some assumptions about the types of people to be included. It may seem that we are pre-judging the issue if we make assumptions about the types of people to be included in the research from the beginning. Few markets however are so wide that 'everybody' is involved, and in most markets we can make some fairly sound assumptions about the types of people we need to approach in order to obtain information. Hence for information about types of food consumed by families in the home, the person who does most of the catering or cooking is the obvious target for research, but further refinement of the target group may follow if we are looking at the market for baby food, health foods, high price speciality foods and so forth. If we are looking at the market for main-frame computers there are grounds for believing that most of the executives concerned will be in large industrial or service organisations. If we do not make some assumptions such as these we are likely to waste much of our research effort in studying people who have nothing to offer us. However, it is important that the boundaries of our research are not drawn too tightly too soon, and that we remain aware of potential users and purchasers outside the obvious segments.

The dimensions or ways in which we describe consumer profiles will vary according to the characteristics of the market, but the following lists cover the more general factors used:

In consumer markets
   Sex
   Age
   Socio-economic class
   Family size and composition
   Terminal age of education
   Life-style
   Rate of purchase or consumption of the product
   Readership/viewing habits

In commercial/industrial markets
   Nature of business (Standard Industrial Classification)
   Size – annual turnover
         number of employees
         number of items consumed a year
         number of sites occupied
   Geographic location

Form of ownership/control
Position of informant(s)
Informant's qualifications
Informant's business/professional reading

Identifying the profiles of consumers, whether individuals or companies, is important for a number of reasons, which may vary from one market to another, but which will generally include the following:

Linking research findings with outside sources of data
Indicating potential market size
Providing a basis for designing samples for further research
Providing broad indications of targets for product development, advertising, promotions and other activities
Providing indications of useful advertising media
Providing images of typical consumers

The collection of profile data and its analysis and interpretation is the basis for the application of modern segmentation practices in marketing. Market segmentation will be discussed in detail in Chapter 6, but the basic idea lies in the concept of reference groups to which we all belong in some ways.

(ii) *Consumer attitudes and behaviour*

It is not enough simply to *describe* the people who are in the market for a product or service. For marketing action more information is needed about them and their buying patterns and motives. We can start with fairly simple factual data about whether they currently use the product or when they last used it, how often they use it, and what they use it for. After dealing with the product we can find out which brands people use or can remember, and then move to the more complex areas of *why* they use or buy one brand rather than another, and in short the whole range of factors which *motivate* purchase and use.

Understanding buyer behaviour is a perplexing but essential task especially in current market and economic conditions. Difficulties arise because of the heterogeneity of the different buying or customer groups and the individuals comprising a group. Behavioural studies have therefore to identify the attitudes, opinions, desires and reactions to marketing offerings at different periods of time. This means that variables such as price, product features, corporate image and promotional activities, including personal selling, affect buyers. The economic, sociological and psychological aspects have to be studied.

These studies try to establish how customers identify a need for a product or service, the pre-purchase activity they follow (e.g. seeking information on the proposed purchase, watching advertisements, talking to friends and so on), the use they plan to make of the purchase item and their post-purchase feelings (e.g. are they satisfied, partly satisfied or dissatisfied with their acquisition). All will help to establish the usefulness of products on offer while the use that customers would make of any item helps to decide the total quantities and pack sizes that should be considered. For example will users' purchases be limited or occasional or frequent and do they prefer buying small quantities or large? Their pre-purchase activity can also indicate what cues have to be put their way by the marketing effort in order to get customers to proceed to the 'right' decision or response, the purchase of the firm's products.

Demand refers to consumers' willingness and ability to buy and buyer behaviour indicates how willingness can be enhanced, thus leading to the making of a sale. Behavioural studies indicate how marketing operations can be planned to affect or shape demand by causing changes in buyer preferences and reactions. They also help to bring products and services more into line with customer needs. They assist when decisions on product modification, rationalisation and new product development have to be taken and not just with decisions concerning promotional, personal selling, pricing and distribution matters. With industrial products, internal influences within the buying organisation, as shown in Figure 1.1, are also dominant.

When the need to conduct research into people's motives for buying was first realised this was seen as a separate arm of market research, and called motivational research. Today the term has largely been dropped although the need for the information remains. Research into motivation and the reasons people have for buying or not buying products or brands has been assimilated into research programmes generally, particularly on the qualitative side.

The area of research involved can be described as the measurement of attitudes and preferences which can be shown to affect consumption of a product or service, using indirect questioning techniques borrowed from the behavioural sciences. It helps to identify what customers want, why they want it and the images of products, brand names and companies. Findings from it have been successfully applied to the design and specification of modified and new products, packaging, advertising, sales promotions, selection of retail or point-of-sale outlets and pricing decisions.

Through the application of psychological and psycho-analytical methods and interviews in considerable depth, the research tries to determine why customers behave as they do, Yet intelligence on motives is not easily obtained. The respondent may not know why he or she behaves in a certain way and might not want to admit to it! Ridicule, insecurity and social disapproval may all be inhibitors. Consumers may not be able to express reactions in clear language and terms, nor be consciously aware they do react in a specified way. Further, motives may change before the intelligence gathered can be used and they certainly change in time as various circumstances also change. Finally, it may be difficult to obtain intelligence about stimuli below the level of consciousness and hence the resultant motivation. The intelligence can also be difficult to translate into correct action.

In behavioural and motivational studies, the research has to establish how far basic needs are being met and how much purchasing decisions depend on the desire for status, self-actualisation and esteem. It must try to establish how behaviour as a result of motivation affects an individual's perception of the posed problem or product offering. It must also indicate how attitudes change and how the learning process changes behaviour as a result of knowledge and experience.

To summarise, the main factors influencing human behaviour and character are listed below.

Primary factors
Family background and life-style
Social background and reference group to which person belongs
Education and work groups
Race or nationality and religion (if any)

Secondary factors
Profession or work status
Income
Social status in community
Social and other aspirations or expectations

External personalised factors
Information and knowledge on the subject requiring decision
Relevant (and sometimes irrelevant) experience
Fears, doubts, uncertainties on the decision to be made
Ignorance – the decision to be made is an entirely new one
Taboos and prejudices

Irrelevant experience refers to the fact that people will sometimes believe that what are facts totally irrelevant to their pending decision do have bearing or significance on the decision to be made. For example, knowledge and experience of holidays in Spain may be used incorrectly to arrive at decisions about a holiday in Southeast Asia. This mistake is likely to occur most frequently when the consumer is ignorant about the matter, as interpreted above.

(iii) *Reference groups*

This approach is an attempt to categorise and identify potential buyers into mutually exclusive groups whose responses to marketing effort display a high degree of homogeneity. That is, each member of the group has similar behaviour characteristics *as buyers*, which may be summarised as 'life-style'. Their other personality characteristics, which do not affect buying responses, could be quite diverse. Each group is said to have certain behavioural characteristics which are seen as the norms or standard of behaviour of the group. Establishing these characteristics for the different groups comprising a total market helps executives to select the most effective marketing operations for the groups that form the targets of their marketing activities. It helps also in the selection of these target groups.

Most consumers do in fact relate to a number of different reference groups. Their background, including their profession, job status, educational standards, social class and family, will give them a variety of behaviour patterns according to the buying decision involved. For example in Britain we can identify groups within the population who have some common attributes in their life-styles which lead to groupings, often with popular labels attached, such as the Yuppies (Young upwardly mobiles), Woopies (Well-off older people) or Dinkies (Double income no kids).

Identification of such groups is of great importance for all types of marketing activity, but is increasingly so for Direct Marketing. Here analysis of Census and other data has enabled links to be established between types of consumer and type of housing occupied. Since houses tend to be similar within small areas it is possible to identify the dominant types of housing within each postcode area. Hence knowledge of a consumer's postcode alone may provide valuable guidance about likely consumption patterns, credit worthiness, and so forth. The results of these analyses are available commercially under a variety of names, while this general area of research is now called geodemography.

(iv) *Opinion leaders*

Every reference group has a few 'members' who are considered by others as being opinion leaders or trend-setters. Usually they are people who are more ready to make new purchases (i.e. buy new products) or who have greater knowledge and experience and are thus more self-assured and ready to experiment. A few may have had this reputation pinned to them when in fact their knowledge and experience may not be greater than the others or which may not be relevant to the decision in question. For example, some years ago in India, when attitudes towards family planning were being researched, in almost every village the oldest male member of the village, their leader, was allowed to be the opinion leader on this subject. Yet most knew nothing about it and were biased by their religious or other beliefs. The true opinion leader should have been a woman, whose experience and knowledge were most relevant to the subject.

These people's opinions are respected and often sought after. Because of their importance, their views have to be canvassed. They are also useful in helping to distribute advice and information. If they can be convinced that a particular marketing offering is worthwhile, their acceptance of it should mean that others in their group will also respond favourably.

However, it is not always easy to identify opinion leaders or early adopters of new ideas or presentations. They tend to be innovative in some areas but not others. For example, senior executives may normally dress conservatively but are ready to try unfamiliar foods. When their behaviour characteristics are known, more effective marketing communications (personal selling and promotional activities) can be planned. In particular their known media habits and attitudes to advertising can be used to increase the firm's marketing effectiveness.

4.5 Planning the research

As stated in the opening remarks to this chapter (fifth paragraph in particular) it is necessary for each research project to be carefully planned. Then the results of the study are likely to prove most relevant and useful to the problem that has to be resolved. In addition the whole marketing research programme should form an integral part of the entire marketing operation and be consistent with marketing and corporate objectives. It may prove just a waste of money for a firm to embark on any research just when the executives feel like it, especially if a grandiose research project is intended. For example, a few years ago, the chief executive of a company in the civil engineering business, making pre-stressed, reinforced concrete products in a limited range, wanted an extensive study done in *all* markets for *all* such products used in civil engineering structures (roads, railways, bridges, culverts, tunnels and so on). Even with the most careful planning, over one hundred questions would have been necessary. Some 80 per cent of the information requested had no relevance at all to the firm's current and future operations. It would just have been filed away. The cost of the study in 1993 terms, would have been about £700,000. There was difficulty in persuading him that this would be just a waste. Only when he was told that the information would be obsolescent in three months and the work would have to be done four times a year if its value was to be maintained did he reluctantly agree that the work should not be done. In fact studies from time to time on a much more limited area, costing about £10,000, would have been most relevant to current and future activities. These were initiated and helped the firm to improve its profitability substantially over several years.

(a) Designing a research project

There are several steps that have to be taken in the design of any project and there is a logical sequence for them. These are set out in Table 4.3. Table 4.4 indicates the questions that should be considered when designing any research. These points are relevant to all projects, consumer goods and durables, industrial products and capital equipment, as well as services. For industrial products and capital equipment the special characteristics of these markets (see Section 1.9) must be taken into account and smaller samples will be used (see Section 4.6). For services (for example tourism, banking, insurance, transport) the procedures and approach are basically the same as for consumer goods but any special characteristics must also be considered (see Section 11.4)

In some cases, when it is not clear what problem the research must resolve, for example the basic hypothesis may not be clear, it is advisable to embark on short *exploratory studies*. They help to decide what the brief for the main study should be. Specific research questions can then be deduced. It is important in exploratory work that flexibility and versatility are encouraged. This form of study may also be used to uncover sources of secondary information, interview key people with good knowledge of the subject being explored and examine analogous situations.

Exploratory studies and full-scale research are also used to establish the causal relationships between important variables, the reason why certain things that have to be forecast happen under certain stimuli. These are referred to often as *causal studies*. Finally, the real-world environment affects real-world events. The environment establishes the 'rules' that describe the relationships between events. These are referred to as *deterministic causations*.

(b) The research brief

Many research studies fail to satisfy the requirements of executives because their purpose is not clearly defined. Also the executives who need the information may not take the researchers into their confidence. Often the researchers do not probe deeply enough into the objectives or purpose of a study. It may well be that the problem to be solved is not as defined by the executives. For example a product may not be selling well not because there is something wrong with its formula-

Table 4.3   **Basic steps in research design and work**

1   Isolate or identify the problem to be resolved, the purpose of the study, or the hypothesis to be tested.
2   Review relevant literature/published data (secondary data); discuss this with informed and interested people.
3   Design the study, making hypotheses specific to the situation or problem.
4   Design or adapt research methods and techniques necessary for the work; if necessary conduct pilot or exploratory studies to indicate when revision of methods and techniques needed.
5   Decide on nature, type and size of sample; select people to be interviewed.
6   Conduct the fieldwork – (primary) data collection and returns.
7   Process the data, coding responses if necessary.
8   Conduct statistical analysis; test for statistical significance.
9   Assemble results and test hypotheses.
10 Write up results, relating findings to other research and information where available, make interpretations and draw conclusions and recommendations.

Table 4.4   **Key questions to consider when planning research**

1   What is the objective or purpose of the study? What must be known to meet the objective? What problems must be resolved? What variables must be measured? Can this be done? Is the required data/information available or obtainable?
2   What published (secondary) data/information is available?
     How current, relevant and reliable is it? What are the reputations and standing of the sources? How detailed is it? Any key point omitted? What further data/verification is needed?
3   What kind and size of sample should be drawn? Why? How? Are control groups needed? Who should be questioned? More than once?
4   What field studies for primary data/information are needed?
     What sources should be tapped? What is the extent of their knowledge, relevancy and reliability? How reliable are the 'experts'? What accuracy is expected of this data? What amount of raw data will result and how should/can this be processed? Is any scaling necessary?
5   What methods should be used?
     Postal questionnaires, telephoned interviews, personal interviews with/without prompting questionnaires? Use of panels? What should be the work-plan? What are the cost and time constraints? How do these affect the work-plan?
6   How should the total data/information be collated, analysed and presented?
7   Therefore, what should be specified in the brief for the research, in particular the terms of reference for it?

tion. It may be that the selling or promotional support is wrong, or is being aimed at the wrong customers or is wrongly timed. Production and distribution factors may also contribute to the problem. A thorough discussion of the subject should lead to a better understanding of what the problem really is and thus more effective research. Since the marketing problem may have nothing to do with anything being wrong in the marketing area, all the departments of the firm should be involved in this critical preliminary discussion, before the brief can be prepared.

Further, it is essential for the researchers to have sympathetic understanding of the requirements of the sponsors of the study. It should be remembered also that the complexity of marketing problems contributes to the difficulty encountered in defining the purpose of a study. While ideally each study should look into one problem, cost and time constraints may force a study to investigate more than one problem at a time, thus aggravating the difficulties encountered in this work.

Then there is the data/information associated with variables that can change quickly or unexpectedly or are in a state of rapid change (for example declining demand due to a rapidly deteriorating national economy or rising unemployment). The information is perishable in that it can become obsolete in a short time. This problem arises especially with studies that cover long periods of time. In such cases it is vital that researchers make interim reports to their sponsors and this requirement is one which should be in the terms of reference in the brief.

The main items that should be in any brief for a marketing research study are listed in Table 4.5. The brief should mean the same thing to all interested parties and should not ask for irrelevant information. It should define the relevant populations (customers) to be sampled in existing markets, immediate potential markets and those intended for later development. It should indicate the order or priority of the required accuracy of the various analyses to be presented while indicating the

Table 4.5 **Main contents of a research brief**

1 *Objective of the research*
   (i)   Purpose of the study or use to which results will be put.

2 *Terms of reference of study*: includes
   (i)   The data/information required;
   (ii)   the customers/respondents to be interviewed;
   (iii) the size and nature of the sample to be used; or
   (iv)   the degree of accuracy required, or error permitted;
   (v)   timing, including commencement and completion dates;
   (vi)   permitted costs;
   (vii) if interim reports and thus flexibility in the research are needed.

3 *Methods to be used*
   (i)   Amount and nature of secondary data or information to be used;
   (ii)   type of field studies to be employed;
   (iii) detailed breakdown of composition of sample;
   (iv)   what follow-up interviews would be undertaken, when and under what circumstances;
   (v)   how the data/information collected will be collated, analysed and presented.

4 *The report*
   (i)   Nature and contents;
   (ii)   conclusions that would be drawn;
   (iii) method of presentation and circulation.

5 *Recommendations*
   (i)   Whether these will be made;
   (ii)   probable nature and extent of them.

required accuracy of the main results. It should not prejudge the selection of research techniques and procedures nor prejudice nor prejudge the results.

(c) Desk research
This refers to the detailed study that should be made by researchers 'at their desks', of all secondary data and information relevant to the project, before any field studies are contemplated. It is not only done when some specific research is to be undertaken. It should form a regular part of the information collection and analysis that form the normal ongoing work of any marketing information system, in order to keep the collected data and information as up-to-date as possible.

If desk research is to be done effectively, the research team must have a good knowledge of the sources of relevant secondary data. They should know also how reliable such sources are and the usual dependence that can be placed on the information provided by them. The researchers must be able to convert 'raw' data into intelligence relevant to the firm's marketing needs as well as any specific problems that may be under study.

(d) Field studies
Field studies are essentially concerned with the collection of primary data from sources outside the organisation. This may be collected by observation, as in measuring the flows of goods through the distribution system, or of people through a shopping centre or store. It may be done through discussion groups, focus groups or individual face-to-face or telephone interviews to obtain attitude, opinion or usage information. Often basic, usually factual, data can be collected using postal questionnaires, guarantee returns, offer applications and so forth. While these last two methods do not involve research techniques as such, the information generated should not be ignored – but it may need care in interpretation.

Some studies will call for the use of large samples of contacts, while others may be completed using only small numbers of people, individually or in groups. The method used will depend on the nature of the study and its complexity, the precision needed in the results, the ease of reaching people, and how much we know already. The amount of time or money available also has effects. The main methods used in these field studies are discussed in the following sections.

(i) *Postal questionnaires*
The advantages and disadvantages of these are summarised in Table 4.6, but some additional comments are advisable. First, the relative cheapness of the method may be misleading since the response rate is usually lower than by other methods. For consumer goods surveys, the response rate can be less than 20 per cent. With industrial products, this author has experienced rates of 10 per cent and less. Where the total sample has to be heavily stratified (i.e. several groups or types of respondents make up the whole), low response may mean that so few replies are received from one or more sub-group that the data is statistically dubious for those groups and perhaps the whole survey. Some or all of the disadvantages listed could also mean that follow-up questionnaires

Table 4.6   **Postal questionnaires**

ADVANTAGES:	
Cheap distribution	Economical costs, but see *Disadvantages*. Widespread distribution of questionnaire is possible, useful when customers are widely dispersed geographically; within limits, costs not increased because respondents are widely dispersed.
Anonymity	Respondents assured of remaining anonymous, provided forms are not 'keyed'.
Time	Gives respondents time to check data etc. with records, reports and for consultations with others; better accuracy possible.
Contact	Some important respondents, by definition, are difficult to contact personally; work and responsibilities require them to travel extensively etc.; they may not have time for interview but might be more willing to complete mailed questionnaire.
DISADVANTAGES:	
Questionnaire	Few respondents prepared to complete long questionnaire (some allergic to them anyway), so must be kept short; problems of design, selection of questions etc. (see Section 4.7).
Unstructured	No control over respondents actually completing the form; they can read whole thing first and so prejudice the answers given to individual questions.
Questions	Must be simple; no one present to answer queries on complex questions which put many respondents off anyway.
Observation	Researchers not present so cannot observe respondent's attitudes and background.
Response	Response rate is usually low. Initial answers cannot be probed at the time.

may have to be sent, or telephone interviews conducted, to clarify doubts and uncertainties that arise from the initial answers. This all adds to the total cost.

The point about anonymity is also doubted by some respondents, especially with industrial products surveys. They know that the questionnaires can be 'coded', that is have numbers or letters on them, or bits snipped out of the edges. These can indicate to the researcher who or what type of respondent has completed the form. Some people will not return the forms if they feel that true anonymity is not being maintained.

Finally, with industrial products surveys, experience shows that questionnaires posted on Mondays and Tuesdays tend to be seen by more executives. Those posted on Wednesdays are less likely to be redirected to the right executive while those posted on Thursdays are most likely to be destroyed! (In Britain this assumes that first class mail is used and delivery is made within twenty-four hours. If deliveries take longer then only the Monday/Tuesday mailings seem assured of some sort of response).

CUSTOMER SURVEY

This survey is being conducted on behalf of Royal Mail by Research International, an independent market research company. It relates to the collection and delivery service of letters and small packets in the UK. (*It does not cover parcels or post office counters as these are now separate businesses.*)

The questionnaire has been designed to obtain an accurate picture of the service you receive from Royal Mail and to provide information about how the existing service could be improved. All the information requested will be treated in the strictest confidence.

Thank you for your time and help in completing the questionnaire.

SECTION 1

1   First of all, we would like to ask how many letters and cards you personally send in a typical month, **excluding** Christmas?
Tick one box.
(7)

1 - 10 ☐₁   11 - 20 ☐₂   21 - 40 ☐₃   41+ ☐₄   None ☐₅

2   How many letters and cards do you receive in a typical month, **excluding** birthdays and Christmas?
Tick one box.
(8)

1 - 10 ☐₁   11 - 20 ☐₂   21 - 40 ☐₃   41+ ☐₄   None ☐₅

3   Do you run (and receive mail for) any business from this address?
Tick one box.
(9)

Yes ☐₁   No ☐₂

4   How often do you normally see the postman/postwoman who delivers your mail?
Tick one box.
(10)

Every week   Every 2-4 weeks   Less than once a month   Never
☐₁   ☐₂   ☐₃   ☐₄

Front page of a questionnaire, carefully designed to encourage response by stating the reasons for the survey, and providing an easily followed method of completion

(ii) *Telephone interviews*

Telephone interviews permit controlled contact on a personal level with a selected sample of respondents. It is a more expensive method than postal questionnaires, but much cheaper than personal interviews. The main advantages and disadvantages are summarised in Table 4.7. While postal questionnaires are best

Table 4.7 **Telephone interviews**

	ADVANTAGES:
Cost	Still cheaper than personal interviews but more expensive than mailing.
Time	Survey can be completed much more quickly than with personal interviews and give time saving over postal surveys.
Response	Very good response rates possible.
Contact	Important respondents can be contacted more easily, even if not available on first call, not so disruptive as with personal interviews where a wasted visit can increase total cost of survey.
Undemanding	Respondents view this method as less demanding of them, time-saving etc.
Follow-up	Complex, difficult answers can be probed immediately and difficult points can be explained to respondent at the time.
Inhibitions	Some respondents inhibited by face-to-face interviews; not so over the telephone. Usually feel free to respond without seeking authorisation of a superior.
Anonymity	Respondents can be assured on this.
	DISADVANTAGES:
Questions	Best kept to those that can be answered off the top of the head, i.e. instantly; no chance to consult others except if a second call is agreed. Not always possible to comprehend importance of answer immediately.
Observation	Not possible. Also personal rapport not always easy to establish.
Interruption	Call can be interrupted or terminated before all points covered.

when limited straightforward information is needed or blanket coverage is acceptable (respondents are not identified specifically) telephone interviews can probe more deeply into important aspects. For industrial products surveys, this method has proved most effective in establishing who uses a product, the use made of it and the level and timing of purchases.

Telephone interviews are useful as a follow-up to other survey methods and for validating quantitative and qualitative information from other sources. If the intelligence obtained is not carefully recorded at the time of the call, accidental interviewer bias can result from later analysis. Finally, it can be difficult to identify the status of the respondent answering the call and, with industrial surveys, what the firm makes, its industrial classification and that of its main customers.

The use of telephone interviews for consumer work has increased greatly in recent years. This has been due to two major developments:

(a)   the more widespread use of domestic phones, with over 85 per cent of households with one or more.

(b)   the development of more specific facilities for conducting surveys by phone.

The limitation that only 85 per cent or so of the population may be reached directly by phone is still a potential source of bias in some contexts, as it is the older and/or the poorer sections of the community who will be under-represented. However in general the spread of phones in the UK is now wide enough to avoid such problems. This is also true for most developed countries, but there will still be reservations about the extent of cover in many other areas.

The development of more specific interviewing facilities has followed two main lines, which are closely linked. One has concerned the installation by research companies of banks of telephones in central locations where interviewers can work in good conditions, where they can be supervised and the quality of their work monitored. This leads to rapid completion of surveys to a uniform high standard. The second development has been in the 'software', under the general heading of 'Computer Assisted Telephone Interviewing' or CATI. Here the questions are stored in a computer program. The interviewer sits at a terminal which shows the next question to be asked, and which accepts answers through the keyboard. The program can check back that each new answer is consistent with previous ones, and raise queries if necessary. It will also select the next appropriate question for display to the interviewer, depending on information already obtained. Since by the end of the interview all the information from the respondent has been entered, there is little need for subsequent editing or coding. Analysis can proceed, at least on a 'top-line' basis, as fast as interviews are completed. (With the development of cheap lap-top computers these programs have been adapted for use in face-to-face interviews as well with similar benefits).

One problem which is tending to reduce the response rate in telephone surveys is the increasing use of selling by phone. This is often done under the pretence that the caller is carrying out research. (The term 'sugging' is often used in research circles to cover this process of 'Selling Under the Guise of ...'.) This is not a new device, and has been used for decades by door-to-door salesmen. However while in a face-to-face interview it is usually possible, by provision of identity cards and so forth, to persuade people about the validity of the research, and to continue with an interview, it is more difficult to deal with the problem by phone. To ensure a high response rate in telephone surveys extra care and skill are needed in phrasing the introduction to avoid immediate replacement of the phone by the contact.

(iii)   *Personal interviews*
While this is the most expensive and time-consuming of the methods available, it offers many advantages. The amount of information obtained by a single interview can be considerable. Complex matters can be dealt with efficiently and the responses can be probed deeply. The structure or nature of the interview can be altered according to the responses being obtained and the interviewer can observe the attitude of respondents and the environment in which they live (consumer goods) or work (industrial products). If a questionnaire is used, complex

questions can be explained. If respondents read ambiguity into any question, this too can be cleared up before the answer is given by the interviewee. The great flexibility of this method is perhaps its greatest advantage since field surveys can be adjusted quickly and cheaply, especially when the early answers indicate that some hypothesis of the survey may not be correct. Faults in method or approach can be spotted early enough to avoid having to redo the survey later. Finally, the respondents are more easily identified and, with industrial products, the activities of the responding firms can be more accurately gauged.

The main disadvantage is the cost. This requires the sample to be kept as small as possible. If too small, however, doubts may arise about the statistical validity of the results. Then, especially with industrial products research, the executives who must be interviewed may have difficulty in making the time available. Even when an appointment is granted, something urgent may arise which takes the respondent out of his or her office. The visit is wasted and all the problems of trying to arrange another will arise. Further, the interviewers must be skilled in the work involved. With industrial studies, often they must have more than superficial knowledge of the business and technology of the respondents and, frequently, of their major customers. Balancing these disadvantages is the fact that a very high rate of response is achieved, especially where respondents can be assured of anonymity.

The cost aspect means also that a wide geographical spread of the survey has to be avoided. This problem is partially overcome for consumer studies by conducting the survey in regions known to be reasonably representative of the nation as a whole. However, doubts exist whether all these zones really are 'typical' and the researchers can never be certain that changes taking place in them are occurring at the same rate nationally, or are indeed occurring elsewhere at all. For industrial products, where specific industries have to be studied, the locations of the firms in them are known. Also industries tend to collect in a few geographical regions for historical reasons or because important sources of supply or major markets are located nearby.

(iv) *Discussion groups*

Discussion groups or focus groups are a major method of gathering qualitative research information. Groups of between six and twelve people selected from the target population are brought together in a suitable location, to discuss specific topics for an hour or more.

In many cases well-conducted discussion groups, with adequate representation of the major segments in the target group, may provide all the information needed to solve the immediate problem.

More generally groups are often used as a preliminary stage to a larger quantified survey. Here the objective is to gain information about usage, attitudes, opinions and even the terms which consumers use in different markets. This information provides a basis for deciding which topics should be covered in a wider survey, and for designing a questionnaire. In many cases the information about the words which consumers use in talking about products and their use is vital in refining the wording of questions to make them respondent-friendly.

4.6 Sampling

In this book the word 'sampling' refers to the selection of groups of contacts for the purpose of a marketing research study. It does not mean the alternative interpretation: the free distribution of a product to obtain further sales. The main terms and their meanings are summarised in Table 4.8. Some further comments are made here.

The definition of the population to be sampled is of prime importance, because until this is clear it is not possible to draw an unbiased sample. When conducting research among people it is important to define the geographic boundaries of the research; to decide whether we need to sample individuals, as for a survey on political opinions or consumption of confectionary; or housewives as for a survey on cooking; or households as for a survey on ownership of durable goods. For more specific areas we may define the population in such terms as 'Mothers with at least one child under five years of age, living in Great Britain'.

In industrial or commercial surveys the population may be defined in terms of the Standard Industrial Classification, but we may need to decide whether we should design a sample of organisations, such as ICI or Sainsbury, or establishments such as individual ICI factories or Sainsbury stores. Even then there may need to be decisions about factories or stores which are operated jointly with organisations outside the defined population.

The *sampling frame* is technically a list of all elements in the defined population. For random sampling (see Table 4.8) it is necessary to have some form of sampling frame, but this may range from a list of all elements in the population to a means of identifying locations in terms of grid squares on a map. In some cases lists of surrogates can be used, such as members of a professional body, but care needs to be taken to ensure that an unbiased sample of the desired elements can be obtained from these sources. For consumer work the electoral roll is often used as a sampling frame, but again care is needed to ensure that samples selected are not biased by the form and limitations of the rolls. Since for most market research work random samples are not used, the need for detailed sampling frames is reduced, but there is still a need for detailed knowledge of the composition of the target population so that appropriate quotas can be developed.

While there are numerous ways of selecting a sample, whether in consumer or industrial research, there are two fundamental types of sample. The first is a sample drawn on a strictly scientific basis, where each component of the sample is selected without any human intervention. These are commonly known as random or probability samples. The second is a sample drawn by the researcher or the field worker selecting components which are judged to fit certain criteria, which may range from being of a certain age/sex/class group to fill a quota, to having specialist knowledge of value to the researcher.

Samples of the first kind should not suffer from bias when they are selected, although different response rates between segments within the sample may lead to bias in the final sample of respondents. Further, since the probabilities of selection will be known, calculations can be made of the sampling errors to which results

Table 4.8   **Sampling: terms and meaning**

Sampling unit	The defined types of people, families, organisations, establishments, etc. among whom we intend to carry out our research.
Universe or population	The whole collection of our sampling units within our defined geographic boundaries.
Random sample	A sub-group drawn so that every unit in the universe has a known, but not necessarily equal, chance of selection.
Stratified sample	The universe is first divided into identifiable subgroups, e.g. males and females; customers in Northern, Central, Southern sales areas; large, medium or small organisations etc. A separate sample is then drawn from each segment, thus assuring proper representation in the full combined sample. This procedure normally improves the precision of the results.
Weighted sample	Units are selected in different proportions from the various strata – e.g. one in five of large organisations, but only one in twenty of the small ones. The results from the strata are weighted during analysis before being combined. This procedure again will normally increase the precision of the results.
Cluster sample *Multi-stage sample*	In research involving face-to-face interviews, random selection will lead to a wide scatter of contacts, and high costs. This can be overcome if instead of selecting, say, 1000 contacts individually at random, 100 'clusters' are selected at the first stage, and ten contacts selected within each cluster at the second stage. This reduces the precision of the results, but is cost-effective and widely used in commercial or political research.
Quota sample	Units are selected by interviewers to fit into specified categories – e.g. under 35, 36 to 55, over 55 years of age. When all the 'quotas' are combined a representative overall sample should be obtained. This is a form of multi-stage sampling which leaves selection at the second stage to human choice, and open to bias.
Sampling error	However well-selected and controlled, different samples from the sample universe will vary in the results obtained, simply through the chance selection of units. The range of error can be estimated, and is usually quoted with the results. For example, in the UK most voting intention surveys, based on around 1000 people, will be quoted as having a range or margin of error of ±3 per cent.

from the sample may be subject, in line with accepted statistical theory. Samples of the second kind may suffer from bias in selection, since human factors are involved; and since the selection was not random, the theory of sampling errors can no longer be assumed to apply – although in general we presume that it does.

The costs of tracing the specific components included in a random or probability sample, whether by mail, phone or personal interview, can be high as numerous follow-up mailings or recalls will be necessary in attempting to contact all those selected for inclusion in the sample. Consequently these types of sample are now used only in social or market research for government, which must be above suspicion, or in some very specific forms of scientific work, such as trials of new drugs. For most commercial research we use the less stringent forms of quota or purposive sampling, but checking the results against all available internal and external evidence before we place our trust in them. When calculating the sampling errors attached to this type of survey we first assume that pure sampling theory can be applied, and then make an allowance for our 'impure' samples, by adding some 50 per cent to the theoretical margins of error. However we still need to be aware of the risks of bias in our results.

4.7   Questionnaire design

There are basically three forms of questionnaires:

unstructured,
semi-structured and
structured.

Unstructured questionnaires are really just notes to the interviewer of the key points that should be investigated in depth. They are really interview guides and prompts. This approach is very useful where very complex technical and other factors are being investigated, especially when there is uncertainty about the underlying hypotheses. They are also very useful where free but very detailed discussion is sought of a major factor and the respondents should not be influenced or deflected by having to answer specific questions.

Usually this 'questionnaire' is used for only a limited number of interviews and often for exploratory work prior to a survey to establish the correct basis for the major study. The free-flowing verbal answers are difficult to analyse and interpret. Worse, if the responses cannot be recorded at the time of the interview, the opinions have to be committed to memory and recalled later. The danger of incorrect interpretation of the responses is increased. Also no two interviews need be compatible; many are downright incompatible. Finally, if the interviewer is not very experienced in, and knowledgeable about, the subject, important questions may not be asked because the interview has wandered off the main objective of the exercise. The comments may seem important at the time but on later analysis may be found to be irrelevant to the subject.

Semi-structured questionnaires have been described as a series of standard questions used by the interviewer with a set of operating instructions designed to cope with most response pattern situations. That is, the questions are designed to provide the basic or important answers but when an interviewer finds responses are varying from what was expected, certain freedom is given to the interviewer to ask alternative or supplementary questions. This permits flexibility in the research as does the use of open-ended and multiple-choice questions (explained a little later). With these questionnaires, interviewers are more in control of the interviews and there is ease of tabulation and recording of the responses. Subsequent analysis is also easier. The fact that part of the questionnaire is structured forces the research planners to consider deeply just what information is needed and how the questions would be best put to draw relevant information easily from the respondents. Open-ended questions with their usual verbal answers, though sometimes difficult to classify and analyse, add colour and meaning to the interpretation of the many statistics obtained by the rest of the interview.

Structured questionnaires are those where all the answers are expected to fall into a pre-selected pattern reflected in the format and layout of the questionnaire. They give a rigid interpretation of the subject or questions. They are useful where simple, straightforward information is required, with postal surveys where the respondents have to complete the forms on their own and in Computer Assisted Telephone Interviewing. Where a complex situation exists, or where the inter-relationships of the variables are complex, as with major industrial products, they are not of much use.

(a) Design considerations

Table 4.9 lists some of the questions that have to be considered before a questionnaire can be designed. Frequently surveys and their questionnaires are not designed or planned at all. Executives get carried away by what seems to them to be an exciting activity. They do not realise that questionnaire design in particular is not an easy task. It calls for great skill, experience and understanding of human behaviour and motivation. Many marketing executives who have been tempted to go it alone discover the error of their ways only when they have implemented plans based on their faulty research and have paid the penalty. The work calls for not only a great deal of technical knowledge but also a prolonged and arduous intellectual exercise.

Surveys and their questionnaires must aim for results which are free from ambiguity and bias, and which make a sound contribution to management action through logical development and efficient execution. Poorly designed research may not only fail to provide valid results, but may provide flawed information leading to faulty conclusions and inappropriate or even disastrous plans and actions.

(b) Questions

Basically there are three types of questions. First, there is the *dichotomous question* which is meant to provide a simple 'yes'/'no' answer. Alternatively, the respondents have to choose between only two clear-cut answers. Second, there is

Table 4.9   Questionnaire design: questions to consider

1	What topics need to be covered in the questionnaire?
2	What information is required from respondents?
3	Who is to be contacted?
4	At what level can questions be pitched?
5	How are contacts to be approached – mail, phone, in person?
6	What limitations are there on length of questionnaire?
7	Will most answers be factual, or are opinions and attitudes involved?
8	In what order should topics be introduced?
9	What classification questions are needed?
10	Will there be any subsequent contacts with respondents?

the *multiple-choice question*. Here respondents have to choose one answer from several indicated possibilities. There are a number of variants on the form of these questions, which include:

Ticking the appropriate box to show the age or income etc. of the respondent.
Ranking a set of alternatives, e.g. holiday resorts, in order of preference.
Indicating on a scale the contact's opinion about a particular topic.

One form of this latter type of question offers a statement and asks respondents to indicate their own positions on a scale ranging from 'Agree strongly' to 'Disagree strongly'. Others use different formats for similar purposes. Such questions are often put in groups, each question approaching a topic from a different angle, with the answers providing a basis for multi-dimensional analysis of attitudes and opinions.

Choosing the appropriate form of multiple-choice question is important since information can easily be lost, and bias may be introduced into the results. If the options given are too narrow to cover the full range of possible responses, some answers may be forced into inappropriate boxes; while if too many options are provided the respondent becomes confused. The problems may be overcome through careful exploratory research involving reviewing any previous work in the area, running discussion groups, talking to experts, and so forth. There are also ways of covering the less common responses by including an 'Others (please state)' option for potential answers outside the main stream, but again care and thought are needed.

Finally there is the *open-ended question*. In this the question is put and respondents are left to answer verbally in any manner they choose. Although in the past these were more difficult to collate and analyse, much of this problem has been solved with the use of computer packages. There are two main uses. First, in many research areas where attitudes, opinions and experience with the use of a product are being studied, greater richness and depth of information is achieved when respondents are able to express their own thoughts and ideas. The appropriate use of open-ended questions should draw out this information, but the development of the wording of the questions which will lead to unbiased results is a skilled undertaking. The second use is to maintain the interest of a respondent through a questionnaire, which may of necessity contain mainly dichotomous or multiple-choice questions. Here the injection of an open-ended question may provide a change of pace and an opportunity for the respondent to elaborate on an answer, or just to let off steam, which will help to maintain interest in the rest of the questions.

Apart from the form of the questions there is a division between types of question depending on their purpose. Most of the questions asked will normally relate to the subject of the research, but in addition there will be some which provide *classification data*. This will cover details of the age, sex, occupation, etc. of individuals, or numbers employed, main product or service, ownership and so forth of industrial or commercial units. These questions need to be very carefully formulated as any failure to collect the required information may put at risk the whole analysis of the survey results. One way of ensuring that appropriate classification data is collected is to draft the form of the tables or other analyses which will eventually be required to make use of the results, filling in the details of the sub-groups which will be examined separately, and thus ensuring that the details needed will be provided by the research.

It should also be remembered that the questions should orientate and stimulate respondents to co-operate correctly in the study. Further, because of the complexities of modern life and the interrelationships of the variables influencing the subject under consideration, many respondents may genuinely not know which answer to give. Provision should be made with all three types of questions for interviewees to give a 'Don't know' answer. This is as valid and useful an answer as any apparently more positive one.

(c) Pilot work

Whenever a questionnaire is being used for the first time it is important to conduct a *pilot survey* among a dozen or so contacts from the defined population, to check that it works properly, and that questions are intelligible to respondents, convey the right meaning and elicit the required information. Even when a questionnaire has been used successfully in previous surveys it may still be advisable to pilot it again before embarking on the major survey. The contexts in which topics are viewed, and even the meanings of words, can change very rapidly today, and an out-of-date question can throw doubt on the whole survey (see Table 4.10).

4.8   Bias

The reader will realise by now that there are many opportunities for unintentional and unwanted bias to be injected in any marketing research project. The more common causes are listed in Table 4.11. Such bias should be avoided, but if this is not possible the degree of bias present should be known and allowances made for it in the collation and analyses of the results of the survey.

It is important to distinguish between bias and sampling error. The latter is inherent in sampling procedures, and while it can be modified by changing the sample size or using more refined sampling methods, it cannot be avoided – but it can normally be calculated and allowed for. Bias is a more difficult problem because it may arise at a number of points in a research programme, its presence may be quite unexpected, and its effects may be unpredictable. Often the only way of detecting its presence is through comparison of the research results with other information, such as data from other surveys, figures of known factory shipments or volumes of services provided, import or export figures and so forth. Here the value of an up-to-date marketing information system becomes apparent, as all new data, not only from market research, can immediately be put into an appropriate context and an assessment made of its validity.

Table 4.10   **Question formulation: points to remember**

1 *Avoid poor question construction by avoiding*
   (i)   ambiguity,
   (ii) lack of mutual exclusiveness,
   (iii) lack of meaningfulness,
   in the questions.

2 *Follow a logical sequence in the questioning.*

3 *Keep questions as simple as possible.*

4 *Avoid complex words or phrases.*

5 *Avoid words which would be unfamiliar to respondents.*

6 *Avoid leading questions and emotionally loaded words which would appear to respondents as hinting at the answer required.*

7 *Avoid questions that the respondents' background, experience etc. does not equip them to answer correctly.*

8 *Do not use questions, or choice of answers, where one answer may appear to respondents to confer some status to them, or make them appear to have a higher standing than they do.* (The interviewees will tend to pick that answer whether it is true or not in their case.)

9 *With all questions provide a space where respondents can answer 'don't know'.* (If this is a genuine view, encourage them to select this answer rather than guess at an answer or give an incorrect one.)

10 *Avoid questions that tax the memory too much* (or which respondents do not wish to answer because they think it belittles them).

11 *Avoid too wide a choice of answers.*

12 *Do not narrow the choice so that answers are not fully representative of the main possibilities.*

(Point 9 above, Table 4.10, itself suggests many causes of bias.)

Table 4.11   **Common causes of bias in research results**

Bias in sampling
1 Use of a faulty sampling frame – incomplete, multiple entries etc.
2 Use of faulty sampling methods – human element in selection.
3 Differential non-response or non-contact rates not allowed for in planning.

Bias in interviewing or schedule completion
1 Ambiguity in questions or responses.
2 Leading questions or hidden prompts.
3 Unintentional interview bias – over-stressing words, prompting.
4 Respondent bias – under- or over-stating in answers.
5 Errors in completing pre-coded answers.

Bias in analysis or interpretation
1 Errors in coding – ambiguity, too few categories, false definitions.
2 Incorrect specifications in computer analysis.
3 Intrusion of researcher's or client's own expectations.

4.9   Marketing information systems

Marketing information or intelligence systems (MIS) have four interrelated functions to perform, as described in Section 4.1. In conjunction with the control systems in operation, executives should also be able to monitor results being obtained, check them against plans and targets and so gain further insight into programme modifications that are necessary. In practical terms the MIS has the prime task of informing executives of what is happening in markets (current and future) of interest to them, what influences are at work and therefore what is likely to happen in the future. Further, it should indicate what the rewards are likely to be for specific inputs of effort and other resources. MIS and control systems jointly have two aims: first, to assist executives to control the present and forecast short-term events and, second, to forecast and plan for the long term.

Therefore, before a MIS can be constructed, the basic questions shown in Table 4.12 should be considered. These in fact require a full-scale review and appraisal of the entire marketing operation, its organisation, strategies and policies. The responsibilities of the executives must be defined to establish how the information should be circulated and when this should be done. The ability of executives to use a MIS and the degree of their sophistication in this respect should be gauged. Further, there must be explicit statements on the planning, decision-making and control processes and procedures that will be used. Finally, the support of management at all levels must be obtained. They should not only be enthusiastic about the system and its potential but be prepared also to assist in, and oversee, its development and evolution.

As firms grow in size and the complexity of their activities, executives become further removed from immediate contact with the scenes of the marketing action. They have to rely increasingly on second-hand information and an increasing amount of it. It is necessary therefore that once a MIS has been developed *rigor mortis* should not be allowed to develop. There must be flexibility of thought and approach that permits the modification of the MIS as the firm's business environment and executives' needs change. Happily the availability of computers, and in particular workstations linked to main-frames or PCs linked in networks, have removed many of the barriers to the rapid retrieval and effective use

Table 4.12   **Key question that determine the nature of the marketing information system required**

1	What types of decision are involved?
2	What types of information are required?
3	From what sources, and how often?
4	What quantities of data are required, and in what form?
5	What access facilities will be required – by whom?
6	What security considerations apply?
7	What non-routine requests are likely to arise for information?
8	What analyses of stored data are likely to be needed?
9	What expansion capability needs to be provided?
10	What budget is needed? What is available?

of data. There are still dangers of the uncritical use of data, of being over-whelmed by the amount of information available, of 'analysis paralysis' in which every facet of a decision is analysed but no decision is ever reached. But the efficient marketing managers can gain greatly from judicious use of an efficient MIS.

Assignments

For your chosen organisation select an area where a market research survey might be useful. Write a brief for a research agency in which you define the problem area to be investigated, the population to be covered in the survey, the method you think appropriate for collecting the data, and provide an outline of the questions or topics to be covered.

What external sources of published data might be useful to the organisa-tion? What information would they provide?

What internal sources of data do you think should be fed into a market-ing information system? What information would then be produced?

⑤ Managing products

A perennial argument amongst marketing academics is: 'Which comes first, the product or the market?' Acceptance of the product–market concept discussed in Section 1.7(b) should terminate the argument, since it acknowledges the joint and equal importance of both subjects. Provided the concept is followed it does not matter if marketing teams study markets or products first. However, since most firms these days are working with restricted resources, because of their cost, it may be more appropriate to start with the product. Here as elsewhere we use 'product' to cover services as well.

This is not reverting to the old idea 'first find your product and then go and look for a market'. Nor is it tacit agreement with those who should know better but maintain that 'a good product sells itself'. It is just that with limited resources priorities have to be set and it makes sense to study the most difficult area first.

Consider, for example, a firm making high pressure, high head pumps for non-corrosive fluids. If it is tuned in to its markets in its normal activities, it will realise that these products are too expensive for applications where high pressures are not involved. It has some idea of what market opportunities exist, but it should first find out what low pressure, high head pumps it could make. It would then study its markets to see which of the new pumps would sell in sufficient quantity at a profit and revenue which would be acceptable. It can also study which markets of its total market mix would be interested. The ultimate choice would depend on the firm's capacity and other resources.

5.1 Product–market strategies

Four basic product–market strategies are available.

(i)   *Market penetration*: the firm tries to increase sales of its current products in its present markets by using more aggressive selling, promotions and distribution;
(ii) *Market development*: the firm increases its sales by opening up new markets for its current products;
(iii) *Product development*: the company tries to increase its sales by developing new or improved products;
(iv) *Diversification*: the firm seeks to increase sales by developing new products for new markets.

It is assumed that these increased sales will result in increased profit. Most major corporations and smaller ones needing substantial growth could be active in all four areas at the same time. They would, however, be implementing an agreed product–market policy and not following the above strategies haphazardly. The degree of difficulty and risk involved is least for (i) and gets progressively greater as a firm progresses through (ii) and (iii). Item (iv) carries the greatest risks and uncertainties. This is because the development of a new product is more costly, difficult and uncertain than opening up a new market. If a firm jumps around in random order in this work, it suggests it is not following any carefully thought out long-term plan. Rather it is responding to the urgent needs of each problem or product need that arises.

Taking the financial services market as an illustration, there have been numerous examples of companies following the different strategies. The high street banks have followed policies of market penetration in cross-selling their existing services to their existing clients, approaching current account holders with details of insurance and so forth. They have pursued market development by targeting younger age groups, and by attracting blue-collar workers as well as their traditional white-collar sectors. Building societies have developed current and other accounts in addition to their traditional savings and share accounts. Both banks and building societies sought to diversify into estate agency – often with disastrous results.

One interesting aspect of the diversification strategy is that cycles can be detected in some companies which have been through phases of diversification followed by phases of retrenchment and concentration on their 'core' business. This can often be traced back to problems of longer-term management of new products in new markets outside the firm's range of expertise, so that any early gains from pioneering efforts are lost in subsequent fire-fighting.

5.2   What is a product?

This may seem a superfluous question but successful marketing executives know that a product is not just the physical thing that is seen, touched, smelt, tasted, used or consumed. Every product possesses symbolic and psychological attributes to the consumer. All have to be catered for, as far as is possible, if a high degree of customer satisfaction is to be maintained.

For example, consider the case of a camera. To persons not interested in photography it is just a lens, with various moving parts encased in metal and plastic. It may be to them an expensive, unnecessary luxury. To the child in its early teens it may be a more grown-up substitute for toys. It is 'fun' snapping this and that and the main attribute in this case is pleasure. To the serious amateur photographer it is a precision instrument. With it they make time stand still (capture photos of the baby at various ages, holiday capers etc.) and record moments for posterity (at weddings and silver or golden anniversaries or other events). For the professional it is a vital tool of the trade whereby records are taken to satisfy their customers' needs and all their psychological and status pretensions. So products also seem different things to different people.

Take the car for a further example. To the manufacturer it is a collection of parts to be correctly assembled and sold to earn their profit. To the distributor it is an inanimate object that must be sold if he is to earn his living. To the 'young blood' it may be a means to woo (or seduce!) the heart's desire of the moment. To a family it is a means of transport for them and often also the means whereby the wage earner travels to and from work. Which attributes predominate at any time will determine how buyers make their buying decisions and thus the marketing mix that should be used.

For both cameras and cars, and for virtually all other products and services, brands will have 'images' associated with them. Some makes of car or camera are seen to have a 'quality' image while others are more basic. Different banks, airlines, schools, restaurants, colleges have different images, which may make them more attractive to some customer groups, or less attractive to others. A product or service will develop an image anyway; so it becomes important to ensure that it will contribute to the marketing effort of the organisation, not work against it.

(a) Basic terms and meanings

There are various standard terms used in product planning and management work. These are summarised in Table 5.1.

Table 5.1 **Product management: some terms and meanings**

Product item	A single product (e.g. a Jaguar XJ6, 3.2 car).
Product line	A number of related products (items) that satisfy a specific need, or are used together, or are within a price range, or are sold to the same customer groups being marketed through similar types of outlets (e.g. all the Jaguar XJ6 cars in that marque).
Product group	All the product lines forming a related group of products (e.g. all Jaguar cars – XJ6, XJ12, etc. – produced by Jaguar Cars.
Product mix	All the products offered for sale by a firm (e.g. all the cars produced by Ford), and the quantities of each to be sold (see also Glossary).
Product management	All the management activities involved in looking after a firm's products; includes *Product planning*; planning items, lines and ranges, prices, etc.
Width	of the product mix, i.e. how many different product lines are produced by a company.
Depth	of the product mix, i.e. the average number of items offered in each product line.
Consistency	of the product mix refers to how closely related the product lines are in end-use, production requirements, distribution methods, etc.
Product positioning	Putting the product into an appropriate slot in its market to gain maximum appeal among the chosen target group.
Brand image	The collection of associations and ideas attributed to a brand by people in the market, whether for an industrial or consumer context, or for goods or services.

(b) Services

As economies develop and income levels rise, there is increasing demand for services of all kinds. This ranges from banking and insurance to transportation (national, international) for people and goods to leisure (holidays, excursions), recreation, education, medical care and so on. The basic techniques and principles of marketing apply here also, except that their special characteristics have to be taken into account. These are summarised in Table 5.2. Most services basically follow the approach needed for consumer goods but some (e.g. transportation of goods and some aspects of banking and insurance) may be more effectively sold if methods used for industrial products are followed. For service industries the services they provide are their 'products'.

Services can have physical as well as pure service elements in them, just as many products contain service elements. Travel agents provide services to business or private travellers, and the services they provide are often bought on trust. In choosing an agent, or the travel arrangements they offer, customers will be influenced by the personnel serving them or answering the phone; by the ease with which enquiries or bookings are processed; and by the physical evidence in the office, in documents and so forth that this is an efficient organisation. Hence apart from the basic four Ps the additional three of People, Process and Physical evidence come into play. Equally in buying life assurance (in reality this is death insurance but who would buy it under that name?) the personality or the selling technique of the agent, the ease of obtaining information and completing the formalities, the layout of documents and so forth may all play a part in reaching the final decision.

There is then a close relationship between customer and staff in all service organisations, from fast-food outlets to five-star hotels, and from travel agents to financial advisers or banks and insurance companies. Because of this, organisations have to ensure a uniform high standard of service from all their staff, involving care in the selection and training of personnel. Further, many service organisations strive for recognition by unofficial or official bodies to enhance their reputations with potential purchasers. Hence the star grading of hotels, the registration or 'bonding' of travel agents and financial institutions, and so on.

Some aspects of service industries have an impact on their marketing and planning. The fact that services cannot be stored, for example, leads to a need for more detailed forecasting and planning through time if excess capacity is to be avoided, or sales lost through inability to supply.

Next, the facilities are relatively inflexible. Insurance experts in life insurance, for example, are not usually able to handle with the same efficiency matters to do with fire insurance. So if demand for the former is not as great as expected, 'spare capacity' will exist and will erode the firm's profitability. An hotel once built is not easy or cheap to convert to other uses. A holiday firm, overestimating demand for holidays in Spain, cannot switch quickly to Italy, Greece or the Far East. Couriers fluent in Spanish and knowing Spain may not have any abilities suited to these other countries. Also, since forward bookings have to be made, it may be eighteen to twenty-four months before the holiday firm can switch its main operations.

Table 5.2   **Special characteristics of services**

Intangibility	Services cannot be touched, tasted, seen or heard, i.e. they do not exist in normal physical form. Cannot be sampled. Potential buyers cannot judge quality before use. Thus reputation of seller plays key role in the buying decision.
Perishability	Their utility is short-lived. They cannot usually be made ahead of time of demand nor stored for peak demand periods. Hotels, transport seats, tourism services, utilities are typical examples affected by these two characteristics.
Standardisation	Difficult if not impossible, for offerings of the same service by different suppliers. Nor can any one seller guarantee consistency in the services offered. Potential customers have difficulty in making definitive evaluations, hence have trouble with making a choice and buying decisions. Creative marketing needed to show how any service meets the unique needs of individual buyers.
Buyer involvement	Sellers must ensure that buyers clearly specify what they want and that these statements are correctly interpreted. For example, what do different people mean when they specify a 'quiet' holiday? Some mean exactly that with lazing on sunny beaches; others may want a few or several trouble-free excursions etc.
Value	Because of the above, it is difficult for customers to judge 'value' before purchase decision and consumption.
Heterogeneity	Services are usually designed around the specialised needs of individuals or firms (e.g. insurance policies; business travel for each executive; etc.) hence heterogeneity of most services. However some services are capable of standardisation (tour operators sell a standard set of holidays to all; public transport services operated on set schedules, available to all) but customers' individualised needs still result in heterogeneity.
Inseparability	For many services, production and consumption occur at the same time (e.g. bank executives 'sell' credit, loans, advice etc. to their customers and the items sold are utilised (consumed) by the latter at the same time). Travel agents, insurance brokers, franchisees have in some cases been able to inject standardisation into the services they sell by offering a limited number of (sometimes specialised) travel facilities, insurance policies and so on.
Ownership (Lack of)	With services, use of a facility does not mean that ownership of it passes to the user. The aircraft seat, hotel room, computer or photocopying service are in fact only hired for a specific time, or specific use (e.g. to photocopy papers). They remain the property of the proprietors.

Source: (Adapted or summarised from: L. E. Boon and D. L. Kurtz, *Contemporary Marketing*, 3rd edn (Dryden Press, 1980); D. W. Foster, *Planning for Products and Markets* (Longman, 1972); P. Kotler, *Marketing Management*, 4th edn (Prentice-Hall, 1980).)

Service companies must therefore have more accurate and detailed knowledge of their markets, customers and demand. Since buying decisions are normally subjective and greatly influenced by personal views and traits, knowledge of human behaviour and motivation and how they affect their business is necessary. Sales staff must be thoroughly knowledgeable about the services they have to sell. Finally, greater care is needed in the selection of marketing techniques used and in their adaptation to the needs of their services. In other words, greater innovation is essential.

5.3   Product management

Product management is involved in the adjustment of manufacturing capacity and technology and the efficient use of these resources and skills to match customer wants as efficiently and profitably as possible. What the work involves is sketched out in Figure 5.1. Note that the work evolves from agreed marketing objectives and strategies. These in turn are a result of agreed corporate objectives and strategy. Also the co-operation needed with the management of the market side of the firm is indicated, as in the important contribution made by costing and pricing decisions. Note also that double-headed arrows are used to illustrate that co-operation and communications must flow in both directions in every link associated with the work.

(a) Product strategy and policy
Events throughout history have shown that the factors affecting the business environment are subject to change, often sudden, sometimes unpredictable. Executives realise that their firms' strategies and policies, including those concerned with the product-market situation, must be modified and changed from time to time. Static, unchanging ones usually spell trouble if not outright disaster. Examples are all the cases of business failures, small and large. Dynamic strategies and policies are essential if profit, growth and survival are to be assured.

Product strategy is concerned with decisions on the range of products a firm must offer to achieve target profit, growth and market shares consistent with total demand and business conditions. This involves studying present and future prospects and the allocation of scarce resources between conflicting and competing objectives. The associated policies will specify the action plans or programmes that would be implemented to achieve the strategy. Policies can be permissive or restrictive. They can be good or bad. A firm that neither defines nor understands its business properly can end up with very ineffective policies. Those that do know their business may adopt similar policies but as they would have been more correctly chosen in relation to the firm's skills and capabilities, they will turn out to be good policies for the company. Also changing circumstances can make what are good and sound policies now into bad policies at some future time. Thus watchfulness and flexibility are required also in product management.

The objectives of dynamic strategies and policies are listed in Table 5.3, with a few summarised notes. What this means in terms of practical work is stated in Table 5.4 in the sub-section that follows.

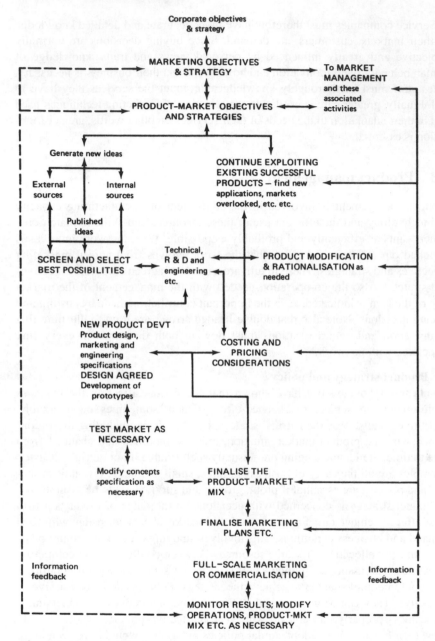

Fig. 5.1   The product management process

(b) Product planning

Through product planning executives shape the entire range of products for their selected markets. Their decisions should be based on consideration of the points in Table 5.4. It is a team operation that involves all departments of a firm at certain periods of the work. It is not confined only to the marketing specialists

Table 5.3   **Product strategies: objectives**

Growth
To improve total performance, counter competition more effectively and market saturation with current products. Exploit or create attractive opportunities. Stimulate sales of basic products. Attack competition before the company is itself attacked.

Survival
Vital for all firms, especially in difficult times. Need to offset obsolescence of current products, declining demand and profitability due to increasing competition and changes in other market factors.

Resource utilisation
Need for better utilisation of all resources: better use of raw materials, plant, labour and of by-products or waste and use of spare capacity. Firm should make full use of management resources also. Greater use of all special skills, assets. Improve innovative ability and competitive capabilities. Exploit prestige, product quality, reputation, market position and standing.

Stability
Firm must attain some stability for its business: profit, sales, return, earnings per share. Must avoid excessive fluctuations or recession.

Flexibility
So that customers' changing needs can be met. Must also adapt to changes in government regulations, laws.

Profit
Firm must strive to improve profit through improving performance of all products in all markets.

charged with responsibility for this activity. The basic steps are shown in Figure 5.2.

There are several factors which tend to broaden a company's product range. First, a growing number of firms may require products specially designed for their needs. They will not accept 'standard' items. Then most firms now split their purchases between more than one supplier to safeguard deliveries. Thus a company may add to its product range to take advantage of this or balance loss of business for their established lines. Or when a sales force is under-utilised, additional products which can be sold profitably may be introduced. The same may happen to absorb any spare manufacturing capacity. However, executives must tread a careful path through these often conflicting factors and arrive at a balance which produces optimum long-term profit. Otherwise the firm could end up with an extended product mix which over-extends the company's resources.

(i) *Product/brand or market managers*
In most situations there is a need to make one person responsible for the planning, development and monitoring of a brand, a product or group of related products. In both industrial and consumer markets there may be a need to make one person responsible for a specific market, or even for handling one specific customer. Hence in one dimension there may be a manager responsible for handling a group of products sold through supermarkets, but another manager responsible

Table 5.4   **Product planning: points to consider**

Profit, growth, stability
How may these strategy objectives be achieved? Usually involves detailed analyses of all aspects of product operations; aims to improve performance of laggard products.

Scope of product range
Requires regular review of product range and product mix to ensure they are meeting customer needs properly, in all respects. All items should also support and enhance sales of each other. Should ensure that all items in a product line help to optimise sales and profit of the whole line.

Marketing and manufacturing efficiency
If the utilisation objective of strategy is to be met, product planning must aim to optimise the efficiency of all marketing and manufacturing activities. Standards for unit costs, quality, output, reliability etc. must be practicable and achieved consistently. Total Quality Management (TQM) emerged out of a need to meet customer expectations at all levels.

Price and value
These must be in accord with customers' expectations. Should also be considered in relation to what competitors are offering. *Quality* should also be what customers expect, no more and no less. Excessive quality is costly and may not reap any additional benefits to the firm.

Competition
Competitive activity must not only be met but also anticipated, including reaction by them to any actions initiated by the company. Changes in competition (firms leaving a market, new competitors entering and hitherto insignificant ones developing into major threats) must be considered.

Service
Nature and standards required by customers (after-sales, maintenance and technical advice) should also be taken into account.

---

for communications and negotiations with each major supermarket chain. The first will be known as a brand manager or product or product group manager and be responsible for recommendations on product development, on pricing, on mass advertising, and so forth. The second will be known as a market manager or co-ordinator, and be responsible for operating profitably in a specific market, whether defined by geographic area or type of customer. A particular type of market manager is the key account manager, found in both consumer and industrial markets. This manager is responsible for profitably meeting the demands of major customers, including specific product development or modification, delivery requirements, assistance with selling-on whether of equipment or consumer goods, and so forth. Such divisions of functions may extend from breakfast cereals to major industrial projects and components, and ways in which responsibilities are divided will depend very much on the nature of the industry and the objectives of the organisation. Basically, however, all aspects of market planning and the satisfaction of customer needs must be covered by the management structure adopted, and these must be coordinated by an appropriate superstructure up to Board level.

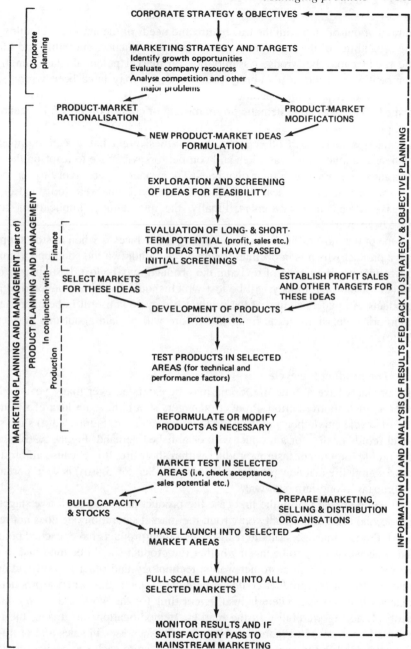

Fig. 5.2   Activities of product planning and relationship with other planning

(c) Why products fail

Products do from time to time fail to achieve their sales and profit targets. There are many reasons. The basic concept, proposition or specification may have been at fault or out-of-step with the true nature and needs of the market, technology or the capabilities of the firm. Or the price, size, performance, durability and life of the product may be wrong. Assumptions on market potential, the strength of competition and the firm's ability to counter this may have been wrong. The whole product planning operation may have been badly staffed, organised or rushed. There was no systematic programming or control of the work. Technical and production aspects may have been rushed, problems may have been missed or under-estimated. All other research activities might have been skimped or rushed. Too much time was taken and competitors were able to leapfrog the new idea into the market with their own ones. The products were 'ivory tower' ones, i.e. satisfied the firm's ideas on technical excellence but were too good or expensive for potential customers. Finally, the international implications could have been overlooked.

One of the most difficult decisions management faces is when to stop supporting a product which is in decline. If support is withdrawn too soon opportunities for further profit, or even of reviving the product, may be lost. If support is continued for too long money will be lost which should have been devoted to new products. An understanding of the product life cycle is useful in helping to take appropriate decisions at the right time. More will be said about this in Section 5.4(c).

(d) The product life cycle

All products have a finite life. Some may be extended over many years, others over a much shorter period. Product managers should have an idea of where on the life cycle curve their products are at any given time. Figure 5.3(a) shows the ideal profile or that for a product with established demand. Figure 5.3(b) shows the profile for a fad or fashion product with a short life. It is because all products have a finite life that new product development (Section 5.4(d)) is so important to a company's long-term survival.

It will be noted that in the first case the product passes through five stages. In the second there are virtually only four, the market saturation one does not really exist. Product managers should realise when their products have reached point A. Then decisions have to be taken whether the product should be modified to take account of changes in customer wants, technology and other market factors so that the life of the product could be extended. Doing this when a product has reached B is too late. There is insufficient time for the work and the product is probably losing credibility in the market. If modifications are made, the ideal profile becomes as in Figure 5.4. Note that the increases in sales and profit and the extended life for each modification diminish with each successive modification. Thus there is a limit to the number of times this can be done. The cost of the work may also increase as each successive modification becomes more difficult to do.

Although we call this the 'product' life cycle it can be used at a number of levels from the total market through to individual brands or pack sizes. The life cycle for the car market began around the beginning of this century, and is now probably in the saturation stage in Western markets, but still developing in many

(a) Basic product life cycle

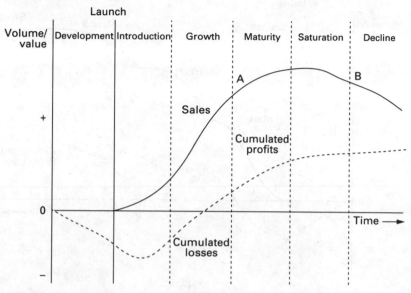

(b) Product life cycle for a fad or fashion product

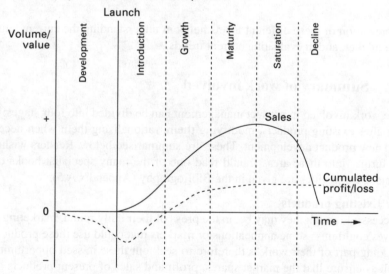

Fig. 5.3   Product life cycle

others. Under its umbrella there have been several life cycles for product groups, such as steam cars, the domination of the present market by petrol and diesel cars, and the potential rise of electric cars. Again under the umbrella there have been many 'brands' which have grown and fallen away; and each model or marque may have only a limited life cycle covering ten or fifteen years. An

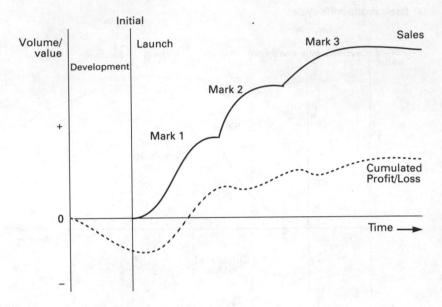

Fig. 5.4   Extended product life cycle

appreciation of these different levels helps in understanding the current situation in a market, and in evaluating current trends.

5.4   Summary of work involved

The work involved in product management can be divided into four stages: looking after existing products, modifying them, rationalising them when necessary and new product development. These are summarised below. Readers wishing to go further into these areas should read one of the many specialist books on the subject. Some titles are given in the Bibliography (Appendix A.5).

(a) Existing products

Successful though they may be, in the press of their daily round, marketing executives could miss some applications or markets that could use these products. An ongoing part of their work is therefore to seek out these missed opportunities as well as ensure that the market shares, profit and sales of present products are on target. However, they should not push products beyond their 'point of diminishing return'. This is when each incremental increase in sales is producing a decreasing incremental addition to profit. Also the incremental costs involved may be rising. Eventually, overall profit can be reduced. The effort could be more profitably put into other activities.

(b) Product modification

Because customer needs, competition, legislation and other market factors change, or because the original specification was inaccurate, even successful products need modification at times. While the product manager should normally be responsible for initiating change, the work is best assigned to a group of executives drawn from all departments who study the possibilities. A detailed account of the work involved is also given in the books listed in the Bibliography.

It is sufficient here to note that modifications can be of three types: improvement in quality, feature and style. Quality modifications seek to improve the performance, durability, reliability or life of the product. Improvement in perceived value by customers because of these changes or improvement in unit cost is another benefit.

Whisky, showing earliest label (top left), 1909 brands (top right) and 1880–1993 sequence (bottom). The central part of the label has moved from 'Old Highland Whisky' to 'Old Scotch Whisky' to 'Red Label'. The words Johnnie Walker, and the figure of The Walker feature only on the last two versions. But through all this the pattern set by the third version is still maintained today

Feature improvements aim at achieving a number of real user benefits. These may offer greater efficiency, safety, versatility, convenience or redesign which can enhance the usage customers can make of the product. Improvements in style aim at increasing the aesthetic appeal of the product, as is the case with modifications to existing marques of cars. The aim here is to achieve or reinforce a unique identity for the company and its products. This helps the firm to achieve a durable share of the market. Style improvements can eventually eliminate the original product, since to sell these new styles sales of the original might be damaged. With some consumer goods, such as detergents or shampoos, a large company may market a range of similar products under a variety of different brand names. In this way they can maintain a high overall level of demand for their product by securing sales in each major market segment through appropriate variations in the basic specification. Some small companies of course can create effective niche positions by selecting segments too small or too specialised for the major operators to service, and matching the specific segment needs.

(c) Product rationalisation

All goods and products have a finite life. Fashion products tend to measure their 'lives' in months. At the other end of the scale, houses, capital equipment, hotels, major industrial products have useful lives measured in (many) years. Yet some old and ailing products, beloved by the executives of their firms, or representing some major point of development of the company, like old soldiers, never die. Sometimes they are very slow in fading away even when they are no longer making profits. During this process of reluctant withdrawal, such products can consume a disproportionate amount of managerial time and other resources. They do in fact drain away profits earned by other activities. They add to costs, especially in accumulating inventories and all the price cuts that are needed to move these stocks. The continuance of products past their prime (obsolete really) can damage the company's image and inhibit the sales of other items. Recent examples include car manufacturers who, for various reasons, continued to make and market obsolete designs and marques.

There really is no room for sentimentality in modern business conditions. When a product fails to earn sufficient profit and it is impossible or too costly to carry out any further modifications to it, or customer demand has declined or switched to other (often new) products, or when it is not still helping to sell other profitable products whose profits far exceed the cost of continuing with the obsolete item, or economic and technical changes have outdated the ailing product, there is only one real answer, rationalisation. That is, it should be phased out of the firm's product mix. However, rationalisation has to be carefully planned and phased-in also with the new product development programme.

Considerable thought has to be given to how and when a product should be rationalised. If too many are deleted quickly or at once, without new items taking their places in the product mix, the total cash-flow position can be seriously affected. While these products may not be earning profits they will still be making some contribution to overhead costs. If other items are not available to take over this load, the overhead costs will fall more heavily on the products remaining in the mix. The profitability of the surviving products will be reduced as will the overall profitability of the firm. While it is not possible to plan product rationalisation and new product development exactly (some new items will be delayed in their launch because of difficulties encountered in their development) it is essential to keep these two programmes in step with each other as much as is practicable.

Table 5.5 **Product rationalisation**

Basic steps

1 The team of executives responsible meet to determine the objectives and procedures for the work.
2 They review, study and analyse the position for all products seen as possible candidates for rationalisation.
3 Their initial findings are compared with the firm's immediate and long-term objectives and strategies, especially plans for the future development of the company into new technologies and markets.
4 They consider also the effects that rationalisation of the 'candidates' would have on surviving products' sales and profitability, the resources that would be released for other activities and so on.
5 The team will then make recommendations on which obsolescent products should be rationalised and when and how this will be done.
6 The priorities will be established and a plan of action will then be prepared.

Questions considered

The key questions considered will include the following.
1 How have the products' sales changed in relation to total demand for them?
2 What new or substitute products have eroded the 'candidates'' positions? How has this affected the expectations (life, sales, profit) for them?
3 How has the competitive position changed and how will it change further in the future?
4 How have the demand patterns in the affected markets changed? What will be the future patterns?
5 What gross profit margins and overhead contributions are achieved by these products? How will this slack be taken up if the products are rationalised?
6 What will be the total cost of the proposed rationalisation?

Again, the detailed work involved is fully discussed in some of the books in the Bibliography. It is only necessary here to summarise the basic approach in Table 5.5 and to make a few further comments. A team of executives, drawn from the major departments, is charged with the task of doing the planning. In most cases it may be the same team that is involved with product modification. They will be the first to identify possible 'candidates' and should possess the basic information needed to arrive at correct decisions. Finally, not all the 'candidates' will be rationalised immediately or even for some time. Decisions will depend upon the overall product–market situation and the full implications of the proposals. Some of the latter have been mentioned at the beginning of this section. Obviously if a 'candidate' is still helping to sell other profitable items and the total gain is advantageous, or if it is keeping out competition in an area sensitive to the firm's future development, its rationalisation will be delayed. However, if it is making no useful contribution, whatever this may be, to the company's business then rationalisation is the only decision.

The classification of existing products introduced by the Boston Consulting Group can be useful when considering a company's 'portfolio' of products. There are four categories:

(i)   *Question marks* – products in high growth areas but with little market share. Most products start here and need much initial investment before becoming profitable as stars or cash cows.

(ii)   *Stars* – successful question marks, with increasing shares in expanding markets. Stars still need investment, but should become profitable.

(iii) *Cash cows* – products with a large share of a mature market, still earning good returns, and needing little investment. They provide the cash flow to support question marks and developing stars.

(iv)   *Dogs* – products with weak shares of markets with low growth prospects. Unless there is some reasonable prospect of progress these should be dropped.

Companies should aim to have a balanced portfolio of question marks, stars and cash cows, backed by a programme of new product development. Dogs, which often claim a large share of management time for no real return, should generally be closed down.

(d) New product development
The detailed work involved under this heading is also discussed fully in the books in the Bibliography. It should be noted here though that new product development is essential to the survival, growth and profitability of a firm. It counters the effects of the inevitable obsolescence of existing products that arises from natural processes or development or through competition. It helps to improve the overall profitability of the firm and to ensure full utilisation of resources and, as stated, it allows sustained growth and expansion that would not be possible with static or ageing product mixes.

The work involves the entire resources of a firm at different times but some (e.g. product managers or their assigns) are involved throughout the process. A high degree of co-operation and co-ordination is necessary between the team members and all the operating divisions of the company. The team itself is drawn from these departments as necessary and must obviously include marketing and product management executives (Figure 5.5) with representatives from manufacturing and financial departments. It should have a dynamic chairman who is interested in the group achieving its agreed objectives and who will drive them on at a good pace. He or she should be senior enough to be able to persuade the directors of other departments to give the work their wholehearted support and assistance. There should also be a secretary who will be responsible for all the paper-work, making sure it is produced and circulated in time and so on.

New product development can cover a range of activities, as shown in Table 5.6. Some new products involving only minor technological or market development may simply be evolutionary changes from existing products. New flavours, colours and designs of existing products involve comparatively little work or risk. At the other end of the scale there are revolutionary products involving both new techniques and new markets which can demand massive inputs of resources, and involve high levels of risk. New pharmaceutical or aeronautical products often come into this category, involving years of development work and vast financial investment.

OBJECTIVES – PRODUCT / MARKET OBJECTIVNESS	TECHNICAL NEWNESS ⟶		
	NO TECHNOLOGICAL CHANGE	IMPROVED TECHNOLOGY Better use of firm's skills, know-how etc.	NEW TECHNOLOGY Acquire new tech., production & other skills
NO MARKET CHANGE	(Current business)	REFORMULATION To optimise balance of cost, quality, performance of current range of products	REPLACEMENT Seek new & better materials etc. for present products in new technology
STRENGTHENED MARKET Exploit present markets for current products more fully	REMERCHANDISING Increase sales to customers of types now being served by the firm	IMPROVED PRODUCT For greater utility and acceptance by customers	PRODUCT LINE EXTENSION Broaden line on offer to customers thro' use of new technology
NEW MARKET To increase no. of types or classes of customer served	NEW USE To find new classes of customer who can use current products of the firm	MARKET EXTENSION To reach new classes of customer by modifying current products	DIVERSIFI-CATION To add to the classes of customer served by developing new techn. knowledge & new products

(The left axis is labelled MARKET NEWNESS ⟶)

Source: Adapted from S.C. Johnson and C. Jones, 'How to organize for new products', *Harvard Business Review* (May–June 1957).

Fig. 5.5   New product–market activities classified by product and market objectives

The development of new products of an evolutionary nature can often be undertaken through the normal management structure, with perhaps a single manager in charge to co-ordinate activities. The management of developments at the revolutionary end of the scale, however, will normally involve dedicated teams of managers and specialists free from other duties.

(i) *Venture management teams*
These teams are sometimes used instead of the new product-development group or committee discussed above. They are comprised of executives drawn from the main operating departments and have the same general responsibilities.

122   *Mastering Marketing*

Table 5.6 **Practical stages in new product development**

1   Prepare long-range forecasts for profit and sales revenue of existing product–market activities based on user requirements, competition and other external factors.
2   Prepare long-range profit plan from the corporate objectives that have been set.
3   Establish profit gap by comparing 2 with 1.
4   From this target (3), which has to be met by new and modified products, select products which can be modified and estimate the profit to be earned by new products if the profit gap is to be filled.
5   Prepare objectives for the new products and make an audit of the company's total resources.
6   From 5, select the new products that seem to be good possibilities from the list of prospects and determine the product–market strategy that would be needed and the markets that would be involved.
7   If necessary, prepare a statement of revised corporate objectives necessitated by the new products.
8   While the above is being done, the work of identifying, assessing and evaluating new product ideas will have progressed, leading to the preparation of a short list of new products that will be developed and the timing for this (i.e. products for immediate, intermediate and long-term development).
9   With these, prepare a long-range profit plan.
10   Assign responsibility for the design, development, manufacturing, launch and marketing of the new products approved in 8. (Adjustments will be needed in 8, 9 and 10, if unforseen difficulties, new market and competitive developments prevent the original ideas from being developed or delay them.)
11   When launched, evaluate the performance of the new products so that any necessary modifications can be made.
12   If the launch of them is successful, incorporate the new products into the main marketing plans/operations.

However, they are usually assigned to one task and when the new product or venture has been approved or agreed, they remain together to manage and plan the launch and initial marketing of it. Usually they only hand over to the departments when the product has been successfully established and can be moved into the main marketing and manufacturing operations. They are in effect an autonomous section responsible for achieving target profits, sales, market shares and so on for the activity in their charge.

It is an attempt to make innovation more predictable and to minimise the risk involved. It is a corporate effort to manage new developments (products or business) as a perennial activity rather than an *ad hoc*, sporadic or crash operation at times of urgent need. It is also designed to achieve significant developments into new activities.

(ii) *Sources for ideas*
Given the need for new products and the fact that many new ideas, for many reasons, may not achieve profitable commercialisation, a firm needs a substantial steady stream of ideas if its new product development programme is to be successful. Thus it must tap all possible sources for new ideas. These range from

customers, distributors, research and trade associations to competitors, published information on new technological advances and product ideas.

Every department can make a worthwhile contribution. Obviously marketing and distribution executives will be the main source but manufacturing colleagues can come up with ideas based on thoughts on cost reduction, improved quality or performance, use of better alternative materials and so on. Financial colleagues can contribute ideas developed from thoughts on how costs could be reduced, prices increased, cash flow and liquidity improvements and better utilisation of funds. In some cases ideas will come from the market or the potential users indicating a need or a gap which a new product could fill. Sometimes an invention or concept may be developed first, and then a market sought for it. A progressing company will ensure that all sources of potential new ideas are tapped and encouraged.

(iii) *Screening*
With a large number of ideas to select from, the development team must have some method for assessing for feasibility and prospects of the ideas. This can be done by screening the ideas graphically or statistically. The latter seems easier to assess objectively (see Appendix A.2). Figure 5.6(a) illustrates the high mortality rate for new product ideas and stresses the need for a continuous supply of ideas if a successful new product development programme is to be sustained. Figure 5.6(b) shows the time/cost relationship. This indicates why it is vital to screen out all the unlikely or doubtful product ideas before the serious design and development stage is reached. It is at this time that total development costs increase very substantially.

Development of the ideas that have passed the second screening can begin. Those set aside can be reconsidered at a later date. Figure 5.7 indicates the process in practice. As the figure indicates, if the idea, concept, proposed specification or performance does not accord with the agreed standards, the new product proposal can be referred back to an appropriate stage in the process for further study. Or it can be set aside for future reconsideration.

Traditionally the stages in new product development have tended to be sequential, ideas being passed from one department to another as successive stages are reached. Many companies are now following what has been described as the rugby scrum approach, where people from the different departments or disciplines work together on the project from the start. This avoids, for example, finance or marketing spending time evaluating potential costs or markets for a device which production cannot make!

Another recent development which has speeded up new product development in complex areas, such as the car market, has been to use off-the-shelf components as far as possible. Previously the design of a new car had involved new everything, from wiper blades to engines and body panels. Now components which do not impinge directly on the new design are taken from the existing range of components in use, thus saving substantial amounts of development time and other resources.

(iv) *Market research for new products*

In mass markets, and in many smaller ones, the penalties in making a wrong
decision in modifying existing products or launching new ones can be high. This

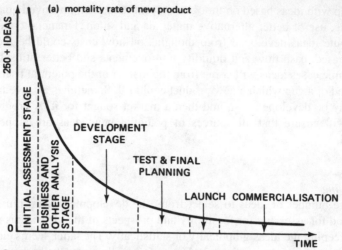

(a) **mortality rate of new product**

250 + IDEAS

INITIAL ASSESSMENT STAGE

BUSINESS AND OTHER ANALYSIS STAGE

DEVELOPMENT STAGE

TEST & FINAL PLANNING

LAUNCH COMMERCIALISATION

0

TIME

Source: Douglas Foster, 'Most new products die young', *Financial Times* (London)
29 July 1969.

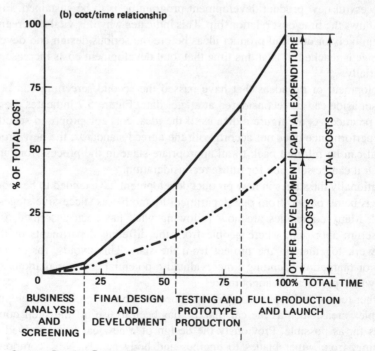

(b) **cost/time relationship**

% OF TOTAL COST

100

75

50

25

0   25   50   75   100% TOTAL TIME

CAPITAL EXPENDITURE

OTHER DEVELOPMENT COSTS

TOTAL COSTS

BUSINESS ANALYSIS AND SCREENING | FINAL DESIGN AND DEVELOPMENT | TESTING AND PROTOTYPE PRODUCTION | FULL PRODUCTION AND LAUNCH

Source: Douglas Foster, *Planning for Products and Markets* (Longman, 1972)
fig 5.10

Fig. 5.6   New product development

Idea generation
External – trade, customers, suppliers, inventors etc.
Internal – market research, sales force, R&D etc.

Initial screening
Does it fit our company?
Does it fit our market?
Can we make it?
Can we market it?
Can our existing sales force sell it?
Is it likely to produce a viable volume of business?
Is it likely to yield an acceptable level of RoI or profit?
Can we raise the necessary finance/other resources?
Will it have any detrimental or beneficial effects on our other business?

Market research
Concept testing
Initial product testing
Modified product testing
Testing of pack, promotion, price etc. as appropriate

Commercialisation
Store or area testing
Area or rolling launch
Full commercial launch

Monitoring
Effects of launch activities, promotion etc.
Acceptance by trade, consumer trial and repeat purchase
Rate of returns, complaints etc.

Fig. 5.7 Stages in new product screening, development and launching

is an area in which properly designed, executed and interpreted market research can be effective, and some uses have already been mentioned in Chapter 4. There are situations of course when total security has to be maintained if the organisation is to keep any competitive advantage expected from the development. Then it may not be possible to carry out any research at all, but whenever possible some feed-back from the prospective target group should be sought as an insurance against wasting resources on developments that the market will not appreciate or accept.

Market Research may often be used for both industrial and consumer products and services, from the time when the new development is only at the *Concept stage*, through to an *Experimental launch* of the new product or variation on the market. In concept testing only the basic idea is put before potential purchasers, sometimes in words, sometimes with diagrams or a mock-up. Would people respond positively to the idea if it was put on the market – or can they suggest modifications, weaknesses and so forth? The number of people interviewed is usually small, perhaps only a single large customer in an industrial market, or a few individuals or focus groups in consumer markets. Results at this stage may encourage development work to be started, or they may show that there are severe weaknesses calling for the project to be abandoned or modified.

After the concept stage research will be geared to the vital areas in the development process, subject to the physical constraints in the situation. Thus while it is usually not difficult to produce small quantities of consumer goods for product testing, this cannot normally be done for more complex products. However the 'product testing' stage may not be needed in industrial markets as products are often developed or modified in conjunction with one or two major customers.

With consumer goods and services the related factors such as packaging and advertising may need to be tested in the development stages. Various specialised techniques are used here, with the intention of ensuring that the message to be conveyed is put across, that these aspects help in correctly positioning the innovation in the market place, and so forth.

The final pre-launch research with many consumer products is a test or experimental launch, where the whole marketing plan is put into operation in a small part of the market to check that all is well before the costs of a wider launch are committed. The scope of these tests can range from single stores – often mobile shops specially maintained by research companies for such testing – through to complete television areas. The scale will be governed by the details of the marketing plan, the degree of novelty in the new offering and the downside risks or the costs of failure. The timing is also vital, as in most consumer markets the critical factor for success is the rate at which those who try the product at all come back to repurchase. Apart from obvious seasonal problems, time must be allowed for repurchase to take place which may be many months for items such as shaving cream or furniture polish, but much less for items in weekly shopping lists.

Three vital points need to be kept in mind when planning research into new products. One is that any extension of the 'critical path' for the launch due to extended market research will increase the risks of pre-emption, or of having a competitor get to the market first. The second is that the research results, even for an experimental launch, will have been obtained under abnormal conditions. Hence while favourable results will encourage progress, they cannot be taken as guarantees that all will be well in the eventual major launch. Much can happen to change tastes, fashions and even spending power in the time between research and launch, as well as in the competitive position in a market. The third point is that good research needs a good brief, setting out the specific objectives, and, where appropriate, with agreed criteria laid down in advance for decisions to proceed, modify or abandon the project.

Assignments

How important is new product development in your chosen market? How *NEW* are new products in this market? Is this a market where there are high rewards for innovation? How many really new products have been introduced in the past five years? Ten years?

Where on the Product Life-Cycle are the organisation's products or services? Is there a good balance across the life-cycle?

Does the division between products and services apply in your market? How much service is involved with products, or tangible offerings with services?

Market management and planning

'Market' can be described simply as a group of people able and willing to buy a particular product or service. While with consumer goods and durables 'people' means the consumers, with industrial products and capital equipment the 'people' are in fact commercial firms and business enterprises. Modern usage has given several meanings to the word 'market'. There are definitions based on the type of person buying the product or service (e.g. above, the 'consumer market' and the 'industrial market'). Markets may also be defined by the type of service used (e.g. the 'electrical contracting market') and the product in the selling-buying exchange process (e.g. the 'refrigerator market' or the 'car market'). It can also be designated in money terms (e.g. the market for Product X is £Y million).

To the stockbroker, his or her market is all the customers who deal through him or her but *the* Market in this case is the Stock Exchange, where the transactions are made. To the sales manager the word means the areas and regions of his sales territory, the different types of customers to be served, the different technologies involved and the use to which the products are put. For the accountant the market is all individuals and organisations using or needing these services. To the economist a 'market' is the total universe comprising it. However, for marketing executives the market is not only present customers but *all those persons and organisations who may be persuaded to buy the products or services they offer.* Table 6.1 lists the various classifications of markets used today and gives examples of the products involved. It will be noted that some items can feature in more than one definition, the deciding factor being the use and the properties of the goods in question. The marketing mix used will differ according to the target market.

6.1 Emergence of mass markets

The history of marketing and the development of markets as we know them today follow closely the history of civilisation and has been discussed in Section 1.7(c). In modern times social changes led to the development of potential mass markets. However, mass markets do not usually occur spontaneously. They have to be stimulated into reality and can sometimes be created by positive marketing effort. As competition increased economies moved from being essentially that of 'sellers' markets' to that of 'buyers' markets'. This required greater sophistication of marketing operations. Studies were needed of such things as the output aspects of the economy, buying power of markets and how this was distributed between customer classes, the expenditure patterns for goods and services and the stability of business activity.

Table 6.1   **Present-day classification of markets**

Consumer goods: goods and services destined for use by the consumer (individuals) or households which do not require further commercial processing.

Mass market: the above that are purchased in some quantity and could be purchased by everyone. Usually these are purchased frequently or on more than one occasion in a trading year, i.e. there is substantial repeat buying.

Convenience goods: Consumer goods purchased frequently, immediately and with the minimum of effort in comparison and buying, i.e. a sub-classification of mass markets (e.g. many food products, soaps and detergents, newspapers, magazines, tobacco products etc.).

Speciality goods: Consumer goods with unique features or characteristics and/or brand identification for which a significant group of buyers will make a special purchasing effort (e.g. specific types and brands of fancy goods, photographic and sporting equipment, hi-fi products and special clothing).

Shopping goods: Consumer goods where in the process of selection and purchase consumers make comparisons based on quality, price, style and suitability (e.g. shoes, women's dress goods, millinery, major appliances, cars, furniture).

Durable goods: tangible goods which survive many uses and have a relatively long life (e.g. refrigerators, washing machines, radio, TV etc.).

Non-durable goods: tangible goods which are normally consumed or used in one or a few uses.

Industrial markets: products, raw materials and consumable items (e.g. cleaning fluids, fuel) primarily for producing other goods or rendering some service or other. Include equipment, components, raw materials, and supplies for maintenance or repair purposes.

Services market: benefits, activities and satisfactions not involving the exchange of tangible products, which are offered for sale (e.g. laundry, transport, travel and tourism services, banking, insurance, hotel and catering facilities).

Government markets: all products and services bought by government departments and agencies for their own use.

Defence markets: all items bought by defence organisations (government departments, army, navy, air force etc.) for use in defence of their countries.

In many markets the simple division between suppliers and buyers becomes more complex. Manufacturers of fast moving consumer goods (fmcgs) or suppliers of family services may need to reach an ultimate market of millions of housewives, or holiday makers, or whatever. However to reach these mass markets suppliers have first to sell their goods and ideas to distributors, who may be individual retailers, or may be powerful chains of outlets. In the UK most producers of mass-market foods need to sell their products to powerful retail chains before housewives have any chance of buying their products. Similarly suppliers of toiletries, consumer durables, home electronics, package holidays and so forth have to sell through appropriate channels, many with powerful influences on what shall and what shall not be offered to the public. While it is frequently stated that selling industrial goods involves dealing with expert buyers, the retail chains also have expert buyers who will evaluate all aspects of a product or service before allowing it into their 'listings'. Without these listings products will not be available through that channel's outlets, and so marketing and selling need to take place on a number of levels.

(a) Effects of technological developments

The Industrial Revolution has never ended though at times economic recessions have slowed it down. The present day is sometimes referred to as the 'Age of Automation' and it has had two major effects on economies of relevance to marketing management as explained in Section 1.7(c). The present age is one of surplus and as this increases so does the need for marketing.

Technological developments also have wide reaching effects on economic and marketing activities. Consider, for example, the development of computers for commercial purposes in 1951 and their present-day widespread use. New factories, equipment and engineering were needed. New and better-paying jobs resulted and additional marketing facilities and concepts were required to sell, lease and distribute the machines and their associated software. New markets were created for magnetic tape, disks, paper and other supplies. New facilities were needed for the training of technicians and there was increased interest in knowledge and applications of sophisticated statistical methods to business and marketing. Inventory control was simplified and made more effective, while general record keeping was made more efficient, faster and could be more detailed in the facts recorded.

Companies providing credit services were able to expand and speed up their operations. Design engineering of all kinds (cars, planes, capital equipment and major industrial products, durables etc.) could be done more quickly. Production methods could be simulated and the most appropriate selected, thus improving manufacturing efficiency. Enquiries, reservations and confirmations for travel and hotel facilities could be provided very quickly and more efficiently.

The modern car and public conveyances improved the transport infrastructures and helped to create major cities and increase leisure and business travel. Trucks expedited the delivery of goods. The modern aircraft speeded up internal and international travel, bringing the latter, and associated tourism, to millions who otherwise did not have the time or money for the more traditional and slower methods of transportation. Planes also improved the transportation of goods internationally, necessitated new material handling methods and, because of the latter, reduced the damage and pollution of goods in transit and losses due to pilfering and other reasons. Satellite communications revolutionised international communication links. The availability of instant colour TV transmissions from remote parts of the world extended consumer interests into learning more about these world areas and stimulated interest in long-distance travel and holidays. Xerography and data transfer also revolutionised office procedures and met reprographic needs that businesses and colleges may not even have realised existed.

All of these and many others contributed greatly to the growth of economies and in marketing opportunities for business. Despite the periodic recessions of the 20th Century, technological advances will continue, if more slowly and carefully. More new opportunities for marketing should flow and in their wake, further development of the economies of most countries. The effect of technological changes cannot be ignored by marketing executives. Some may bring indirect benefits (e.g. the computer and its effect on travel and tourism through improved information handling). Remember that improved technology has brought benefits over a wide range of products. These include plastics, transistors, microprocessors, frozen foods and microwave ovens, packaging materials, power brakes and steering with automatic transmission for vehicles, air conditioners, tape recorders and antibiotics, to mention just a few at random.

While the European Community is opening up wider mass markets, new design, manufacturing and distributive facilities are making many aspects of niche markets economically viable and attractive. Markets therefore tend to be in a state of change and flux, and those who first perceive significant changes will benefit. However there needs to be stability in some aspects of any market if anything beyond short-term opportunism is to be developed.

(b) Stability of markets
Without some confidence that a 'market' will still exist once current plans have reached fruition there can be little market planning. However the rates of change in design, processes, products and ways of marketing are all tending to increase. While *product* life cycles, for types of food, cars, home entertainment, holidays and so forth may run for decades, the life cycles of brands or of variants within brands is becoming shorter and shorter. Beyond that the size and shape of markets may be changing.

Some changes in markets are gradual but some may be more sudden. Refrigerators came into home use gradually over several decades, and the frozen food market only grew slowly. Micro-wave ovens came into homes far more rapidly, and the development of micro-wave meals was equally rapid. Television spread more rapidly than did radio when that was introduced. Video recorders have penetrated the market far more quickly than either – although so far the spread of satellite dish aerials seems to be moving more slowly. In the main however these changes have been gradual to a greater or lesser extent.

Some changes are generated within specific markets, such as the deliberate attempts by ice-cream manufacturers to spread consumption through the year instead of being confined to the summer months. Other changes follow from changes in other fields, such as the moves to lighter clothing generally in the UK following the spread of home central heating, which itself was fostered by North Sea gas discoveries. Even the structure of families is now changing with effects on many consumer markets.

Market changes of a more drastic nature may arise suddenly, and may be far less foreseeable. Concern about the ozone layer has led to rapid changes in the formulation of refrigerants and propellants. Concern for the greenhouse effects and acid rain has brought in legislation about car exhaust gases and engine efficiency, as well as efforts to conserve heat in homes, offices and industry. The arms industries have suffered heavily from the end of the Cold War, which was sudden and virtually unforeseen.

6.2   Market strategies, objectives and mix

Marketing executives have a number of strategies they can choose, but it is essential that choices are related back to the organisation's corporate strategy. In some major conglomerates the overall corporate strategy may be set in financial terms, but at some stage this is brought to the level of the operating unit or business. Hence the term Strategic Business Unit (or SBU).

At the level of the SBU, strategies will be decided which will apply to all its products and three options are generally recognised. These have been described by Michael Porter who has suggested that a company can achieve success through aiming to:

(i)   provide basic goods or services at *low cost*;
(ii)   incur higher costs but produce *differentiated* or unique products selling at premium prices;
(iii) *focus* on a small specialised niche in a market.

Examples of all three strategies are common, but in the computer market Amstrad has provided an example of the first kind, which caused major shifts in demand. In the car market there are examples of all three strategies run concurrently by different companies. In many food markets some companies follow the first strategy and concentrate on Own Label products; some produce distinctive branded products at higher prices; some supply specialised diet or health products to meet the special needs of small sectors of little interest to the other groups.

Within each corporate strategy there is still a choice of four specific marketing strategies, described by Igor Ansoff. The first of these is market retention, concentrating on marketing a company's existing products in their current markets, using existing expertise and knowledge to gain a competitive edge. Normally product development is vital, but it is low-risk evolutionary development, or Old Product Development, simply to keep abreast of changes within an existing market.

The second option is for expansion by taking existing products into new markets. This may mean exporting to other countries, a method of increasing importance within the European Community after 1992. Here the company has the assurance that it knows and understands its products, but it is venturing into new markets, with some degree of risk. However it may only mean marketing existing products to new segments in the home market, such as selling office equipment to domestic users, or rooms in holiday hotels to conference organisers. Here the new segments need to be carefully studied as some product modifications may be needed for success, but the company is still handling a familiar product.

The third option is similar, providing for expansion within a company's existing market by introducing new products. Here risks are again kept low, as the company continues to work in familiar markets, but by introducing products with which it is not familiar.

The fourth option is the diversification strategy, in which a firm launches new products into unfamiliar markets. This is a high-risk strategy as both product and market elements are new, and there are also risks that so much effort will be allocated to the new venture that existing products and existing markets suffer.

(a) The product–market portfolio

Once a firm moves beyond a single product in a single market it will have a 'portfolio' or a range of product–market operations. Some of these may be at early stages in their life cycle; others may be in decline. Some may be earning good returns; some may still be costing more in development and promotion than they are achieving in revenue. It is vital for the long-term health of the company that there is a balance, within the portfolio, of old and new products or markets. A review or screening process must be regularly undertaken covering all areas in which the firm is interested. Too few new or emerging products may mean that there is nothing to replace the current earners as they become obsolete. Too many new products in the range may place a heavy burden on management, on cash flows, and resources generally which may drag the firm down. Too much concentration in declining markets spells risks of one kind. Too much commitment to new markets may be equally risky but in a different way. A balance needs to be struck, and to be maintained by a careful review of current earnings, forecasts and potential returns. Products or markets with no future need to be closed down. Current earners need to be managed for maximum results. Those with growth potential need to be fostered. Research & development need to be focused. Securing a balance between all these factors in the market is one of the most critical activities in marketing management.

(b) Identifying market opportunities

Before the market and product-market screening take place market opportunities and characteristics must be identified. The work needed here is summarised in Table 6.2.

6.3   Market segmentation

Except in special circumstances (e.g. a small, very specialised market, or where the firm has a monopoly through a unique product) it is no longer economically possible to serve total markets. So the need to segment markets has become a reality for executives. Apart from preventing a firm from attempting the impossible and spreading limited resources on too wide a front, market segmentation tries to determine the differences among potential buyers (e.g. buying habits and patterns, preferences etc.) that are consequential to their buying decisions. The rationale is that a total market is not homogeneous (i.e. is not similar) with respect to customer response and preferences for products, price, promotional strategies or the channels of distribution used.

Ideally, total markets should be divided so as to give maximum heterogeneity (dissimilarity) between segments and complete homogeneity (similarity) within each segment. Thus responses to marketing variables will vary more between segments than within them. If this is to be done well, executives must have clear and detailed definitions of the market in terms of consumer needs, wants and problems they are trying to resolve by their purchases. Executives must also understand other problems, however irrelevant they may seem, if these are deemed to influence consumers' buying decisions.

Table 6.2 **Identifying market opportunities and characteristics with marketing research**

Stage		Activities
Identifying markets and market segments		1 *Identifying markets and discrete market segments* estimating total demand or market size; identifying significant segments of total market; measuring the coverage of the market by existing products or services (to deduce the new or revised/modified activities the company could consider).
		2 *Market projections* projections into the future (for 5, 10 or more years) to evaluate growth or decline of existing markets; or changes in customer requirements, preferences, etc; or changes in economic, social, political, technological, ethical and other environmental factors which affect market conditions or the services being offered.
	Determining characteristics	3 *Characteristics of market* services required by customers; function or usage of service or products; essential features which the service or product must have; methods used by customers in searching for services/products; competitive position, including share of markets, costs/prices, etc. (should include projections as (2) above); range of services to be offered; functions critical to the success of operations offering services to selected markets; commercial conditions and terms expected by customers; cost/price relationship; price sensitivity; possible pricing policy.
Selecting marketing strategy. Markets and marketing operations + control information feedback		4 *Available market share* estimate of market shares available; projections of market shares as per (2) above; company and competitors' strengths and weaknesses and how these may affect market shares; how to modify marketing operations to improve profitability and gain increased market shares.
		5 *Marketing strategy and market selection* selection of strategy and operations (tactics) to be followed; selection of markets and market segments to be attacked; possible mix to be offered; deciding the resultant marketing plans to be implemented; implementation and control of marketing operations, including analysis of results being obtained, feeding new information and data into marketing planning activities and assessments.

The demand characteristics of each segment have to be identified and this requires study of the way different consumer groups perceive the basic need to be satisfied or the problem that has to be overcome. For example, the purchase of expensive capital equipment would be viewed differently by the large firm and a small one. In the consumer market, the need to shave is viewed differently by old and young men. To the former it is a necessity of civilised living. To the latter it may just be a chore to be avoided as much as possible. If they do they could be relatively insignificant buyers of shaving requisites.

Then, how a product's attributes relate to customer preferences and how concern or interest in various aspects of the product lead to a buying decision must be known. Next, what trends the different demand characteristics of each target segment are taking should be known and accurate forecasts made of where these would take demand (i.e. nature, size etc. of demand) into some specified future period. Finally, the worth or size of each segment has to be estimated.

Table 6.3 shows the different variables that can be used to segment consumer goods and industrial products markets. Tables 6.4 and 6.5 indicate how two service industries (travel/tourism and investment services) may be segmented, using their special characteristics to arrive at the final groupings. These special features influence potential customers' buying decisions. Figure 6.1 illustrates the use of the family life-cycle concept mentioned in Table 6.3. Finally, Figure 6.2 gives brief descriptions of the different classifications used in the case of the individual consumer and the sort of products and services that would normally appeal to them.

(a) Segmentation resulting from marketing strategy

How a market is segmented is also determined by the type of marketing strategy followed. There are three basic strategies that could be followed.

Table 6.3   **Market segmentation variables**

[*Variables*]

For people	*For organisations*
Age	Nature of activity, SIC etc.
Sex	Financial/legal structure:
Working/not working:	Sole trader
Part/full time	Partnership
Occupation	Single company
Income	Subsidiary
Home ownership	Holding company
Family composition	Charity
Education	Government Department
Socio-economic class	Local Government
Media exposure:	QUANGO
Reading habits	etc.
TV viewing	Numbers employed
Radio listening	Turnover
Personality:	When founded
Innovative/traditional	
Introvert/extrovert	*For both*
etc.	
Life style:	Geographic area
'Yuppies'	Urban/rural situation
'Dinkies'	Time in present premises
'Woopies'	Usage patterns
etc	

Many of the 'people' variables can usefully be applied to managers interviewed in industrial surveys.

Table 6.4 **Segmenting the travel and tourist market**

Segment	Sub-segment
Holiday tourist	fully inclusive package partly inclusive package independent traveller booked via travel agent independent traveller booked privately

Business traveller	booked via travel agent
	booked by employer's travel dept. or individually
	(the above could also be divided to show those who go
	    solely for business purposes and those who tag on a
	    short holiday at one end of such trips)

Special or common *interest traveller*	hobby cultural (art, music etc.). religious archaeological and ancient history ethnic and anthropological flora and fauna

Table 6.5 **Market segmentation variables modified for the marketing of investment services**

Standard variable	Special sub-classification
1 *Income groups*	(a) Expected return required (b) Degree of risk acceptable (c) Current investment and amounts and incidence of new funds for investment
2 *Social groups* *(A,B,C1,C2,D,E)*	(a) (b) } As above. (See Figure 6.2 also) (c) (d) Personal characteristics and attitudes to investment and portfolios (e) Possible response patterns to offerings, or marketing and promotional activities

3 *Geographical*	(a) The home locations: region
	    size of community
	    type of community

4 *Personality*	(As standard variables in as far as they condition response)
5 *Buyer behaviour*	(As standard if not taken into full account by 2(e) above)

The first is *undifferentiated marketing*, involving the firm marketing one product to all markets using the same marketing mix. The second is *differentiated marketing*, in which the firm markets many products with different marketing mixes designed to satisfy smaller market segments. Third is *concentrated marketing*, where the firm is concentrating all marketing resources on a small segment of the total market.

Bachelor stage: young single people not living at home	Newly married couples: young, no children	Full nest I: youngest child under six	Full nest II: youngest child six or over six	Full nest III: older married couples with dependent children	Empty nest I: older married couples, no children living with them, in labor force	Empty nest II: older married couples, no children living at home, head retired	Solitary survivor in labor force	Solitary survivor retired
Few financial burdens. Fashion opinion leaders. Recreation oriented. Buy: Basic kitchen equipment, basic furniture, cars, equipment for the mating game, vacations.	Better off financially than they will be in the near future. Highest purchase rate and highest average purchase of durables. Buy: Cars, refrigerators, stoves, sensible and durable furniture, vacations.	Home purchasing at peak. Liquid assets low. Dissatisfied with financial position and amount of money saved. Interested in new products. Like advertised products. Buy: Washers, dryers, TV, baby food, chest rubs and cough medicine, vitamins, dolls, wagons, sleds, skates.	Financial position better. Some wives work. Less influenced by advertising. Buy larger sized packages, multiple-unit deals. Buy: Many foods, cleaning materials, bicycles, music lessons, pianos.	Financial position still better. More wives work. Some children get jobs. Hard to influence with advertising. High average purchase of durables. Buy: New more tasteful furniture, auto travel, non-necessary appliances, boats, dental services, magazines.	Home ownership at peak. Most satisfied with financial position and money saved. Interested in travel, recreation, self-education. Make gifts and contributions. Not interested in new products. Buy: Vacations, luxuries, home improvements.	Drastic cut in income. Keep home. Buy: Medical appliances, medical care, products which aid health, sleep, and digestion.	Income still good but likely to sell home.	Same medical and product needs as the other retired groups, drastic cut in income. Special need for attention, affection, and security.

Fig. 6.1   Life-cycle of a family

The system of classifying people by 'Socio-economic Class' is open to many criticisms. However it is still in general use, partly because it is easily understood, partly because many organisations have large amounts of historic data based on it; and partly because much media research still uses the system. The main UK definitions are those used by the National Readership Survey, whereby members of a household are normally classified by the occupation of the 'head of the household'. The definitions are:

Socio-economic class	Percent of population	Status	HoH Occupation or vocation
A	3	Upper-middle class	Higher managerial, administrative or professional
B	14	Middle class	Intermediate managerial, administrative or professional
C₁	26	Lower middle class	Supervisory, clerical, junior admin. or professional
C₂	25	Skilled working class	Skilled manual workers
D	19	Working class	Semi-skilled and unskilled manual workers
E	13	Lowest levels of subsistence	State pensioners, casual workers

Fig. 6.2   Socio-economic classification

The first strategy is not widely practised now and the inherent danger of it lies in the effort to satisfy everyone. The firm is open to intensive competition from companies offering specialised products to smaller market segments. When competitors hold substantial market shares this strategy becomes unworkable. Where marketing to foreign countries is concerned, there is the added hazard that tastes, preferences and needs will vary. So one product formulation would not be acceptable.

With differentiated marketing greater satisfaction in numerous market segments may be achieved but the costs are greater. With shorter production runs and increased inventories, manufacturing costs are increased. The use of different marketing mixes for each product–market situation increases the time and effort needed from executives and usually requires a larger marketing department with attendant higher costs and greater promotional costs. While concentrating on a single market segment often gives a profitable operation, should total demand in that segment decline, the supplier can experience a critical drop in business volume with subsequent financial trouble.

Some firms do concentrate on very specific market segments – e.g. Lotus, Jaguar or Rolls Royce cars – accepting the risks which have been very evident in the recession of 1991–93. Some spread the risk by covering a wide range of products and markets and accept the increased costs and efforts of managing the spread. An example here is Ford with models for different segments from the Fiesta for the sales representative to the Grenada for the senior executive. Some companies mix their strategies, such as Kelloggs offering Corn Flakes to a large segment covering most ages and classes, and a range of more specialised and costly products to consumers with concerns about health or weight.

In all segments the vital need is to 'position' the product in terms of value, design, price and other attributes so that the whole image of the brand meets with the approval of the target group. Integrated marketing should ensure that every aspect from the name to the way in which the product or service is delivered form a coherent and consistent whole. Matching the firm's offerings to the expectations of the chosen segments is vital.

(b) Segmentation strategies

Again there are two basic approaches or strategies. The first is the *consumer segmentation* method where potential customers are grouped according to personal characteristics and product attributes or properties are compared with the former. The second strategy is *product segmentation*, a term open to misunderstanding by newcomers to marketing. In this, product benefits and attributes are first defined and then consumers' personal characteristics are compared against them. The two approaches are not competitive but complementary. The first helps to answer which consumer groups should form the target markets. The second is useful in market definition. It is of particular value to consumer goods as it illustrates what the *brand structure* of a market is and how the different brands are perceived by potential consumers.

(c) Advantages and disadvantages

The purposes of market segmentation are to improve the competitive position of brands and products, attain a more effective position for them in limited markets, identify gaps in the market (unsatisfied needs etc.) which represent new product opportunities and find new customers for existing products. Despite the basic logic of the approach, doubts have been raised as to the viability of the concept. Some markets do not have sufficient heterogeneity of needs. They may have only a need for product variety. Markets can also be too small for efficient segmentation. Further, since three rules have to be satisfied to ensure sound segmentation and these cannot always be met, segmentation can be difficult. The three concern the different consumer groups that could form the basis of segmentation. The groups must be clearly identified (physically and in terms of their needs), they must be easily located and it must be possible to mount specifically designed marketing mixes to appeal to their wants, preferences and so on.

In practice this means that segments must be accessible. It must be possible to focus marketing activities on the segments chosen though this is not possible in every case. Using mass media, such as newspapers or television, may not permit advertising of a product to be very closely focused on the prime target group, and much of the effort will fall outside this prime area. However in the past it was often more economic to reach the target group through mass media than to use more specialised and more costly means. Recent advances in the analysis of information about consumers or industrial users have however led to the development of databases or lists identifying members of very specific segments. This has led to growth in Direct Marketing operations using mail or telephone calls to reach very limited target groups. In these ways accessibility to some segments has been greatly increased.

Then the segment must be substantial, that is, it is large enough to warrant the design and launch of separate and distinctive marketing activities for it. With many products in both industrial and consumer markets major segments offer potential for substantial volumes of sales, leading to profitable operations. Marketing to smaller segments however can be more risky because of the more limited potential, but the willingness of some people to pay more for something which meets their needs more closely can ensure profitability. Linked to the methods of direct marketing which will be developed later (see Chapter 9), quite small and demanding segments can now offer substantial earnings.

Finally it should be possible to measure the key aspects of a market segment. Some of the characteristics listed in Table 6.3 and in Figures 6.1 and 6.2 can easily be assessed, but some are more difficult. Life-styles or corporate styles may be more important in some segments but assessment and classification may be difficult. However not all classification and assessment need be highly scientific. Labels may come and go, but most people will recognise a Yuppie or a Woopie or their current equivalents when they see them. Products aimed specifically at the first group may not have a long life cycle, but properly positioned they can be highly profitable for a while. Products aimed at the second group may have longer lives, but only if they are very carefully positioned in the first place. Different travel agents have segmented the markets carefully, and few retired people will be found in Club-Med resorts, or many young executives on holidays designed for the elderly.

One development of great interest to those seeking to contact smaller segments is the analysis of Census data down to quite small units, such as the enumeration districts. Basic housing characteristics picked up during the Census are known to provide useful correlations with life-styles. When linked with postcodes these analyses are used to identify and reach members of important but small segments more effectively than can be achieved with broader media.

Despite the great advances in analysis and in methods of reaching members of segments now available through computers, good judgement is still needed in handling market segmentation. In fact computers may make it easier to end up with false or incorrect segmentation. For example, the market for housing may be thought to segment into demand for houses, flats (apartments) and bungalows but no specific customer group is interested in only one of these. There are no significant differences in their consumer characteristics except for the elderly and disabled, who will prefer apartments and bungalows designed specially for them. Prices and locations are usually the critical factors so segmenting the housing market by price and region would be more correct and practical.

Next, it is possible to overlook or forget a segment or two, in the rush to carry out segmentation. In almost every marketing situation there is always a customer group or two that could use the product in question but who do not know of its existence. For example there was the firm that developed special gas-tight ceramics for the envelopes of large valves, klystrons and so on used in TV and long-distance communications. Every effort was put into this. It was not until enquiries were received from other manufacturers in the electronics industry for the new ceramic for their own special uses (e.g. for transistors and as bases for micro-miniature circuitry) that the executives realised a much wider market, consisting of many segments, was available for the new product.

Finally, there is the aspect of product variety. Some consumer goods firms believe they have achieved market segmentation through offering a variety of brands. If a brand offers some unique benefit or point of interest to one or two customer groups but not all, then true segmentation may result. However, where there is no real difference in the benefits offered, then consumer preference may just be influenced by the fact that one brand may be 'new' and therefore worth a try. Brand switching and lack of brand loyalty may be the only results. The snack market, which saw few product changes until a few years ago, is now one where a major segment of consumers will move to new variations. While the basic recipe may remain unchanged the flavours, shapes or textures will be subject to frequent change to appeal to this important segment. Brand switching and a lack of brand loyalty may be the only results for the industry, but failure to keep up with changing demand can erode sales of individual brands.

The advantages from true segmentation range from a firm's ability to spot opportunities more quickly and accurately and so compare more precisely the marketing possibilities that exist. Then, marketing effort and expenditure can be more profitably deployed on a selective, narrower front. Fine adjustments to products and marketing appeals can be made. The total effect is the improvement of the firm's competitive stance and more effective market positioning of products and brands. Gaps in the market, or consumer satisfaction should be more easily and accurately identified.

(d) Evaluating market segments

If market segmentation, the identification of gaps in consumer satisfaction and the selection of appropriate segments is to be well done, careful evaluation of the turnover, profit (if possible) and future trends in demand are necessary. Assuming the necessary data is available, simple grids can be used for this purpose. Figure 6.3 illustrates one approach.

In Figure 6.3 (a) a general grid shows what the total purchases of different groups of customers are for specified product groups. Figure 6.3 (b) is a more detailed grid showing how different products in a product group are selling currently to one of the customer groups. A further column shows the estimates of future sales for some specified period and the last one indicates the trend. (See also Section 10.3). If possible, and it is not always so, profit figures can be shown. Then subject to the marketing targets for sales, profit, future growth and development, the appropriate product–market segment mix can be selected to fit with the cost constraints applying for the period being planned. A further grid, showing the channels of distribution to be used and the promotional activities

(a) **the product-customer group grid for the total market**

Mix	CUSTOMER GROUPS			
PRODUCT GROUPS / Customers \ Product	Group 'A'	Group 'B'	Group 'C'	Total
Product 'X'				
Product 'Y'				
Product 'Z'				

(b) *grid for a product-customer group*

	CUSTOMER GROUP 'A'			
PRODUCT GROUP 'X' / Estimates of Product	Current sales & profit (if poss.)	Future sales & profit	Trends (%)
X1	£	£	
X2			
X3			
X4			
X5			

Source: Douglas Foster, *Planning for Products and Markets* (Longman, 1972).

Fig. 6.3   Evaluating market segments

needed, with estimated costs, can also be used to help with the planning of the marketing mix for the selected product–market segments. Such grids will normally be set up on a computer using a spreadsheet, into which will be loaded relevant data from the marketing information system, and which will be linked with the budgeting and accounting systems.

The benefits of this approach include forcing executives to think systematically about market selection and segmentation and to treat each segment as a distinct entity. They can also make sound decisions on the marketing mix to be used and whether the expected return from a segment justifies the costs. The selection of the correct marketing strategy is more clearly defined and targets and expenditure budgets are in fact built from the bottom up. Strategies and targets are not first imposed and then marketing executives have to struggle to make them fit into the programmes for what is practical.

6.4   Market planning

Market planning has to define the markets to be served, the declining markets to be dropped, what new markets should be introduced and the various programmes that

Marketing management depends on teamwork and communications. A planning meeting should ensure that everyone is kept up to date and involved in decisions. Careful preparation is needed however if meetings are to be useful and economical

would be needed to achieve agreed objectives. There are three stages. First, the market strategies relevant to corporate objectives and corporate Strengths and Weaknesses must be decided. Second, from all the alternatives available those offering the greatest Opportunities or avoiding the greatest Threats must be selected. In this process what is commonly called a SWOT analysis will be undertaken, looking inwards for the first two headings, and outside the organisation for the last two. Finally, on the basis of the earlier decisions, action plans for both the short and longer terms can be developed, with their appropriate forecasts, budgets and controls.

The critical questions that have to be answered in market planning are listed in Table 6.6. The answers will be needed both in terms of market requirements and of the firm's capacity to meet those requirements. For example, two new markets may be available, one involving the existing sales force and channels known to the company, the other demanding a new sales force and unfamiliar outlets. The responses could be widely different depending on the overall strategy of the organisation, loads on different departments and so forth.

In some firms there may be separate market managers (or departments) in the way that there are for product management. In other cases the detailed work will be done by product managers in the normal course of their product studies, since they are the ones most likely to obtain and be able to analyse correctly the

Table 6.6   **Market planning: key questions**

Marketing
Which markets/market segments are available and which selected? What products to be sold?
What sales methods and channels will be used, including sales aids, brochures, point-of-sale materials, exhibitions etc.?
What advertising required (kind, media, quantity and quality)?
What kind of sales force is required? What market shares required?

Pricing
What pricing policies are available and which will be used?
What trade terms and discount policies will be used?
What pricing structure will be followed for products, spare parts and servicing?
What ratios of turnover and costs are required?

Physical distribution
What channels and method of distribution will be used?
What standards will be set for delivery times etc.?
What forms of transportation will be used?
Where will depots be located and what size is in mind for the inventory levels for the different products?
Where and what products can be stored? Should inventories be held at own depots and/or with distributors and sales outlets?
How will the dispatch be organised?

Other
What support services are needed?
Will these be provided by the firm or the trade?
What personnel are needed?
What will be the cost of all the above?

intelligence available on this subject. When specialist aspects, such as pricing, physical distribution, costs and so on are involved, other colleagues will assist them. For critical or important matters the marketing manager, marketing and other directors will be involved in the decision-making area if not the detailed work.

When planning for *consumer markets*, executives have to identify the individual consumer or household buyer and the supermarket chains or wholesalers, retailers and other middlemen in the distribution channel. Increasingly the first need in any consumer market is to convince the highly skilled buyers in the distribution channels to handle the product. Some firms find it profitable to appoint specialist 'key account managers' to concentrate on these parts of their market. With *industrial products markets* the ultimate user, often sub-classified by end-use, technology, size of company or potential demand, has to be identified together with the middlemen who will be used. The latter are specialists too and deal with specific industries for which they have the contacts and technical knowledge. Usually they can also provide limited back-up services such as repair and maintenance.

In the case of *'government markets'*, market planning should differentiate between central government, local or state government and quasi-official markets. The last include the 'defence market'. In every case the product offerings have to be matched against needs. These offerings cover the good or product itself, back-up services, brand and packaging (for consumer goods), price aspects including credit terms, all distribution methods to be used and the promotional and personal selling activities in mind.

For *service industries* the customers are either consumers or business enterprises. Often both are potential buyers as in the case of transport services. The planning approach will follow either that for consumer or industrial markets, whichever is appropriate. (The marketing activities will do likewise.) However, the special characteristics of services (see Sections 5.2 and 11.4) have to be taken into account. It must also be remembered that industrial buyers keep in mind the profit requirements of their own firms when they make their buying decisions.

(a) Market share

All marketing operations rightly aim to achieve specified market shares. It permits comparison of the firm's performance against that of competitors. It is in fact a comparison *with the average* of all other companies in the industry or market and avoids comparison with just one enterprise. If the latter is the very best firm, direct comparison would underrate the company's performance; if it is the worst, the company would be led to believe it was doing better than it really was.

Market share comparisons also help to indicate whether changes in sales were due to uncontrollable external forces or some weakness in the marketing operations. If market shares are dropping and there are no external reasons for this, then the firm's marketing mix, or its execution, can be judged to be at fault somewhere.

A company that is able to build up its market share is more likely to be able to match, or turn away, the effects of competition. Or conversely, if a firm has a reasonable market share it can safeguard its position. However if it becomes greedy and goes for too large a slice of the total potential available, as mentioned before, it can become vulnerable to competition from smaller companies.

For every operation there is a minimum share that must be held if the operation is to remain viable over a reasonable period of time. What that level is will depend on the industry, products or services, markets, total demand, prices, profit margins and competition at any time. It is not a question of maximising market shares but of optimising them. Executives have to get the right balance for all the company's activities, taking into account the conflicting needs of long- and short-term requirements. At the same time they must obtain sufficient immediate profit without jeopardising long-term survival and growth.

(b) Market leadership

Market planning must also take into account the market image a company wishes to achieve. It can be measured in quality of the products or services offered, the 'value for money' aspect, technological innovation, reliability and performance. It can also be measured by the views customers hold of the fact that the firm is playing fair by them. That is, its prices are more than reasonable for the dependability provided and that unjust demands are not being made. That is, when costs increase, the resultant price is not raised by more than is necessary, nor before existing stocks at old costs have been sold. For firms operating overseas, especially in developing countries, strict adherence to the letter *and the spirit* of the law, no matter how inconvenient, is something else that is appreciated by the general public and can lead to the reinforcing of the firm's market image or standing.

Market image can be lost when marketing plans and actions are not kept up-to-date and when firms are run on outmoded ideas and methods stemming from obsolete experience and maintained prejudices. It can also be lost when the wrong type of executive is allowed to gain control of any of the firm's operations and gain dominance for his or her ideas regardless of their relevance to the conditions and requirements of the market-place. Failure to design and produce products or services in accordance with market needs will also erode the market leadership being enjoyed by a firm. Ignoring any of the points mentioned earlier will also prove disastrous here.

6.5   Managing markets

The work of managing markets parallels, or mirrors, that of managing products. First, existing profitable markets must be looked after so that they continue to be so for a reasonable length of time. Next, when performance is dropping off because of some change in market factors – especially consumer preference or customer needs – market modification is required. If it is not possible to do anything on modification, or it would prove too costly, or provide insufficient increased profitability, then market rationalisation may be needed. Finally, if growth is to be achieved and the losses resulting from rationalisation are to be balanced, then a continuous development of new markets is required. Again, as with products, sources for ideas on possible new markets are many, but in this case Marketing and Distribution departments, with middlemen in the distribution network, will usually be the main sources.

(a) Existing markets

Part of the 'looking after' process is making sure that all customers who should be offered the products are being well covered by the marketing activities and that no little, forgotten pockets of potential users exist. Another is to make sure that market share, growth of sales and profit targets are also being met. Then there is the question of improving the profitability of these markets or market segments.

The work could start by taking the total statistics for the market or segment and splitting them down stage after stage, to the smallest denominator if possible to see where performance is falling below target. It is possible for a market segment to be producing the required results in total but some parts of it are not, while others are exceeding expectations. The procedure is similar to that for evaluating new market segments (Figure 6.3). Executives can then investigate the poor performing areas to see what could be done to improve matters.

Perhaps too much marketing effort is being used for the potential demand or market share available, in which case marketing costs would be too high. Or perhaps insufficient effort is being made, or competition is more severe than estimated. Or distribution may be too elaborate and costly, or too slow and losing the firm business and goodwill. Or customers may be switching to 'Just In Time' deliveries. Or prices may be too high so that cost reductions may have to be achieved. There are many others but identifying which one is the culprit will indicate steps that can be taken to improve the profitability of a market.

(b) Market modification and rationalisation

There will be occasions when market performance cannot be improved in the ways mentioned above. Perhaps some groups of customers in a market or segment have changed needs or preferences, or are not buying in the quantities anticipated. Then it may be necessary to make modifications to the market by finding other or extra groups of customers in the segment who could be persuaded to buy the products. Perhaps the promotional campaigns may also have to be changed or modified?

However, all markets have finite lives like products though the time-scale is often much longer. So eventually a firm would have to withdraw from a market when demand has fallen too low or competition has intensified too much. Again, as with products, withdrawal has to be carefully planned so that the abandonment of a segment does not jeopardise the total potential of important products. The resources saved can be put to the development of new markets or segments offering better long-term potential.

(c) New market development

New markets have to be found, assessed and exploited if the company's long-term objectives for growth are to be realised. All ideas have to be studied and their potential, probable competition, estimated profitability, ease of access and ease of penetration have to be gauged. With these priorities in mind, a list of prospects can be prepared and these follow similar assessment and screening processes as is used for products (see Appendix A.3). Of course during the work executives bear in mind the market objectives and mix that should be achieved. Sometimes new markets that are not immediately profitable or capable of achieving profit targets will have to be developed if they represent areas in which the company believes its future prosperity and survival will be. Or some scarcely profitable markets may be developed if by so doing, the firms prevents, hinders or frustrates the growth intentions of major competitors, or ones who might become so in the future.

6.6   Market costs

The bulk of the costs that could be ascribed to market management are in fact incurred by selling, promotional, market research and physical distribution activities. Most of these will be discussed in their appropriate chapters but one or two points should be noted here.

First, by operating in a market a firm incurs various costs, the sum total of which can be equal to or greater than manufacturing costs. Therefore there is need for effective cost control and realistic assessments of the benefits that any expenditure would bring to the company's business. Second, it is always possible for some executive to get carried away by the concepts of promotional activities, market research or physical distribution. Then the executive could commit the company to unnecessarily extensive and costly promotions or research. Or a distribution system could be constructed that was far too elaborate for the firm's needs and thus results in unnecessary expenditures.

Marketing executives responsible for market management work of any sort must remain aware of the cost generation of being in a market. Although the various cost items are the direct responsibility of other line departments, it is beneficial if whoever does the market management work adopts an overseeing role for them. If this person is the product/brand manager or executive, this role would be a natural one since this staff member fulfils a similar one in product management.

Linked to the need to control costs is a need to check on the effects of different types of marketing expenditure. If money is spent on advertising or promotions it is logical to set up methods of monitoring the response. In many cases simple methods are available, such as coding coupons in advertisements or asking telephone enquirers how or where they heard of the company. In other cases, as with mass advertising to major market segments, specialist research through 'tracking studies' may be needed to monitor the effects of TV advertising on awareness, attitudes and so forth. Here while the research costs can amount to thousands of pounds, the advertising costs may run into millions, so the expenditure may be justified as a check on the effectiveness of the advertising, and cutting the costs may be a false economy. Equally, cutting costs on packaging, distribution and so forth may lead to false economies if customers become unhappy and begin to buy elsewhere. Again controlled spending on market research to identify the importance which those in the market place on these and other aspects of the marketing effort should be cost-effective.

With computers and spreadsheets widely available, and effective networks established between market research, market intelligence, product managers, market or key account managers and accounting services, it should be possible to monitor costs and results with a minimum of effort. However it is vital that someone in the organisation is given responsibility for managing information sources and flows across all areas of marketing, and again with a view to the cost-effectiveness of their activities.

6.7   Competition

This subject has been discussed in other chapters where relevant and appropriate. A few general comments here are advisable.

Competition is desirable because it tends to improve marketing efficiency. It requires firms to follow dynamic policies and strategies specially evolved for specific conditions. Thus competition promotes greater innovation and the intro-duction of new products (though all the latter of recent decades have not been seen by everyone as being beneficial to society). It should result (but does not always) in better service to customers. Unregulated monopolies, in comparison, tend to encourage higher prices, discourage innovation, tolerate lower quality of service and product and permit slothful management.

Competition occurs at all levels of business and in all functional areas. Price is not the sole criterion. Non-price competition in product quality and design, pro-motions, merchandising, delivery and so on is also important. How successful the firm is in these areas will none the less influence the price levels possible. Thus competition can be classified into two types. The first has been called *commodity competition*, where the supply–demand forces of markets establish the nature and extent of competition and hence the prices to apply. The other has been called *enterprise competition*, where the price and non-price factors mentioned above are in play. The latter is normally what is implied when the word 'competition' is used.

The *principle of competitive differential advantage* interprets competition as complex interactions in which a firm's operations are affected not only by its own actions but by the strategies and actions of competitive firms. It is a sequence of initiatory moves by a firm and counteracting responses by com-petitors and others with which it deals, including customers, its work-force, suppliers and distributors. Thus when a firm offers its customers better prices or quality, or anything else, in order to improve sales volume at the expense of competitors, the latter will retaliate. They do this to redress the balance of sales or to minimise their losses. Competitors try to neutralise or counteract the ini-tiating firm's advantages by offering customers inducements that are as good as, or better than, the initiator's and hopefully increase or improve their own marketing advantages. The time-lag between action and reaction can be a mat-ter of days or years. It depends on the industry and technology, the nature of the markets and the resources of the firms concerned. Instantaneous reactions are more usual in fast-moving, mass market consumer goods. Slowness is unavoidable in high technology products or capital equipment because of the time needed to work out and test product responses. Some new design or concept may be involved and this must be subject to tests prior to offering it to customers. For companies with limited resources, it will take longer for even simple changes to be planned, checked and executed.

Assignments

How many of Porter's alternative strategies are evident among competitors in your market? What advantages if any might be obtained by following, or changing to, any of the alternatives?

Is your market segmented in any way? If so, along what lines? Is the trend now towards more segmentation or less? What differentiates the products or services offered in different segments?

Can you identify one or more leaders in your market? If so, what characteristics have given them leadership?

Prices, revenue and profits

Setting an appropriate price for a product is a complex matter with different implications for different people. In the marketing context price is known to affect the ways in which a product is seen by potential buyers. In many markets some people will take relative prices as a measure of quality, with higher prices linked to better quality. In these markets putting too low a price on a product may signify poor quality rather than a bargain. In fashion markets a high price may indicate exclusiveness, and set a garment above something almost identical in the mass market. In other markets if a supplier sets a price for a brand only slightly above the 'going rate' this will seriously reduce sales, either because the ultimate users will not pay the extra money, or because middlemen will refuse to carry the product at all.

Where there are middlemen, such as factors, wholesalers or retailers, a chain of prices and price margins may need to be considered. In consumer markets where taxes such as VAT are involved this chain must still leave the final selling price, including VAT, at an acceptable level.

Pricing factors also need to be considered right through the development of a product. An early decision is needed between designing a product up to a standard and then considering price, or designing down to a price from the beginning. An aero engine will be designed to a specification from the beginning, to meet stringent standards of performance and reliability. If the price that is needed to make a profit is uncompetitive, cost cutting may be considered but it is more likely that the product may never reach the market. For most fmcgs a price, or at least a ceiling price, will be built into the initial brief for product development, and the product will be designed or formulated down to that price. If initial plans do not meet the target price, even after cost reduction exercises, again the product is unlikely to be launched.

People outside marketing may have different perceptions of price. To a salesman or a potential buyer a selling price may be the starting point for negotiations. If a logical policy on discounts is not thought through, and sales people are not properly briefed, a determined buyer may obtain a price which is unprofitable to the company. People at the 'sharp end' of selling will normally press their company to set the lowest possible price. To some accountants price may simply be the figure by which volume sales are multiplied to arrive at gross sales revenue. They may see a price increase mainly as a simple and immediate way of increasing revenue and profits.

To marketing people price has a number of dimensions. It may play a part in determining the way in which potential buyers see product quality, or place a brand on a scale from luxury to utility or cheap and nasty, as well as being the

Müller
Fruit Corner Yogurt
(all varieties)
Each
37p
31p

Fresh
Whole Trout
(pre-packed & loose)
Per lb
£2.38 £1.88
SAVE 50p
Per lb

Brussels Sprouts
(loose) Per lb
35p
29p

48p per lb.
(An early Xmas present from Tesco.)

Tesco Frozen
Cooked & Peeled Prawns
400g Pack
£4.99 £2.99
SAVE £2

Tesco
Frozen Tiramisu
£2.39 £1.59
SAVE 80p

Fresh
Bone-in Leg
Joint of Pork
Per lb
£1.49 £1.09
SAVE 40p
Per lb

TESCO FROZEN TURKEYS
PER LB
76p 48p
SAVE 28p
PER LB
(BASTED, QUICK FROZEN AND
FREE RANGE TURKEYS
AVAILABLE AT OTHER PRICES)

Tesco
Pure Orange Juice
3 Litre Bottle
£2.89 £1.98
SAVE 91p

CROSSED OUT PRICES WERE PREVIOUSLY CHARGED AT MOST TESCO STORES.

COUPON NEWS!
Tesco will now give you the same money
off your shopping bill if you present
any money off coupons issued by other
major food retailers in the local area.

Offer available until further notice. Subject to the same coupon redemption
conditions, excluding secondary offers. Featured product must be
purchased or an equivalent product where not stocked. Offer excludes gift
vouchers and any money off vouchers without a spending requirement.

District Shopping Centre, Chineham.
OPENING HOURS:
Monday-Thursday 8.30am-8pm. Friday 8.30am-9pm.
Saturday 8.30am-8pm. Sunday 9am-6pm.*
OPEN SUNDAY 9am-6pm.*

TESCO

DELTA MasterCard VISA

Offers end Saturday 30th October, 1993 or Sunday 31st October, 1993.
All offers subject to availability at the above store(s) only. Switch available in scanning stores only excluding purchases from Tobacco Kiosk, Coffee Shop, Pharmacy and Garden Centre
where applicable. MasterCard, Visa welcome at all stores excluding purchases from Tobacco Kiosk. *Beers, Wines and Spirits open 12noon-2.55pm.

Temporary price reductions play a major part in retail advertising and are a common way of promoting specific lines or the stores in general. This advertisement was placed on a Wednesday and the offers were valid until the week-end

basis of all financial calculations. While a whole range of factors will be considered when deciding on prices, the expected financial outcomes will always be vital to the company. Hence it is impossible to discuss pricing without calculating revenues and comparing them with costs. As there are often many alternative prices which might be considered in any marketing situation, then comparisons of the expected results will also be needed.

7.1   Some basic calculations

The price at which a company offers its products will affect both the quantity sold and the total revenues and profit. These revenues and the costs of operations can be combined in various ways, and it is useful to look at some definitions in use in the financial area:

(i)   *Gross sales revenue or gross revenue* is all the money nominally coming in from sales, given by units sold × list price = gross sales revenue

(ii)   *Net sales revenue* is gross sales revenue less any discounts given for volume, trade bonuses, advertising contributions, or other reasons. The difference between the gross and net sales revenues needs to be watched closely, as a company can easily get into a situation of trying to maintain sales by giving large discounts at the expense of profits.

(iii)   *Profit* is what is left after all costs and expenses have been deducted from the net sales revenue. These include both fixed and variable costs involved in manufacture and distribution, marketing and sales, and all overheads and other expenses incurred by the company.

(iv)   *Contribution* is a measure favoured by some companies, particularly where there is a wide range of products and there are difficulties in allocating overheads among them. The contribution from a product is measured by the gap between net sales revenue and direct and attributable costs of goods.

Companies may use different terms for some of these sets of figures. Some have more layers, or different definitions, such as taking out all marketing and selling costs to reach net sales revenue. However the general ideas are in common use and need to be kept in mind when deciding on prices for a product or service.

7.2   Breakeven calculations

Two basic ideas are needed to help a company set a price for a product and understand the effects its decisions may have on income and profit. These are the 'breakeven price' and 'price elasticity'.

The *breakeven price* is the one at which a given quantity of product needs to be sold to avoid any loss on the operations. The calculation of this price is a useful exercise since it brings together costs, prices and quantities sold in a simple way. The costs need to be broken down between fixed costs and variable unit costs.

The fixed costs will normally cover such items as rent of space, costs of plant, supervisory staff salaries and so forth. They may also include basic marketing and selling costs, such as advertising or core promotional material. These fixed costs are incurred during the running of any operations, however small or large the quantities produced. Variable unit costs cover raw materials, direct labour, energy, packaging, transport and so forth, which all tend to vary directly with the scale of operations. In practice it is often difficult to draw any precise line between the two sets of costs, but liaison with the cost accountants will usually provide working values.

Given these costs we can either assume a price and calculate the minimum sales needed to break even, or we can assume a sales volume and calculate the price needed to break even. Either way the result will be the same for a given cost structure, but different marketing and production situations will lead to the problem being approached from different directions.

To calculate the breakeven point:

Let fixed costs be f
Let variable costs per unit be v
Let the price per unit be p
Let the number of units be n

In the most basic case the calculations are simple. We calculate the total sales revenue, R, and the total costs, C. That is:

$$R = (n \times p)$$
and $\quad C = f + (n \times v)$

Since the breakeven point is where revenue and costs are equal, then

$$(n \times p) = f + (n \times v)$$

If we divide each side of the equation by n we see that the price needed to break even on a sales volume of n is given by:

$$p = \frac{f}{n} + v$$

Conversely the volume of sales needed to break even at a price of p can be shown to be given by:

$$n = \frac{f}{p - v}$$

Since f and v, the fixed and variable costs, have been estimated already by the accountants there are only two unknown factors, price and volume. If we assume the level of one we can calculate the corresponding level of the other.

Suppose that fixed costs have been estimated at £500,000 per period, of say a year. Variable costs are expected to be £20 per unit, and a factory price of £50 per unit is being considered. Then the calculation of the breakeven level of sales becomes:

$$n = \frac{f}{p - v}$$

$$= \frac{500,000}{50 - 20}$$

$$= 16,667 \text{ units}$$

(or more practically, 17,000 units)

Conversely the calculation can start at the other end, by calculating the breakeven price for a given level of sales, using the second equation shown above.

The same answers can be obtained by graphing the data, and if the calculations are set up in a computer using a spreadsheet, large numbers of alternative assumptions can be evaluated and graphed very quickly.

Figure 7.1 shows the results of the calculations above, with revenue and fixed and variable costs plotted on the vertical axis, against unit sales along the bottom axis. The revenue and total costs line cross at the breakeven level of sales. At smaller volumes than this the gap between revenue and total costs shows the losses incurred at each level of sales. At higher volumes the gap between the two shows the level of profit being achieved. By plotting alternative revenue lines, using different proposed selling prices, the breakeven points and the patterns of profits or losses at different prices can be compared.

This simple chart may not always show the true position. On the basis of Figure 7.1 we might expect that once the breakeven point at 16,667 units had

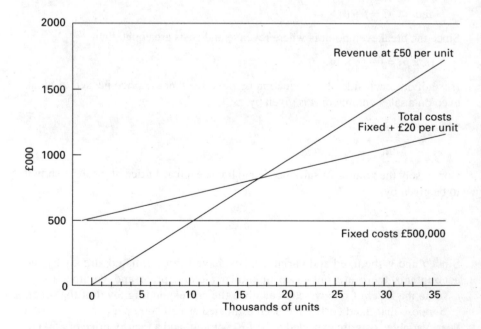

Fig. 7.1   Breakeven pricing

been passed, profits would grow continuously. If 35,000 units were sold profits would reach some £550,000. However further analysis may show that the initial fixed costs of £500,000 would only support production of about 23,000 units per period. Investment in more plant would be needed for larger quantities. Figure 7.2 shows the possible situation if more plant had to be installed, or other fixed costs had to be incurred. With the price still at £50 per unit and variable costs of £20, losses are made on sales levels between 23,000 units and 30,000. Hence a long view needs to be taken to avoid becoming locked into an unfavourable situation. Many companies have suffered because their initial marketing planning was on too limited a scale.

Other factors may pull the pattern of costs and revenues away from the simple situations shown in Figures 7.1 and 7.2. There may for example be economies of scale in the variable costs, due to increased purchasing power for raw materials, improved skills in production, and so forth. Hence the total costs may no longer increase in a straight line, but may bend downwards at higher levels of production, thus boosting profits.

More importantly for market planning, the price at which the product is offered may need to be reduced to gain the higher levels of sales. While it may be expected that sales of 20,000 units can be made at a price of £50, it may be necessary to offer a lower price to reach sales of 40,000 units. This means that the revenue line on the chart will be flattened as volumes increase. This flattening then takes away some of the profit shown on the chart. Alternatively, although the price might be held at the higher volumes it may be necessary to increase

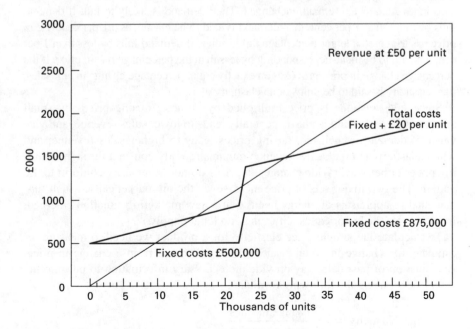

Fig. 7.2   Breakeven pricing: further analysis

advertising expenditures, to increase the sales force, or to make other additions to marketing expenditures.

Often it is necessary to balance any gains which may occur from expanding production against the revenues which accrue at diminished selling prices. In some favourable cases it may be possible to sell different tranches of production to different market segments at different prices, such as cinema or airline seats. Here the revenue line may show marked changes in pattern as segment boundaries are crossed, and skill is needed in allocating seats to segments to maximise the revenue from bookings. Such calculations depend on personal skill and sophisticated computer backing, but in the end the calculations are merely more complex forms of the breakeven charts. The breakeven concept is fundamental to any pricing considerations, but other concepts are involved as well, including price elasticity.

7.3   Price elasticity

Price elasticity shows the extent to which a change in the price of a product or service is expected to affect sales or demand. In terms of brands produced by individual companies, price elasticity can operate at a number of levels. As an example consider the market for a consumer good such as instant coffee – although the same factors generally apply across service and product markets, and for industrial as well as consumer goods.

If the prices of all instant coffees are increased, demand is likely to fall as some users give up, some use less, some switch to other drinks and so on. Suppose the average price of instant coffee is increased by 1 per cent, and the prices of all other substitutes such as tea remain unchanged. Then demand is likely to fall. If demand falls by more than 1 per cent, then demand is said to be elastic, as a 1 per cent rise in price has triggered a larger percentage fall in sales. If demand falls by less than 1 per cent it is said to be inelastic, responding by less than the percentage rise in price. If the percentage change in price provokes an exactly equal percentage change in unit sales, then elasticity is said to be unity, or an elasticity of 1.

Since sales revenue is price multiplied by volume, raising prices by small amounts where demand is elastic generally leads to lower sales revenue, and vice versa. If demand is inelastic, raising prices leads to higher sales revenue; and where elasticity is unity, sales revenue remains roughly constant through changing prices either way. (Wide changes in prices do not necessarily conform to the pattern. The two major sets of price increases in the oil market caused such fundamental re-appraisals of energy needs that a new marketing situation emerged. In such cases the historic elasticities may no longer apply.)

To calculate the simple price elasticity for a product we need to measure, or estimate, the change in volume sales which will result from a change in price. Examination of past data may provide the necessary information to put into the calculations, using the following formula:

$$\text{Price elasticity} = \frac{\% \text{ change in sales}}{\% \text{ change in price}}$$

Two factors can upset this simple relationship. The first is that there are acceptable substitutes for many products and prices are not seen in isolation. If instant coffee prices rise, consumers may drink more tea or other drinks, and most consumer goods are in competition with other similar goods. Hence there may be 'cross-elasticities' so that coffee sales are affected by the relative prices of coffee against tea, milk, squash, and so forth.

The second factor is that within a product group, such as instant coffee, the brands offered by any single manufacturer will be in close competition with other brands. Then if price is increased for only one brand of instant coffee, consumers may switch to other brands. Again there will be 'cross-elasticities' involving the relative prices of brands. The effects of these cross-elasticities will generally be to reduce the effects on a product or brand when all prices rise, but to allow them full scope when the price of only a single brand or a single product group is moved.

Price elasticities lead into some complex areas which we will return to in Chapter 10 on Forecasting where they can become important. However it is vital that when pricing and pricing strategies are being considered, relationships with prices in the market and in adjacent markets are kept in mind. Prices will generally affect volume sales, and in turn changes in volume may affect unit costs in the short term, or even fixed costs in the long run. Hence the importance of understanding price elasticities, and making some attempt to evaluate them.

One possible way of breaking away from cross-elasticities is by creating a strong brand image and identity for a product. Consumers may then be deterred from switching to what they regard as less acceptable alternatives when price changes occur. With physical products, and particularly in industrial markets, there usually needs to be some product differentiation, perhaps maintained through patents. With services this depends on positive identification of some favourable attributes of the brand or house name.

While classical economic theory of price elasticities has been well-developed there are practical areas which do not always conform. Among other things the theory suggests that elasticities work both ways. If a rise of 1 per cent in price causes a fall of x per cent in sales, then a price reduction of 1 per cent should lead to a rise in sales of about the same x per cent. In practice this does not always happen, perhaps because consumers are not aware of changes, or because expectations on prices are important as well as current levels. In many markets buyers are not always aware of prices, especially where unit prices are low as for many fmcgs, and they are not frequent buyers.

In some markets expectations of future price movements may have an influence on decisions, as well as current prices. Here a rise in price may trigger increased buying before prices rise again. Conversely a fall in prices may lead people to expect further falls, and cause a drop in immediate demand. The fall in house prices between 1990 and 1993 did little to encourage demand – although many other factors were involved.

7.4   Pricing decisions

Prices in some markets are set entirely by market forces, and the individual producer or supplier has no option but to accept this price. Such conditions prevail in commodity markets, such as for grain, raw coffee and so forth. In some cases

A direct marketing promotion using a price offer on one product to generate enquiries about a more expensive item

marketing boards or major producing or consuming countries can exert some influence, at least in the short run, but ultimately the'costs of subsidies or market intervention prove prohibitive.

There are a few markets where prices are quoted on the basis of costs of production plus a margin. In some areas, such as civil engineering or contracting, bids may be sought from potential suppliers for specified work. Contracts may be awarded on prices based on expected costs plus a margin. In intermediate markets, such as factoring, wholesaling and retailing, there may be customary rates applied to calculate the mark-up on buying price to get to selling prices. For most initial providers of goods or services other factors are more important than costs in setting prices.

As we saw above, costs feature in the calculation of profits or contribution, and set a lower limit to the price which can profitably be charged. If the market will not pay a price which gives a margin over costs then the company has three main options: the product could be withdrawn (or not launched at all); it could be sold at an overall current loss in the hope of better times to come; it could be sold at a loss to allow time for a profitable replacement to be launched based on lower costs, or achieving a higher price.

When demand is slack, perhaps on a cyclical or seasonal basis, or in a recession expected to end before too long, a company may be prepared to sell at prices above its variable costs but which do not fully cover fixed costs. Then there will be some contribution to the fixed costs which would not be obtained if the chance of sales was declined. Hotels may offer cheaper rooms on certain days, or during their 'off-season'. Builders or contractors may bid low to obtain work to keep a team together. Retailers offer discounts to pensioners to shop during slack periods. However as the fixed costs must be met in full at some time, high volumes of sales at low rates or 'marginal prices' cannot be sustained indefinitely.

Market factors which affect the prices which can be charged include the going rate among competitors, the position which is sought for the product in the market, and the general strategy of the organisation. Where there is little product differentiation competition tends to be on prices, and movement away from the market norm will quickly reveal severe problems with elasticities. Where a brand is deliberately marketed at a lower price it may gain some sales but it may also be perceived by many consumers as an inferior product. In the petrol market in the UK the major producers keep their prices very much together, and if one changes the rest tend to follow within days. There are cut-price brands, but many motorists look on them with some suspicion and are reluctant to risk using them in expensive cars. An interesting exception is the sale of Own Label petrol through some supermarket forecourts. Here it is the good reputation of the stores themselves which becomes attached to the petrol in lieu of a major brand name.

7.5 Pricing a new product

The most difficult problems in pricing probably arise in relation to the introduction of new products or new lines. Here there will be no specific history relating to the new offering, but there will normally be both a history of the market and contemporary information about competitors. In many cases there will be price histories from a company's other offerings in the same market. This pricing information about the market, and existing products in it, sets the context in which the decisions are to be made.

The company will have its own objectives in introducing the new product and in planning its positioning. It may be planned as an extension to an existing range, it may be a replacement for an obsolescent product which the company is withdrawing, or it may be an entry into a new market for the company. If planned as a range extension, then the price set must fit logically with other prices in the company range. Ensuring that all packs or products within a company range have logically related prices is known as 'line pricing'. If planned as a replacement, the price of the obsolete product may be a starting point, but advantage may be taken of the new design or formulation to reposition the product and to raise the price. Wherever a product is introduced into a market where a company is already marketing, the potential effects of pricing decisions must be thought through with regard to the existing products as well as the new one. Wrong pricing within a range can divert custom towards a company's less profitable lines, through substitution or cannibalism, with adverse effects on revenues and profits.

If a company is entering a new market then prices of close competitors will provide a basis for discussion. A price based on competitors' prices, related to the desired positioning of the new product, will then be decided.

Research or experience may lead a company to look at pricing from the out-side in, and to be guided by 'what the market will bear'. The price then set may be markedly different from going rates, and there have been both successes and failures in this area. The risks are that a low price will be taken to indicate inferior quality, and a high price as not worth paying!

Overall, price involves some of the most important decisions which have to be taken when bringing a new product to market. It is usually one of the major factors which determines whether intermediaries will handle the product at all, or whether consumers will eventually buy it. The prices set will have a direct bearing on achieving volume objectives. Setting a price either too high or too low can easily lead to failure of the entire operation.

Entering a market with too low a price, with a need then for subsequent price rises, can cause long-term damage. If the customers gained on the basis of the initial price will not stand the price rise, then a new customer group must be attracted and established at the higher price level. However the product may already have acquired an inferior image due to the low price, and those who might initially have been willing to pay a higher price may now be put off by this image.

Entering at too high a price can equally create problems. Sufficient demand will not be generated to meet original objectives, and price reductions may again mean that the customer base has to be rebuilt. Further, the fall in price may be seen as an open admission that the product was not selling well. Results can be a loss of image, possible de-stocking by distributors, and ultimate withdrawal from the market.

There are often good reasons for setting a price at the going rate or in line with competition or similar products. However at the ends of the price spectrum there are two contrasting ways of pricing a new entry into a market which can be used. These extreme solutions will work under appropriate conditions, but need careful thought before being adopted. At one end of the scale, if there is some new product feature which can be exploited, it may be possible to adopt a high initial price and to reduce this later as competition catches up, or to stimulate further sales. This is known as setting a 'skimming price'. At the other end of the scale, where a product has no specific advantages, and particularly where the economics of mass production require the rapid achievement of high volumes, a low initial price may be set. This is known as setting a 'penetrating price', and is a way of buying initial volume and market share.

(a) Skimming pricing

In order to be able to set a skimming price, the product must have some perceived advantages not offered by competitors. Further, the advantage must be sustainable, through secrecy, through patents or whatever. Two new product introductions illustrate how skimming prices were used, successfully in one case, but not in the other.

The Polaroid camera was introduced in a black-and-white form about 30 years ago, and has since undergone considerable changes, with the introduction of colour, improved quality and timing, and additional facilities. In the first instance however the product was unique in providing instant photographs, although not then of very high quality. The novelty appealed to people in the 'jet-set' and a high price ensured the exclusivity they sought. Competition could not match the product, which was effectively covered by patents. As demand at high prices was filled new models were introduced at lower prices to reach the next layer of buyers. Stage by stage the prices have come down, to the current low levels, but in the process initial research costs were quickly recovered, and high levels of profitability have been maintained.

The photographic market has always been competitive, but none of the competitors was able legally to copy the instant processes of the Polaroid camera. The company could then maintain tight control over supply, and thus over prices. Basically prices were lowered only when demand faltered, and not when competitive products made it necessary.

At about the time of the launch of the first Polaroid camera the first electronic pocket calculators appeared on the market. Originally they also sold at very high prices. However within months the market was flooded with clones at very low prices, and the initiators often failed to recover their research costs. They were unable to protect the supply of products through either secret components or processes, or through patents. Any company which could analyse and imitate one of the initial products could manufacture its own model. Since costs of components and assembly were low, prices fell and there was virtually a commodity market for the initial simple models.

Although dated these examples show some of the benefits and the problems of skimming pricing. A skimming price, by its nature of offering wide profit margins, will encourage competitors to enter the market if they can. The policy can only be maintained while the product and its specific benefits can be protected from imitators and competitors. The speed with which clones or imitations appear on the market then limits the extent to which a company can apply or dictate skimming prices. With the Polaroid camera this lead time has proved to be long standing, through the granting of patents to cover a string of product improvements. In the case of the calculators, the lack of any protection through patents or through technology meant that the lead time of the innovators was short, and gave no chance for the policy to be effective.

(b) Penetration pricing

Many products or services can only be produced economically above some minimum level of operation. This can apply from airlines to hotels, and from industrial goods to fmcgs. Further, if planning is initially on too small a basis the product may be vulnerable to attack from competitors willing to invest and market on a much larger scale – as the Japanese approach to many markets has shown.

To break into an established market with a 'new' product with only minimal differences from those already there will often mean that competition will be largely based on price. Market entry will be based on prices which are below the nearest competitors in order to secure initial distribution or trial. This process of buying market share may lead to little or no profit being made during the introductory phase (although hopefully still making some contribution), but with the prospect of lifting prices to more profitable levels later. This then raises two problems.

The first is where to pitch the long-term price objectives in relation to the market and the immediate competitors. The second is to decide what price reduction can be made, and how it can be applied to achieve maximum impact during its life, and least disruption when it is withdrawn.

In a well-integrated marketing plan price will have been considered at an early stage, and included in the brief for developing the new product. At this stage decisions on formulation and positioning will have been involved, and these will indicate which brands already in the market will be the main competitors. Competition will then set limits to the range of prices which might be charged, and integrated decisions will be made within these limits. The price can then be tested on a breakeven chart or other calculations for profitability. There may then need to be some rethinking on either costs or prices – but except in some special cases of tendering for specific jobs, costs are not a determinant of prices. Costs and prices between them determine profits given the volume sold. Prices and market reaction play a major part in determining the volume sold, but the consumers in the market may show little concern for the profitability of the operation.

Given a price structure which meets company objectives and is expected to lead to profitable long-term sales there remain questions about the launch price. These have to be answered in the context of other marketing activity associated with the launch. How much can the company afford to spend on price cutting, advertising, promotions to trade or consumers, press relations and so forth, in say, the first six months of the product's life? How large will the launch budget be? Will some of this budget be better spent on initial price reductions to tempt trial, on media advertising to generate awareness, on promotions to stimulate immediate purchase, or on other means of gaining attention? What are the trade-offs between a price reduction and media coverage or promotions? Would some form of coupon or money-off offer provide a stronger advertising platform? What is the attitude of retailers to money-off or other promotions, and would they add their own efforts?

Looking further ahead, if a low price is used to penetrate the market, what will be the reaction when the reduction is removed and the product has to face a price rise to achieve the overall marketing objectives? In the late 1980s inflation meant that prices seldom remained stable for very long, and consumers were conditioned to frequent price rises. Removing a launch reduction would not then be very evident. Given low levels of inflation, price changes become less frequent and consequently more noticeable, and thus possibly more detrimental.

(c) The middle path

There is a middle path where pricing is set in the context of building long-term relationships with customers. 'Relationship marketing' involves a co-operative or mutually beneficial approach to trading between supplier and customer, rather than the older confrontational approach. While this applies largely in industrial transactions, it also applies more and more to dealings between manufacturers and wholesalers and major retail chains. Prices and margins are set at levels acceptable to both sides in the expectation of long-term relationships. Purchasers prefer stable prices which will not drive suppliers out of business. Suppliers prefer stable relationships at reasonable rates, rather than constantly seeking new customers or renegotiating with the old.

In these situations the extremes of skimming or penetration pricing determined by the producer will give way to market-based pricing strategies aimed at securing and retaining a stable customer base.

Relationship marketing does not preclude careful negotiation. It does however imply negotiating to obtain maximum mutual long-term benefit which can then be divided, rather than each side seeking its own maximum short-term benefits which may not endure.

7.6 Managing price changes for existing products

Not all suppliers of either goods or services have problems setting or changing their prices. This is true not only in commodity markets, but in many other markets as well, including many branded consumer markets. Some brands can be identified as price leaders who can generally change their prices and expect others to follow. Other brands can be seen to be price followers, where management has little influence on the level of market prices, although they may still have some control over timing.

The characteristics of price leaders will depend on the market. Often price leaders have a significant market share, although not necessarily a dominant one.

They are strongly positioned as a preferred brand – even if most consumers cannot afford them. Linked with these two, they should have assured distribution. Price leadership is often shared among two or more major brands, as in the petrol market. Here if one major brand moves its price the others will follow, but the initial move may come from any of the major brands. If any of the minor brands moves its price within the market it tends to do so alone, and may stay in isolation until it moves back, or conditions cause the price leaders to move.

Two sets of conditions arise in which price changes may be considered. The first is when internal pressures develop which can only be solved by a price change. The second is when external conditions change and threats or opportunities arise from outside the company.

Internal pressures may come from a lack of profits, leading to a price rise being considered, or from a lack of orders when a price reduction may be one solution. In either case it is useful to have some knowledge of expected customer reaction, through price elasticities or cross-elasticities. Knowledge of trade or distributor attitudes or opinions will also be useful, if there are risks of adverse reactions. Insights into the type of management among competitors may also play a part in decisions. Some managements are against taking any risks. Some see risks as the major opportunities to advance or develop. So reactions from competitors may depend on their position on a scale from aggressive to dormant.

When faced with pressures on profits, management should be clear about the source of the pressure before resorting to a price increase. If the cause is one affecting the whole industry, such as a rise in raw material costs, then all firms will be feeling the pressure, and may be expected to raise prices in the near future. However the pressure may come from internal factors, such as incurring heavy labour costs due to obsolete plant while competitors gain from modern equipment. Then a price rise may place the company in a worse position, as competitors will not follow. Market share will be lost, and profits may be squeezed further. The real solution to the problem may be to invest in new plant, or to leave the market before more serious losses are incurred. Alternatively it may be possible to compete in the market on non-price factors, such as delivery, by improving design and so forth. Being locked into competing on price alone can damage a company's wealth!

Pressures for price reductions may develop when demand is below capacity, as has been the case in the UK in the early 1990s. A price reduction may be expected to bring more market share or volume, and again elasticities will indicate the probable net result in cash flows or profits. If a marked change in volume is expected, then retaliation from competitors can be expected too. They will not want to accept reduced volumes, and a price war may result. While there may then be some increase in overall volume of sales, the general effect is for all to suffer from a drop in revenue while still producing at around the previous levels. No-one gains, and most will lose in the end.

Price reductions can sometimes be organised on a limited and temporary basis if that will meet the company's needs. Hence the 'sales' in retail stores, the money-off coupons from fmcg brands, discounts on holidays booked before a given date, and so forth. While these may be appropriate in some cases they may not always be as temporary as their originators had planned, and promotional wars can last for years. 'Special offers' and 'sales' become almost routine, and wily customers never pay the full price.

7.7 The importance of pricing

Price relationships within and between markets may be affected either by changes to existing prices, or through the prices of new products. Any changes to the balance of prices, or the pricing structure within a market, may have long-term effects which detract from any immediate advantage to be gained. Wrong pricing tactics can easily damage the image of a brand, particularly those positioned at the top end of a market. They can inflict damage on a distribution system which can be difficult to redress. They can start price wars which may be difficult to stop. Hence it is essential that pricing policy, pricing tactics and price changes are determined with as much knowledge and experience of the market and their related systems as possible, to avoid causing permanent damage to product acceptance at whatever level.

Price and the positioning of the product or the organisation in the market are far more closely linked than costs. Consumers expect to pay more for high fashion goods, for 5-star hotels, for luxury holidays and so forth. They will accept and pay higher prices for consistent high-quality components or supplies, delivered on time by co-operative companies. Equally they expect to pay basic prices for run-of-the mill products sold through the normal channels of mass distribution. Pricing strategies should reflect the broader marketing objectives and positioning, and should aim for some consistency through time. Short-termism in pricing may provide temporary relief from problems with cash flows or stocks, but may raise longer-term problems by undermining a quality image, or starting a damaging price war.

7.8 A note on the retail price index

In the UK, and in most other countries, monthly measures are taken of the prices being charged for consumer goods and services. These are used to calculate the Retail Price Index (or RPI) applied in many government calculations, in wage and other forms of negotiation, and regarded generally as a measure of inflation.

The basic idea of the index is simple. The average amounts spent by families on housing, drink, food, clothing, travel and so forth are measured in a major survey. This becomes the base for the calculations. The UK RPI is currently based on family expenditures in 1987, using the typical 'basket of goods and services' bought by an average family. Each month prices for the various types of goods and services bought are collected, and the overall price of the basket of goods is worked out. This price is then percentaged on the initial 1987 figure to give the new 'General index of retail prices', which can be found in the press and in *The Monthly Digest of Statistics*.

In the summer of 1993, the index stood at about 140, indicating a rise in consumer prices since 1987 of 40 per cent. In terms of the 1993 level of price increases, or inflation, the rise is about 2 per cent a year.

Apart from the general index other indices are calculated for particular purposes. Because the general index has been subject to wide fluctuations due to the interest on household mortgages, figures are produced excluding this factor, and described as the underlying index covering other goods and services. Within the general index, figures are published for the major components, such as food, transport and vehicles, clothing and footwear, and so forth.

Similar measures of price movements are produced for industry, ranging from indices for materials and fuel to factory-gate prices for finished goods. Separate indices are published for major industrial sectors.

Price indices are useful in assessing how prices of individual brands, or across a market generally, are moving in comparison with wider trends. However certain limitations of price indices need to be kept in mind. The main ones are:

(i)   The long-term general pattern of consumption will change after the base year and before the next revision. Given reasonable revisions, say every five to ten years, this should not be a major problem.

(ii)   In times of boom or slump, patterns of consumption may change temporarily in ways not reflected in the index. Families facing reduced budgets will cut some expenditures and trade down in other areas, while the reverse may happen in more prosperous times. The changes will not be reflected in the general index.

(iii) The calculations are based on average family consumption, and may not apply to the target group of customers. Some specific indices are calculated for particular groups, such as pensioners, but the same problem arises of the 'average pensioner'.

(iv)   The indices are necessarily historic. What is often needed in price decisions is a view of how prices are likely to move in the future. However, knowledge of the indices and some simple comparisons of trends through time can often help, allied to general awareness of the market and wider economic conditions.

Assignments

How far is there evidence of price elasticity in your market – either overall for the product group, or for individual brands?

How does your chosen organisation set its prices? If selling through intermediaries, how far does the organisation have any control over margins?

Is your market subject to VAT or other taxes? If so, at what rates? If not, what effects do you think the imposition of taxes would have on demand, in total or for individual brands or organisations?

8 The mass communications mix

A firm may communicate with its markets on two levels: it may use advertising, public relations or sales promotions to reach a wide target group of people; or it may use personal selling or direct marketing aimed specifically at individual corporate buyers or individual consumers. In this chapter we will consider the first level normally concerned with reaching large numbers of people through the mass media, whether press or electronic, or through distribution channels. In the next chapter we will consider selling activities and the distribution systems generally. The boundary is not absolute, and should not be, as the various activities need to be integrated. Advertising may be planned to introduce a new product to a mass market, but the advertising plans themselves will be used by sales people to persuade retailers to stock the new product. In many markets for both consumer and industrial products, advertising may be used to generate enquiries which are then followed up by sales people. Although then different aspects of a firm's communications with its markets are treated in two chapters, they all need to be co-ordinated in an integrated marketing plan.

8.1 Some definitions

Advertising is any paid form of non-personal presentation of products, services or ideas by an identified sponsor. The sponsor may be the firm manufacturing the item (or product group), the distributor handling it, the retail outlet selling it to the ultimate customer, or any combination of the three. Where the cost of the advertisement is shared between manufacturer and retailer (or wholesaler) it is often referred to as *co-operative advertising*. Where producers organise advertising for a product as a whole this is called *generic advertising*. Other useful terms are *display advertising* which covers the main forms of brand advertising, and *classified advertising* covering the small advertisements for jobs, houses and so forth.

While advertising is strongly associated with branded consumer goods such as food and drink, some of the heaviest advertisers in the UK are retailers and mail order companies, financial services, government and car manufacturers. Total display advertising expenditure in the UK is over £5 billion a year, with press and television each taking over 40 per cent of the total, and the rest spread between outdoor (posters, bus sides etc.), radio and cinema. Advertising expenditure accounts for about $1^1/_4$ per cent of the gross national product, or about $1^3/_4$ per cent of consumer expenditure.

Public relations, also known as press relations or publicity, aims to improve or maintain the image of an organisation, service or product among a target

"I don't approve of taking unnatural substances.

That's why I eat butter."

SALLY GUNNELL

"When you're a world champion you can't afford to take risks.

If my coach caught me eating anything but natural foods, he'd run me into the ground.

You see, under firm orders from my dietician I have to maintain a naturally healthy diet to keep in tip-top condition.

You know, like wholemeal bread and real butter.

Which is fine by me, I absolutely love the stuff. And I'm a big fan of enjoying being healthy.

Anyway, I must dash. Catch you later."

BUTTER

Generic advertising for a product like butter is supported by producers to foster sales in the market generally, for their mutual benefit. Individual brands will then use their own advertising to foster their own shares of the market

FOOD & WINE

Is BUTTER *better?*

The margarine industry spends a lot of time telling us that its product is healthy. It spends a lot less time telling us how it's made. When you find out, you start to have doubts...

KATE CALVERT

FIRST, margarine's ingredients – usually seeds – are heated and crushed using chemical solvents to produce a high yield of crude plant oil.

This is then washed with caustic soda or phosphate and neutralised with sodium carbonate or bicarbonate.

Fullers earth may be added to the resulting oil to bleach it. The oil is then reacted with hydrogen in the presence of a catalyst (usually nickel) to harden it artificially.

The solid fat is filtered before being refined, deodorised and heated to melting point. Then it is usually mixed with fish and animal oils to produce a blended oil.

This is then combined with water, skimmed milk, salt, artificial colour, flavouring and vitamins A and D.

Butter, on the other hand, is in effect a wholefood – as close to its natural state as possible, having been made by the time-honoured system of churning cream.

Fatty acids

Margarine sales soared at the expense of butter with the arrival of dietary theories about fats.

In the 1970s and early 1980s researchers said that eating fats rich in polyunsaturated fatty acids might help reduce blood cholesterol, and these should therefore form a higher proportion of our fat intake.

Margarine manufacturers latched on to this, made sure that they included polyunsaturates in their spreads, and spent a lot of money advertising the idea along with the product.

But nowadays the theory is said to be flawed.

Take the French, for example. They favour saturated fats in butter, cream and countless high-fat cheeses far more than polyunsaturates – and they have fewer heart attacks than we do.

It may be that we don't adhere to the rules strictly enough – margarines "high in polyunsaturates" legally need to be no more than 50 per cent polyunsaturate fat.

But, perhaps most importantly, there's a question over how margarine is made. Regardless of how healthy the ingredients start out, the manufacturing of margarine may damage them, it is claimed.

Industrial hardening of fat uses a process called hydrogenation. This converts unsaturated fats into saturated fats. According to a trial last year in the US, reported in the *Lancet*, the process increases the ratio of substances causing cholesterol to that of substances which drive cholesterol out of the body. Quite the reverse of what you want.

Furthermore, the chemical structure of oils is altered by the high temperatures needed for the crushing process. It is claimed that polyunsaturate fats are unstable at these high temperatures and can easily oxidise and give off molecules held responsible for various problems including cancer.

There has even been a claim from within the margarine industry that most margarines are not good for you.

The comment comes from the producers of the European brand Vitaquell, which has been on sale in UK health food shops for about 15 years and in Germany since the 1950s. Its producer, a family-run firm, claims that it is probably the healthiest margarine in the world.

The margarine is produced by a cold pressing process. Because chemical solvents are not used, the usual subsequent cleaning and neutralising is not required.

Vitaquell, says its producer, "is the only margarine where the healthful effects have not been ruined by the chemical and physical assaults on their integrity".

And that isn't all. In a 12-year research project American nutrition expert Professor Paul Addis has focused on the effects of unstable polyunsaturates when heated in cooking to the point of smoking, or where they have been reused too often.

He says this can lead to blockages in

the flow of blood and so to heart attacks.

Professor Addis believes this is because the unstable molecules can set off a chain reaction in the body's cells, damaging blood vessel walls.

The resultant cell debris attacts other cells and fatty deposits, causing them to cluster and form blockages.

So experts now say that the answer is to cut down on eating fat altogether.

And if you want to include fats in your diet, butter and even lard *may* be a safer bet than margarine.

"We're fighting back," said a spokesman for The Butter Council. ∎

Butter is in effect a wholefood – as close to its natural state as possible.

FAT FACTS

● You need at least 4g a day of essential fatty acids.
● You need about 30g of any fat a day to help absorption of fat soluble vitamins (A, D, E and K).
● The World Health Organisation recommends that total fat consumption should make up a minimum of 10 per cent, maximum of 30 per cent, of total calorie intake.

An example of advertising and PR being used to complement each other. While the advertising shown opposite was being used, a PR campaign ensured that more information about butter and competitive products was being put before the target groups audience. Various methods can be used from simple publicity releases which it is hoped will lead to favourable mention in the press or on radio or TV, through to more sophisticated programmes of visits or events. Lobbying of Members of Parliament or other influential people is often a part of the activities.

Sales promotion covers a range of short-term or one-off activities aimed at traders or purchasers, with the objective of stimulating sales. Trade promotions, designed to 'push' goods down the distribution system, include competitions among retailers, incentives if goods are prominently displayed, rebates if minimum quantities are ordered, and so forth. Consumer promotions, designed to 'pull' goods out of shops, include competitions, money off coupons, free goods for coupons, reduced price offers, banded packs of two-for-the-price-of-one, or of two associated products, and so forth. Some promotions are offered across all distribution channels; some are 'tailor-made' as joint operations between the manufacturer and a specific retail chain. Special offers are not confined to fmcgs but are found in financial services (apply before a set date to gain a discount), holidays and hotels, and in some industrial markets. Even sales of capital goods such as power stations, aircraft or

Table 8.1   **Some popular promotional activities**

Advertising
Air miles
Audio-visual sales aids
Banded packs
Brochures
Catalogues
Company visits
Competitions (for customers and the trade)
Coupons
Design (product and packaging)
Direct mail
Directories
Financial incentives
Free gifts
Free mail-ins
Guarantees
Incentive schemes (trade and own salespersons)
Leaflets (technical and other)
Merchandising
Off-premises displays
Packaging
Point-of-sale displays
Premiums
PR (public and press relations)
Price reductions (and pricing strategy)
Self-liquidators
Special offers
Telephone selling
Tent cards (hotels, restaurants, departmental stores)
Vehicle livery
Year books

defence contracts are often attended by 'inducements' such as beneficial financial arrangements or similar deals.

The items forming this mass communications mix are not mutually exclusive. In many cases the vending firm will require some mixture of two or more of them. This will depend on the type of product being sold, the market conditions applying, especially competition and the type of potential customer forming the target market. The amount of money (budget) available and the other resources of the vendor will also affect the decision. How much total expenditure should be put behind the total effort and what relative usage should be made of the various activities form the substance of this chapter.

In meeting its basic aim, the mass communications mix has to respond to increasing competition in domestic markets. With the increasing internationalisation of business, this domestic competition may come from home-based enterprises, which may be national or foreign in ownership, and direct imports from overseas. Usually it is now a combination of both types. Then if the firm is active itself in overseas markets, foreign competition has also to be met, in those counties. The communications mix used must be modified to counter all forms of competition. Having got the mix 'right' at any point in time for the home market does not mean that marketing executives can sit back and have an easy life. Competition now is volatile and with sudden economic changes can change quickly, often unpredictably. Thus the effectiveness of the entire mix and its components must be reviewed regularly so that modifications to it all can be made as seems necessary. When entering a foreign market for the first time, a mix different from that being used in the home market may be necessary (see Section 11.2). Also, for similar reasons, the effectiveness has to be monitored and the necessary changes made to the mix. It is a very challenging but interesting task.

The development of methods of mass production after the Industrial Revolution led to increasing supplies of goods on both domestic and world markets. At first there was sufficient demand to absorb the new production, but competition quickly became more intensive in many markets. A simple objective of selling what the company made was no longer adequate. A shift began towards what is now called the marketing philosophy, of finding out what the customers want and are willing to pay for, and then producing what can be sold. The mass media evolved to facilitate more effective communications between vendors and buyers. This mass media included the development of TV, commercial radio and the press (national or large regional newspapers, both daily and Sunday editions; magazines; trade and specialist publications).

This development and associated technical advances (colour photography and printing, the computer for commercial uses of all kinds, electronic news gathering and transmission equipment, and so on) allowed new methods of communications to be evolved, especially in new concepts of advertising and sales promotion, until we have today mass communications methods. Mass production predicated mass consumption which in turn predicated mass communications. Any one is not possible without the other two and in a highly competitive economy mass communications, efficiently and effectively used, are vital for business survival. Even with industrial products and capital equipment, the extent and nature of the communications mix used today is more extensive than half a century ago.

8.2   Advertising

Modern commercial advertising is the persuasive force that aims at influencing customers' attitudes and patterns of behaviour to a product or service (by use of the mass communications media) in ways which would be favourable to the vendor. This is necessary since consumers' needs and wants change as their economic position improves and as they pass through the different stages of the family life-cycle (see Figure 6.1). In persuading them that certain products satisfy these changing needs better than others, advertising and the other components of the communications mix provide an effective way of reducing marketing risks by giving greater control over changes in demand.

Advertising, with help from the other components of the mix, also has to develop and establish distinctive or unique product or brand identities or images which will prove attractive to both existing and potential customers. The ideal situation is when these identities are seen by customers as synonymous with quality, dependability and the performance of a particular function. For example Hoover became synonymous with vacuum cleaning using a reliable appliance, so that many housewives still refer to '*hoovering*' their homes even when they are using a different make of appliance. Xerox became synonymous with fast, efficient reprographic services.

Several models of 'how advertising works' have been put forward. Early models followed a sequential pattern as shown in the first three columns of Figure 8.1. Members of the target group seeing the advertising were claimed to move from a state of ignorance through Awareness to Action or a purchase. Empirical evidence for such movement is scarce, but in any case this 'strong' or conversion theory of advertising would only tend to fit some limited situations. Most adver-

AIDA	DAGMAR*	Hierarchy of effects	ATR
Awareness	Awareness	Awareness	Awareness
Interest	Comprehension	Knowledge	Trial
Desire	Conviction	Liking	Repeat
Action	Action	Preference	buying
		Conviction	
		Purchase	

* DAGMAR = Defining advertising goals for measured advertising results.

Fig. 8.1   **AIDA, DAGMAR and other models**

tising expenditure in advanced countries is for established products, whose brand names will be known to most people actively in the market. Here the role of advertising is partly to hold on to existing buyers of a brand, and partly to attract buyers to the brand from competitors. The first role is one of reinforcement, or assuring current buyers of a brand that it is still a good buy, that the brand is still active, and the manufacturers are still in business. This role also extends to the trade, seeking their support in stocking a brand which is still being actively advertised.

The second role may sometimes be helped by a 'new improved' or other promotional message, but it is performed mainly by keeping the name of the brand in the consumer's mind. This should then ensure that if for any reason, such as a bad experience with their normal brand, an out-of-stock situation at the normal retailer, or just an impulse to try something different for a change, a consumer considers switching brands, the advertised brand is included in any list of alternatives in their mind. Awareness in this situation is then an ongoing state, boosted with each new exposure to an advertisement, and encouraging trial, or re-trial, when the opportunity arises. Once trial has been achieved, then given favourable product performance, repeat buying may follow. This Awareness–Trial–Repeat buying or ATR pattern of behaviour was put forward by Ehrenberg in 1974, and is now widely accepted as the most likely way in which mass advertising normally works. However, the discussion about 'how advertising works' still continues among advertising people and researchers.

The three basic aims of advertising for established products are (1) to inform potential customers and users of the existence of the product or service and the benefits they can bestow on the purchaser; (2) to remind established users of the continued existence and/or improvement of the products and services; and (3) to regain lost customers and accounts. The balance between these three objectives will vary during the life of a product or brand. For a new brand or the relaunch of a new/improved old one the informative aspect will be paramount. This aspect may also be used to draw attention to a special offer or other promotional activity for an established brand. However for most established brands the 'reinforcement' aspects will be important, to maintain a positive image and to counteract the effects of competitive communications among users, and hopefully to regain lost customers or accounts. Most advertising for existing products is aimed at maintaining a current market position against competition.

The information aspect of advertising can accelerate the demand for new products by creating customers more quickly than would be possible without advertising. This is vital when it is necessary to gain an early foothold in competitive markets, especially when technological, economic and other changes are occurring at a fast pace. Unless reasonable demand can be created relatively quickly so that profitable levels of business activity result, fewer new or improved products and services could be offered. Thus these promotional activities help a firm to look well beyond the next immediate sale.

The effects of advertising are not necessarily limited to the time when it appears. Indeed good advertising has a long-term, durable effect in that it builds goodwill between the firm, distributors and customers. How well this is done

A chance to win a tropical holiday used to advertise a well-established chain of restaurants. Planned to stimulate custom as competition entries are collected through boxes in the restaurants, plus an offer of a free pancake if other purchases made

depends also on the product not being competitively inferior or failing to match the claims made for it. Bad, misleading or ill-judged advertisements can, however, damage customer goodwill that might have taken years to create and can undermine the entire work of the communications mix (see also Section 8.3).

The second aim of advertising, reminding customers and potential users, is necessary because the total of products and services is changing due to economic and other changes, new incentives to spend money in other ways being devised and the average customer not being able to remember everything or keep abreast of all these developments. Also markets are not static organisms. New potential customers are drawn into them from newly employed, newly married and newly retired persons, from families changing homes and localities or moving into a new stage of the family life-cycle (see Figure 6.1). Further, fresh interests and needs are being created. Without advertisements reminding people of the availability of products (especially mass market ones) or services, demand for any one would soon decline.

(a) Objectives

The general goal is to improve the likelihood of customers buying a particular product or service. The specific objectives will depend on the nature of the product, the stage it has reached in its life cycle, competitors' advertising strategy and the purpose of the proposed advertisement. The more usual purposes are listed in Table 8.2. Objectives will also be influenced by content, type of appeal, intended effect, geographical coverage and other factors. A possible classification is given in Table 8.3.

The setting of advertising objectives is fundamental to the formulation of advertising strategy. Unfortunately, firms have trouble in identifying the correct objectives with precision. There may also be arguments about the real purpose of the campaign. The sales manager will see the prime purpose as helping his people to sell. The chief executive may be preoccupied with creating a good corporate image. The technical directors may wish to see the firm's technical abilities properly put across to potential users. And so it can go on. While having a multiplicity of goals is not of itself harmful, the relative importance of each goal or purpose must be known and made clear to those who have to organise the campaign.

In many markets, and particularly those for fmcgs, there is a secondary side to most advertising. Distributors such as factors, wholesalers or retailers will be more willing to handle lines and place orders when they know there will be advertising support to attract buyers. Brands with advertising support tend to have less difficulty in maintaining distribution than brands without it, and this is a legitimate and profitable objective.

(i) *Consumer goods advertising*

Consumer advertising, sometimes called display advertising to distinguish it from 'small advertisements' (although some current advertising for jobs is anything but 'small'), can be divided in a number of ways. Some is straight factual advertising, that a sale starts on Monday, that a product has only *x* calories. Some is emotive or mood advertising offering happiness or other results from the product or service. Some can be classified as 'soft sell' simply planting ideas in the recipients' minds, while others are hard sell of the 'buy now while stocks last' type. Some advertisements are one-offs in support of some specific 'scheme' or

Table 8.2 **Common purposes of advertising**

To create awareness of	
New products or services	for firms established in a market or newcomers.
New variants on old	new packs, flavours, interest rates, destinations etc.
Price changes	obligatory for changes in some interest rates; 'buy now before prices rise' etc.
Benefits of use or effects	from slimming aids, tools, redecoration etc.
Special offers,promotions, competitions etc.	linking media advertising with promotional activities.
To attract	
Enquiries	for brochures, catalogues etc.
Direct sales	through coupons or phone numbers.
New buyers/lapsed buyers	by emphasis on positive properties, nostalgia etc.
To reinforce	
Use among existing users	to keep users loyal, to assure users that they are still using 'the best for them', to counteract competitive claims etc.
Awareness among potential purchaser or users	especially where need is infrequent as with capital/ durable goods, repair services etc.
To influence distributors	
Wholesalers and retailers	to persuade that company will support them with advertising to 'pull' product or service through into the market – much consumer advertising has this as a secondary purpose.
Original equipment manufacturers	to persuade them to fit firm's components as standard or easy option.

promotion which is being run by the manufacturer, such as a temporary price reduction or a competition of the type discussed in the next chapter. Others support a 'theme' running through a whole series of advertisements, possibly over a period of years, with a common thread or covering a common aspect of the product.

Underlying the creation of an advertisement, and its place in the various categories described above, will be two factors related to the objectives. They can be put in the form of two questions which should be asked by everyone involved in the creation and publication of advertising:

Who are the people we are trying to reach?
What message do we want them to receive from our advertising?

The skills in consumer advertising lie in selecting the appropriate media for the purpose and in ensuring that the planned message is received and properly understood by the target audience. Transmitting what the advertiser wants to say is not enough. The message as understood by the audience is what will matter in conveying information.

Table 8.3   **Classification of advertisements**

By appeal	Factual
	Emotional
By content	Product advertising
	Institutional advertising
By demand influence	Primary product level
	Selective brand level
By geographical spread	National
	Regional
	Local
By intended effect	Direct action
	Delayed action
By sponsor	Manufacturer
	Distributor
	Manufacturer-distributor; co-operative advt
	Joint by two manufacturers
	Retail outlet
By target market	Consumer
	Industry
	Trade
	Government agencies

(ii) *Business buyers*

Advertising under this heading must take into account the four main groups of business involved: industry, trade, the professions and the agricultural community (mainly farms). They are customers for consumer goods, services, industrial products and some capital equipment. In the case of *industrial buyers*, purchases cover all the items required in the conduct of their businesses. The advertisements should stress such qualities as economy, efficiency, durability, reliability, strength, performance of the bought item and convenience of purchase and use. With *trade advertising*, aimed at wholesalers and retailers of all kinds, the objective is to encourage purchase and assist the trade to move the items through the distribution channel. Profitability and advertising or other promotional activity to generate consumer demand are common themes.

In the case of *professional advertisements*, aimed at lawyers, accountants, architects, doctors, dentists and so on, the usage of the bought items and the requirements for quality, dependability and value for money (cost) will indicate what the themes should be. Finally for *agricultural* (or *farm*) *advertising*, the users should be judged to be similar to industrial buyers in their purchase of farm machinery, pesticides, fertilisers, other chemicals and agriculture-related products. The advertisements would stress similar points to those shown for industrial buyers.

(iii) *Industrial products*

Industrial products and services tend to have their own specific advertising needs. The markets are generally smaller in number of potential customers (but not necessarily value) and are more specialised.

The first problem is demonstrating to potential customers that the product or service advertised will decrease costs, increase production, be economical without sacrificing quality below permitted limits, improve the saleability of customers' own products or otherwise increase profits. A product which cannot be demonstrated as helping to improve profitability of the purchaser's operations is a difficult product to advertise and sell.

Another problem arises with a component or raw material which loses its identity in the final end-product. It is then difficult for the supplier of the raw material or component to build a solid 'brand image' with associated 'brand preferences'. Then there is the need to pitch the appeal not only to the primary customer but also to that firm's customers. This is essential for new and improved products where considerable resistance to change may be met, especially if the improved benefits, at first consideration, appear to be marginal. The advertisement should convince the ultimate user of the merits of the product. It should influence that company to specify the new or improved product on new orders for the complete equipment or plant. With expensive products and capital equipment, the importance of them, their high cost, performance, durability, minimal maintenance needs, quality and reliability are all points on which potential buyers have to be convinced.

Thus industrial advertisements should

make clear to the recipient what the sponsor makes or does;
describe the firm's functions and specified product advantages without ambiguity;
stress correctly the competitive advantages of the products; markets seldom know as much about a product as is imagined by the manufacturer; it is not safe to assume that everyone knows and appreciates the attributes of the product or service;
consider long- and short-term objectives for they often clash; quick sales of cheap plant can damage long-term intentions of say establishing the firm's products as leaders in their own field.

These must be taken into account with the other points mentioned earlier about advertisements if effective industrial products advertisements are to result.

(b) Style

The various types and classes of advertisements and their different purposes or goals have been discussed. Consider now the styles that are adopted and the results they are expected to achieve.

(i) *Persuasive advertisements*

These are sometimes referred to as the 'hard sell'. This type forms the greater majority of the advertisements seen daily in non-Communist countries though even the latter use them, if to a lesser degree. (All political advertisements and blandishments on posters and in the press are however, 'persuasive' in nature.) It is the inevitable companion of industrialisation and mass-production societies. There is no point in having production machinery if the output cannot be sold (a reality that quite a few firms do not appear to understand fully). These advertisements' primary aim is to find the markets and, by keeping up demand, help to keep the wheels of industry turning.

These advertisements must perform five functions if they are to attract new users or recapture lapsed buyers. The first is attract attention to the product or service advertised. Second, they must command attention and interest. Third, by so doing, create desire in potential users. Fourth, they must inspire conviction and so, fifth, provoke action. For existing users, particularly of fmcgs but also owners of more durable goods, the need is for an advertisement to reinforce loyalty to the brand, and to reassure users that they are still using the 'best' product despite the appeals of competitors. But good advertising will normally manage to achieve both sets of objectives, although emphasising one more than the other if necessary. The creation of these advertisements calls for a considerable range of skills.

(ii) *Informative advertisements*

Many products and services are bought infrequently, and require careful consideration and thought and often detailed analyses of quite a bit of data and information. There may be need for considerable 'shopping around' and budgeting before a buying decision can be made (e.g. important industrial products or equipment; a car; the next holiday; a new suit or dress; a purchase of a product or service not bought before, for instance life, household or fire insurance). In these instances informative advertisements have to be used inviting readers to obtain more information by obtaining a brochure or leaflet, or discussing the important facts that potential users will want before a decision is taken.

One form is the advertisement which simulates the editorial style of the medium carrying it. Such advertisements are very informative but because they can be mistaken for editorial matter the *British Code of Advertising Practice* stipulates that these must have the heading 'Advertiser's Announcement'.

Advertisements frequently combine the persuasive and informative approaches. Also the former tends to be used on TV and commercial radio and in the popular press, while the later appears in magazines, specialist and trade publications and the Sunday editions of the press. The exceptions are advertisements for those products that are sold on hard facts or where the ethics or self-regulation rules prevent or frown on pure persuasive advertising. Examples include proprietary medicines and treatment where lengthy copy on evidence and testimonials supporting the claims are needed. These then are purely informative advertisements within the definition of them.

(iii) *Institutional advertisements*

These are more usually called *corporate* or *prestige* advertisements. They are used to present and promote a company's image or sometimes the image of its activities and major products. This type is used by oil, chemical and pharmaceutical companies who take space to describe their skills and contribution to society, or their attempts to minimise pollution or support conservation. The aim is to gain increasing support from the public, especially potential users of its products and to tempt young graduates and other skilled workers to join their work-forces.

(c) Designing an advertisement

The first step in designing any advertisement, whether it is a one-off or part of a continuing campaign, is to define its purpose. For simple situations such as advertising a house or a car for sale the purpose is simple – to make potential buyers aware that the object is for sale, where they can contact the seller, and the price. Two related sets of decisions then need to be made. One is concerned with the medium to be employed. To advertise an old car a postcard stuck in a newsagent's window may be appropriate; for a prestige car a quality newspaper; for a vintage car there are specialist magazines. Using the wrong medium will mean that while the message will be *sent* it will not *reach* the appropriate target group. The other is concerned with the pitch of the message. The appropriate pitch for the old car may be short and factual, covering model, year, price and contact point. The executive car may have additional details of engine size, mileage, service history. For a vintage car further details of marque, mileage, ownership, restoration and condition may be needed. In each case the details and the way they are presented will be geared to secure a positive response from the type of person likely to be interested.

For commercial advertising similar conditions apply, and depend on the advertising strategy within the overall marketing strategy. While the ultimate end of the marketing strategy may be sales volume, the part to be played by advertising may range from 'buy now while stocks last' or 'send for our free brochure', through to investing in building a long-term image which will attract custom. In each case it is vital that the right combination of medium and message is used. Table 8.4 lists the key questions involved in developing advertising.

(i) *The creative task*

The answers to many of these questions will already be known, such as the target groups defined by overall marketing strategy. In other cases research may be needed. For example, while the target groups may be known in general terms, by age, class or whatever, little may be known about their knowledge of, or attitudes towards the brand and its competitors. Is the existing image of the product positive and beneficial? Are there problem ares, such as people believing that the brand is 'expensive' or 'old-fashioned'? Only when the existing image can be compared with the ideal which the advertiser is seeking can advertising be developed to attack the problems. The solutions may range from short *bursts* of intensive advertising to more extended low-level *continuous* or *drip* campaigns. The media may range from national coverage in the main media, to local radio, cinema, press or posters.

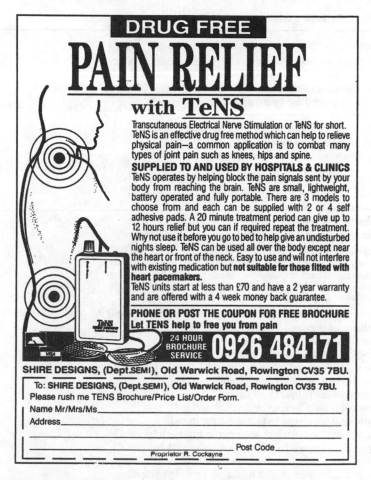

Not all advertising depends on colour or 'hype' to make a point. In some areas a 'no frills' approach can make its own appeal

There are many other factors as well as communications considerations which may affect the final decisions. With small budgets, television may be ruled out because of cost; production costs may rule out the use of colour in press advertising; time constraints may rule out the use of some magazines with long press dates. Legislation may prevent the use of some media (e.g. cigarettes on TV); the Code of Advertising Practice (CAP) places restrictions on advertising for health products, on advertising to children, and so forth; and the media can reject advertisements which they consider not to be truthful etc. Hence the development of advertising depends not only on the ability of the creative people, but on the ability of a whole team of people from market research through to lawyers to work together to achieve an acceptable result.

Table 8.4 **Designing advertising: key decision areas**

What strategic objectives should this advertising meet? For example:

Create direct and immediate response, by phone, coupon etc.
Create awareness of new product/pack etc.
Create awareness of offers, promotions etc.
Reinforce or extend use by existing users
Attract new users for an existing product
Reinforce or change the image of the product
Counter competitive activity
Within which primary and secondary target groups?

What media decisions need to be taken?

What mix of printed or electronic media should be used?
What is the target group?
How can they best be reached?
Will the creative treatment affect the choice of media?
What geographic coverage is needed?
What frequency of exposure will the creative treatment need?
What constraints are imposed by the advertising budget?

What creative decisions need to be taken?

Is the strategy to reinforce, or to change, existing ideas about the product/service?
Is the theme of previous advertising to be used?
How can continuity be combined with freshness?
What new aspects can be introduced?
Is there scope for a radical new approach?
What response is wanted from the audience?
What do we want people to remember?
What do we want people to believe?
What do we want people to feel about the brand?
Should a factual approach or an emotive approach be used?
Will media selection affect the creative approach?
What frequency of exposure will be needed to convey the message?
What constraints are imposed by the advertising budget?

What testing can be undertaken before or during the campaign?

Defining the dimensions to be tested in the light of the strategic advertising objectives
Testing early roughs, storyboards etc.
Testing finished ads prior to publication
Measuring immediate awareness after publication
Assessing longer-term effects

(d) The advertising budget

The advertising budget has to cover two main items of expenditure. In most cases the media costs, for space in print media or for airtime, take most of the budget. However the production costs, for preparing copy and artwork or producing the TV, radio or cinema material can be considerable. Both aspects have to be covered in the budget or 'advertising appropriation'.

There are four main methods of setting the advertising budget, which can also be used for looking at budgets for sales promotion, PR and so forth as well. Briefly these are:

(i)   To cost up the resources needed to achieve the tasks or objectives set for the advertising function. This would mean determining who needs to be reached by the advertising and how often during the budget period, and assessing the costs involved. This is the task approach to budgeting, and can be used for both new and established brands. It has a logical basis, but often the factual basis for calculation is lacking.

(ii) To budget on a fixed proportion of sales revenues. For advertising, where figures are generally available, the proportions are often fixed in relation to the advertising/sales (A/S) ratios of competitors. These may range from minute fractions for industrial products to 25 per cent or more for fashion products with short life cycles. The result can be a reduction of advertising when sales fall, and an increase when sales boom – which may not be logical.

(iii) To budget on a share of advertising or a 'share of voice' basis – often used for new launches, or when seeking to expand a brand's share of sales. Generally to gain market share the share of voice needs to be well above the target share of sales.

(iv) To budget on what the brand can afford. Even when this is not the method for setting the budget it will act as a constraint on other methods.

In practice the marketing executive will keep an eye on competitive activities and the scale of any necessary response, on the effectiveness of his own past expenditure, on the needs of his products in their life cycles, of support for his distributors, and a range of other factors. He may then have to compete with other product or brand managers for a share of the corporate promotional budget, and first bids may be pruned heavily during the annual budgeting round. Here logical justification for the proposed budget may be the vital factor in getting resources.

(e) Measuring effectiveness

The view that advertising should produce increased sales is still valid in some contexts, but in others it must be accepted that advertising is only one factor in the creation of sales. The advertising may be working well, but if the price is wrong, if the season is too hot, too cold, too wet or whatever, if the economy is stagnant, if competitive activity has increased, then sales may not show any immediate response.

The advertising budget, especially for consumer goods and durables, is one of the larger components in the total marketing budget. It is substantial in the communications mix budget, generally being exceeded only by the personal selling costs. So assessment of the effectiveness of the advertising and control of expenditure on it are vital necessities. However, advertising effects are difficult to assess for these purposes.

The problem is that any causal relationship between advertising and sales is limited and often unmeasurable. How far did sales rise because of the new advertising campaign? What would have happened if there had been no advertising? Was the sales increase due to a rise in total demand? Or how did advertising influence total demand? These are some of the questions that need answers. If any answers are to be found there is a need for some method of estimating the effects of the different factors in the environment, the market and the company's marketing mix. This calls for the development of a 'marketing model' bringing together the different causes operating in a market and quantifying their effects. This can be a complex statistical operation, which has only become generally possible during the past 20 years or so, with the development of modern computers. Now using a PC estimates can be made of the effects of the factors on brand sales, including any direct effects of advertising. However the purpose of advertising, as was discussed above, is not always to produce a direct change in sales. Awareness of the product, the development of a favourable image, or simply maintaining existing high levels of these factors are logical advertising objectives which may only affect sales levels in the longer term. Hence other measures may be needed to evaluate the true effects of advertising.

The methods fall into the two categories of pre-testing and of post-testing. Pre-testing involves showing the proposed advertising to samples of people drawn from the target groups. They may then be asked questions generally about the advertisements, whether they liked or disliked them, would buy or not and so forth. But the main information will be about the extent to which the people understood and grasped the message or content. Was the message built into the advertising by the creative people received and understood by the audience? If not, what was received? What was missed or misunderstood? On the basis of the results the advertising can be amended or modified before incurring the media costs. There are problems about the unusual environment in which the advertisements are shown, with respondents being shown commercials in public halls or vans, or press advertisements in dummy publications. There may also be problems because the responses are based on only a single viewing, and so forth. However the method in various forms can provide early warning that an advertisement is failing to meet objectives, even though favourable results cannot guarantee similar responses in natural surroundings.

Post-testing or evaluation of effects can take a wide range of forms, but the essential element is that people are only asked about the advertisement after they have had opportunities to see it in natural surroundings. Once the advertising has been published or broadcast, samples from the target group may be interviewed face-to-face or by phone to discover whether they have seen the appropriate publications or were viewing or listening at times of transmission. Those who have had 'opportunities to see' are than asked about awareness of the advertising, what they remember about it and so forth. The results provide data on the extent to which the advertising is achieving the objectives set, and communicating its message, and possibly with supplementary information on purchasing patterns and intentions. Continuous research in the form of tracking studies can be bought from companies specialising in this work.

8.3   The advertising process

The process normally involves two separate but co-ordinated functions. One is the creation of the advertisements and their preparation for broadcasting or publi-

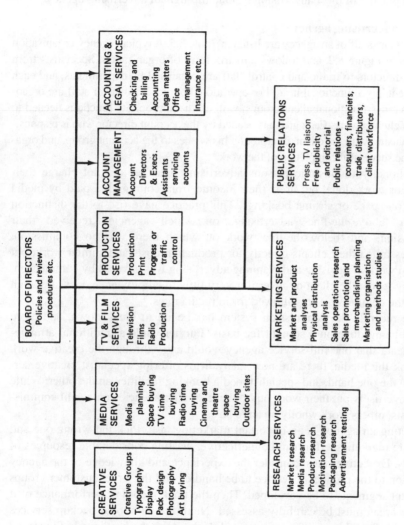

Fig. 8.2 Typical advertising agency organisation

cation. The other is the selection of the appropriate media and the negotiations on timing and costs leading to booking of the space and time. A company will normally make a member of the marketing staff responsible for organising and executing the advertising function. Where there is a need for specialised work, such as detailed technical illustrations, work may be done in-house, but the preparation and placing of most advertising is done through an advertising agency.

(a) The advertising agency

The specialist staff of an agency are listed in Table 8.5. A typical agency organisation is shown in Figure 8.2, and follows a matrix form of organisation. Specialists from account directors to traffic and control staff are organised by departments, and each department has a functional head. For operational purposes however staff are organised into cross-functional client groups, with all the appropriate functions needed to handle a client's work. Each group is headed by the account director who is responsible for liaising with the client, interpreting his wishes to the account group, and organising the successful completion of the work.

Traditionally for historic reasons advertising agencies did not charge their clients for work done, but drew their income from commission paid by media owners on space or airtime bookings. This practice gave rise to the distinction between 'above-the-line' advertising, on which agencies received their commission, and 'below-the-line' work on which there was no commission. Agencies billed their clients directly for production costs and similar work, but the main work of devising and planning advertising was covered by commission. In theory it cost the client or advertiser very little to employ an agency, although clearly the commission was allowed for in media rates.

More recently the commission system has begun to break down, and more work is being done on a straight fee basis. Further while a traditional arrangement meant that one full-service agency would carry through the creative work and book the media, there are now many firms offering specialist creative services on the one hand, and specialist media booking facilities on the other. While some advertisers put their work out to these smaller agencies on a split commission basis, others work wholly on a fee basis.

Selecting an agency is an important marketing task. Pick the wrong one and the entire marketing effort can be ineffective, wasting considerable resources of all kinds. Executives must consider the experience and knowledge of the agency in relation to the product or service to be handled and the target customer groups or market segments to be developed. Then the track record or performance of it in these areas must be carefully assessed. Next, the additional backup services that can be provided must be investigated. Help under the headings in Figure 8.2 of 'Media Services', 'Research', 'Marketing' and 'Public Relations Services' may be crucial to the success of any campaign.

The acceptance of the 'marketing concept' has made executives realise that they must overcome not only problems associated with the manufacture of their products (or services) but also those of presenting products effectively to potential users. Customers, instead of being on the periphery of management thought and planning, secondary to manufacturing aspects, now occupy the centre of the

Table 8.5   **The advertising agency: staff functions**

1   *Account Executive*: has overall responsibility for looking after the client's work within the agency, and for contact between the client and the agency. Looks after the 'business' side of the relationship, and ensures smooth running of the account. On a large account the account executive will probably be a Board Member, and called Account Director, helped by Account Executives or Representatives working on specific areas. Smaller accounts will be serviced by an Account Executive or Representative, probably supervised by a Board Member.

2   *Creative team*: develops the client's or agency's ideas into advertisements. Usually consists of a writer and an artist, dealing with the words and images respectively, whether for print or electronic media. While the writer will normally see the words through from initial ideas to the final version, the artist may simply 'visualise' or doodle the results required and commission the finished product from other people. In particular the work of producing a TV commercial will be put out to a specialised TV production company, working with the creative team, and to the script and brief developed by the agency.

3   *Media team*: recommends where the advertising should appear, and then buys the appropriate facilities. In small agencies one person will cover both the planning and buying aspects of the work, but in large agencies there may be a split between Media Planning and Media Buying. Planning is a strategic function, ranging from the initial selection of the type of medium to be used, through to planning how often, where and when advertisements appear. Media buying is a negotiating function, securing the best rates for the client to meet the plan. The 'media schedule' sets out the details of the plan and is the basis for buying. Close liaison between the two functions is vital to ensure that best use is made of the client's money in carrying through the advertising strategy. There are now some companies which specialise in this area, with work contracted out to them by advertising agencies which can then concentrate their resources on the creative side.

4   *Account planner*: analyses marketing information and research, assesses the strengths, weaknesses, opportunities and threats within particular markets, and makes recommendations on the marketing and advertising strategies. Generally exercises a key role in providing understanding of the market and the client's place in it, and a formal planning base for the agency's activities for a client. In a small organisation the Account Director or Executive may well cover the Account Planning role, but in any case close co-operation between the executive and planner is vital.

5   *Other departments*: will include an accounts department who will pay bills from outside suppliers and the media, and will bill clients. There will be someone responsible for ensuring that deadlines are met, and monitor work in progress; and someone watching the legal and voluntary requirements within the industry. Normally however contact between clients and these areas is through the Account Executive.

stage. This requires firms to have greater and more detailed knowledge of customers. As a result agencies, their functions and services, have had to be developed to meet clients' increased needs. Further it was realised that the many skills involved had to be properly integrated into a balanced whole if the advertisement or campaign was itself to give balanced and integrated support to the rest of the marketing effort. The advertising industry has come a long way from the days when agencies were just space-buying and -filling companies.

The agency plays a very important role, through its specialised skills of providing important practical help and advice to clients on a wide range of marketing problems. It brings an independent mind and considerable expertise to bear on such matters as client's marketing strengths and weaknesses; the effectiveness of the firm's current communications mix, especially personal selling; the level and quality of product mix, product distribution and display; the effectiveness of the distribution system generally; and the effects of specific promotional activities at trade and consumer or customer levels. The agency's involvement in clients' marketing planning and thought on a continuing basis increases the chance of more effective advertising being created and used, while giving greater stability and integration to the client–agency relationship.

Some major organisations have their own advertising departments. Today's costs, however, make it almost certain that in most instances the total cost of what is virtually an in-house advertising agency, cannot be justified. A small department may then be used. The purpose of such departments is to assist marketing colleagues to establish advertising strategy and goals, help to select an appropriate agency, brief it thoroughly on what is required, explain the firm's policies and philosophies to the agency, decide how the total advertising budget should be allocated, monitor operations and make recommendations if results are not as planned. Sometimes one executive, usually called the 'advertising manager' will do all this; at others there may be a few assistants to help with the work.

Once the basic decisions have been taken, on the objectives, the budget or appropriation, and who is to handle the work, the task of developing advertising falls largely into two interlocking parts, the creation of the advertising and the selection of the media to be used. Given an advertising brief which has been agreed with the client, then the creative people and the media planners can develop the detail.

(b) Creating the advertising

Within the context of the advertising objectives and agreement on the media to be used, the creative effort may range from a simple factual statement of product attributes for the technical or trade press through to a whole series of television commercials. Some television advertising almost takes the form of mini soap operas, and the same basic treatment may be used for months or years.

The creative decisions involved will depend on the target audience and the advertising task, and discussions will cover the way the message is to be delivered, hard sell, soft sell, straight factual or with humour, with one advert endlessly repeated or a series developing different aspects of the product, and so forth.

For each type of advertising, from simple press to TV, various production stages and various costs are involved. Budgets may determine the size of print ads, and thus limit their content; or preclude the use of colour or complex illustrations. Budgets may limit the nature and location of 'sets' used in TV, or the number of actors employed. Timing may be vital and affect preparation in all areas. Hence even in this creative area it will be necessary to give due attention to deadlines and costs.

The objectives and purpose of an advertisement or a campaign will be agreed between the client and the agency, whether it is a general agency or a creative specialist shop. The creative people will then develop their ideas in accordance with the brief, but clearly linking with the media planning people to ensure that both sides fit together.

For press advertising a copywriter will be involved, and often a visualiser as well. The precise titles held by the people involved will vary from one agency to another, but between them they will develop ideas for the advertising, with support from typographers, photographers, artists and so forth as necessary. Once the content and the illustrations have been agreed with the client, production specialists become involved to translate the ideas through to the form appropriate for the publications concerned. The use of electronic methods for type-setting and illustrations, and of fax machines for sending images over long distances, have had a marked effect on the production side, and have eased some of the constraints on the creative side.

With electronic media, and particularly TV, greater flexibility leads to more decisions involving more people. For TV advertising a writer will produce an outline script, which may be developed into a story-board showing the visual images at various points in the commercial. If the ideas are accepted and it is decided to go ahead, a producer or production team will become involved, and with the co-operation of the agency people, and often the client as well, will shoot the commercial. For radio the situation is similar but much more simple, with only sound involved.

Whichever media are used there may be a need for testing the ideas during the development of the advertising. More will be said about this later, but it is useful to have a firm understanding between the client and the agency about responsibility for the costs of research and testing. Normally the client will be responsible for general market research leading to the development of strategy and objectives. The agency will normally be responsible for any 'pre-testing' of the advertising during the development stages up to publication or broadcasting; and any subsequent monitoring of results becomes the responsibility of the client. However any of these responsibilities may be subject to negotiation, and proper definition of responsibilities within an agency between creative and administrative personnel is necessary if undue concessions are not to be made.

(c) Planning the media

Decisions on the way in which the advertising is to be put before the target group fall into two parts, decisions on the types of medium to be used, and decisions on the frequency of appearance. The decisions on the media to be used will have been made at a strategic level. Decisions relating to the pattern of advertising within the chosen media fall within media planning.

Some of the main points involved in these two sets of decisions are set out in Tables 8.6 and 8.7. Decisions in the creative area, such as the need for colour in press advertising, will clearly affect the range of publications available, and so forth. Generally however planning the pattern of advertising, which involves selecting the specific print media or radio or TV stations, deciding which days of

A leaflet inserted into a newspaper or magazine may attract more notice than a conventional advertisement, particularly when using colour. Economy of effort may be achieved by arranging for inserts to be restricted to areas served by the advertiser

the week to use, how often the advertisement will appear, and the whole development of what is called the *media schedule* will take the following factors into consideration:

Table 8.6 **Media available**

Newspapers
National daily newspapers
National Sunday newspapers
Regional/local morning, evening or Sunday newspapers
Regional/local weekly newspapers
Local free-sheets
(Any of these may include regular or occasional sections or supplements, which may appeal to specific groups of readers.)

Trade and technical press
Trade newspapers or periodicals, e.g. *Admap*, *The Grocer*
Technical periodicals, e.g. *The Lancet*, *Nature*
Close circulation magazines mailed directly to special interest groups.

Magazines
General, e.g. *Private Eye*, *Reader's Digest*
Women's, e.g. *Woman's Own*, *Family Circle*, *Vogue*
Special interest, e.g. *Motor Sport*, *Angling Times*, numerous PC mags

Electronic media
Commercial television – terrestrial
                     – satellite
                     – cable
                     – oracle
Commercial radio
Video for some in-store purposes

Other media
Cinema advertising
Posters
Transport advertising at bus stops/stations and on vehicles
Direct Mail in a wide variety of formats

---

size of the media budget;
degree of flexibility required;
nature and scale of competitive media activity;
effectiveness of the medium;
the importance of reach and frequency.

Ideally the size of the budget should be such as is necessary to achieve the advertising objectives most economically and effectively. However, for economic and other reasons, this is not always possible. For example the wider the purchase of an item, the more difficult and expensive it is to reach all potential customers. Where colours are needed (as in advertisements for foods, toiletries, fashion and cosmetics) the costs are increased. If primary and secondary media have to be used this also increases total advertising costs.

The degree of flexibility of media planning required is primarily dependent on the nature of the product and its demand. For well-established products having continuous use during any year, the degree of flexibility needed is not great. For products with predictable seasonal peaks (e.g. sun-tan lotion, cold remedies) or

Table 8.7a   **Media selection: points to consider**

THE MEDIA-CREATIVE LINK

The type of media to be used in a campaign and the type of creative treatment used must of course be co-ordinated. In some cases the need to use particular media to achieve object-ives will impact on creative decisions. In other cases the need for a particular creative treatment will condition media selection. Only when all decisions are taken in harmony can a fully effective campaign be developed.

THE TARGET GROUP

Most target groups can be reached by several media types. Major groups can be reached by most media; minor groups may be reached by specialist media, but also as part of the audi-ence to mass media. In reaching decisions many non-tangible factors may be taken into consideration, such as the 'authority' of a publication in a particular area. However, one common denominator is often the 'cost-per-thousand' of reaching the audience through a particular medium. This is the cost of the chosen space or slot related to the numbers expected to be exposed to the advertising. A balance has to be struck between the costs per thousand and the *reach* and *frequency* which will be provided.

REACH AND FREQUENCY

Reach is the number of people, or the proportion of the target group, who will have at least one opportunity-to-see/hear (OTS or OTH) a campaign. The numbers reached will tend to increase as advertisements are repeated in the same or different media, and different media schedules will lead to differing patterns and costs. Reach for a single publication, expressed as a percentage of the target audience, is known as 'penetration'.

Frequency is the average number of OTS members of the target group will have during a campaign. In some cases the objective will be to secure as wide a reach as possible, with minimum duplication of exposure. In other cases the objective will be to ensure that mem-bers of the target group will receive numerous or frequent OTS to meet the advertising objectives.

PROFILE

An analysis by age, region, social class, etc., showing the proportions of people of differ-ent types reached by a publication or station. Essential for matching against the target group, and in building a multi-media schedule.

---

when sources of supply are subject to the vagaries of climate (e.g. fresh fruit and vegetables, imported canned foods) there is greater need for flexibility in media planning. In the case of the appropriateness and effectiveness of media, the factors in Table 8.7 have to be considered. The effective cost (per thousand read-ers/listeners/viewers) of each medium and the effectiveness of the message or copy have also to be taken into account. The *impact* of an advertisement depends also on the following four points.

(d) Reach and frequency

'Reach' refers to the number of potential customers reached by the advertise-ment. 'Frequency' is the number of times the message is exposed to each of these people. Coverage can be increased by adding to the number of media used. Fre-quency is increased by buying more insertions in the media first selected and/or by increasing the media used while keeping the number of insertions per medium unchanged. Given the fact that most persons have short memories and it is neces-sary to keep reminding them of the existence of a product or service, a firm

Table 8.7b   **Media selection: some data sources**

There are a number of sources of media research in most countries. In the UK many of the sources are sponsored and managed by 'Joint Industry Committees', formed from representatives of media owners, advertising agencies and advertisers. Other sources are commercial companies offering specific services. In the UK the main sources are these:

The Audit Bureau of Circulations (ABC) monitors the paid sales of major newspapers and magazines. A subsidiary company, Verified Free Distributions Ltd, monitors the circulation figures of free publications.

The Broadcasters' Audience Research Board (BARB) was formed by the amalgamation of the Joint Industry Committee for Television Research (JICTAR), and the BBC audience research department. It measures the size and composition of all TV audiences using electronic devices attached to sets in a panel of homes. Using separate panels it also provides Audience reaction research on qualitative aspects of programmes.

Joint Industry Committee for National Readership Surveys (JICNARS) measures readership of about 200 major newspapers and magazines through a continuous programme of personal interviews. Reports show the numbers, and characteristics, of people reading each publication.

Joint Industry Committee for Poster Audience Research (JICPAR) provides information on site classification and on the size and composition of poster audiences.

Joint Industry Committee for Radio Audience Research (JICRAR) provides information on the numbers and composition of audiences to local and national radio stations. The research is based on diary panels.

Media Expenditure Analysis Limited (MEAL) is a commercial organisation collating, analysing and publishing estimates of advertising expenditures in the main media by individual brands and organisations.

British Rate and Data (BRAD) is a monthly publication giving details of all media which carry advertising. Data include advertising rates, mechanical/electronic requirements, press dates, audited circulations, etc.

Other research into consumer buying and usage patterns may provide information on reading, viewing and listening habits. Data can be collected through continuous panels or series of successive consumer surveys, and can link media habits directly to product or brand usage.

should achieve the greatest frequency possible within budget limitations and other marketing considerations. However, continuity of advertising is essential and most firms rely on the experience and knowledge of the media planner in their advertising agency to advise them on these two points.

(e) Colour and size
The use of colour in print media, as mentioned, is necessary for some products but is generally advisable for most, where the extra cost can be met. Coloured advertisements attract more attention than black and white, and certain colours

Some publications enhance their own sales of advertising space by tailoring their space to needs of smaller clients. Here a series of one-eighth pages meets the needs of smaller service companies while boosting advertising revenue. Each ad gives address and phone/fax numbers for direct response

produce particular emotional responses. The latter vary with ethnic groups. For example red to a European usually means danger but to some Eastern races it is a very auspicious colour. Gold (rather than yellow) is favourably aspected with most people. The psychology of colour is one that successful advertising executives have found useful to understand.

The size of an advertisement will first depend on the amount of copy that is required, the size of the budget and thus on the creative ability of the advertising agent or department. Large-sized advertisements certainly attract attention and there is a limit as to how small an insert should be. Too small for its purpose or message and it will be overlooked by readers or swamped by competing advertisements. Given that potential users have to be reminded often about the product or service, smaller advertisements placed say weekly or fortnightly into a publication may be disproportionately more effective than one whole- or half-page insert placed once a month or once every two or three months. Each case requires careful consideration by executives expert on the subjects of media effectiveness and related aspects, as every solution could be different.

8.4 Public relations

Public relations is the deliberate, planned and sustained effort to establish and maintain mutual understanding between a firm and its public. This must be founded on correct information and true facts. It is not a casual or *ad hoc* activity and should not be a means of attempting to excuse company failings. The 'public' varies too from consumers and customers to financiers and shareholders, employees and the public at large. Public relations must also inform the company of any changes in public opinion about it or its products. Thus it helps to indicate the implications for company policies and actions.

Public relations influence the opinions of various groups. It can show the firm to be a leader in its industry or as an innovator. Or it can illustrate that the company is public spirited and aware of its social responsibilities or is a vigorous organisation that gets things done (worthwhile ones, that is!). Well thought out public relations activities can enhance employees' sense of pride and so improve their performance, critical in the case of the sales force.

Public relations, although using similar media to advertising,unlike advertising does not normally promote a single theme. It is a highly specialised activity requiring a constant flow of press releases about the company, its operations, products and employees. These releases are adapted to the needs and style of the chosen medium. It is a sophisticated technique of communication to a much wider range of audiences than advertising or sales promotions. Nevertheless it must form an integrated part of the entire communications mix and indirectly support its sister activities in this mix.

In cases when advertising for a product may be prohibited (e.g. cigarettes in Britain, Scotch whisky in France), public relations activities can be useful. Here the release would feature the firm or factory where the product is made, related advances in research and development or some human interest story about the employees. This helps to overcome the difficulty in establishing the brand name for products so afflicted.

Promotion of sporting or artistic events may be part of a continuous PR campaign. Care is needed in linking the activity with the company or its products, but an increasing amount of promotional money is being spent on activities from classical concerts to rock festivals, and from golf to motor racing.

8.5   The promotional mix

The size and nature of the mass promotional mix will depend on many factors, ranging from the type of product or service to the extent of competition. The forms of distribution system and the selling methods, to be discussed in the next chapter, will also need to be considered. Both the communications aspects and the distribution and selling aspects need to be drawn into an integrated marketing operation, taking account of both strategic and tactical objectives.

Where the emphasis should be placed (on selling, or advertising, or public relations, or sales promotions) depends on the nature or type of products (consumer goods or industrial), the target markets involved and the value and profit margins of the products. (The same considerations apply to most services.) For example, low value consumer goods sold on a national basis would normally rely heavily on advertising and sales promotion while the personal selling content would be low, probably restricted to distributors and concentrated on retailers including supermarkets and chain or departmental stores. Consumer goods of high price or value sold into a more limited number of markets could use promotional and selling activities, both to a high but not necessarily equal degree.

An example of the first group is inexpensive processed foods of all kinds. The second group includes expensive escorted tours sold to the 'B' and 'C' social groups. In the latter case, the tour company does the advertising and the retailer (travel agent) does the personal selling, as well as some advertising perhaps in the local press. With the former example, the manufacturer advertises the products and sells into the retail outlets and the only selling involved as far as the consumer is concerned is the availability of the products in the shops or supermarkets they use. The expensive end of women's toiletries can use advertising and personal selling equally, though the emphasis is usually on the former through impressive advertisements in the glossy women's magazines. Personal selling would be by canvassers to the homes and by salesgirls in the more expensive departmental stores.

For screwdrivers and hand tools (relatively low value, industrial products needing national coverage) almost all the expenditure would be on advertising (including a few mail shots). Again the only 'selling' might be the availability of the products at the retailers, with suitable displays. For most other industrial products (high value sold on a more selective basis to various customers having different or specialised needs), the emphasis is usually on personal selling with sufficient advertising to make users aware of the existence of the products. Much of the effort would also be on sales promotions (leaflets, catalogues etc.) especially where considerable technical information is needed by customers. For capital goods or plant and equipment (very expensive items sold almost on a one-off basis and tailored to individual requirements), the communications mix would be comprised of almost all personal selling and negotiations. Advertising would be minimal, again just to keep the firm and its products in the eyes and minds of potential users.

Seldom can there be reliance on one component of the mix. While advertising is probably the most effective for creating overall awareness, personal selling is more effective in some areas in producing conviction in customers' minds that they need the product. Finally, the optimal communications or promotional mix will depend on the stage that a product has reached in its life cycle, the promotional strategy of competitors and the nature of the buying process.

(a) Measuring promotional effectiveness

In many markets a range of competitive promotional activities, as well as other marketing efforts, will be happening at any one time. Trying to establish the effects of any particular activity can therefore be a difficult undertaking.

Where clear objectives have been set for some promotional effort, assessing the effectiveness can be made easier. A good example of the benefit of clear objectives based on knowledge of the market was provided by one old-established consumer product. This was showing declining sales, and after 50 years on the market it seemed that the product had reached the decline stage of its life cycle. Research among housewives however showed that most of them thought the product itself was still alright, but many thought it was only used by:

older housewives set in their ways;
bad cooks to hide their inferior cooking;
poor people who could not afford good food.

Based on these findings the advertising objectives were defined as moving the image of the product away from the pattern shown by the research, to one in which the product was used by young, ABC_1 housewives who were good cooks. A campaign was developed, and subsequent research showed that the objectives had been achieved. The product was Oxo, the time was the mid 1950s, the campaign featured a young middle-class housewife who was a good cook. She was named Katie, and the product is alive today.

In other cases the objective may simply be to maintain a position in the face of competition. Here it may be extremely difficult to show that any of the promotional effort is having an effect, whether on sales, distribution, the product image or anything else. What may be required here, if it is important to assess causes and effects, is an experiment in which the intensity of the promotional effort is changed in one part of the market, while being maintained in the rest. At the extreme the promotional activity is removed entirely from the experimental area. Then in time, and it may take many months for differences to appear in the experimental area, the effects of removing or changing the promotional stimulus may become apparent, and conclusions drawn. (Records exist showing that anything up to eighteen months may pass before any experimental effects can be seen even from complete removal of the activity, so patience is needed.)

A third approach is sometimes possible, but depends heavily on continuous data being available. In most markets this involves data on sales, prices, distribution, advertising and promotions, both for a brand and its competitors. The approach then involves building statistical models of a brand in its market, and attempting to unravel the effects on sales of prices, distribution, promotions, weather or holidays, and so forth. The model building approach will be discussed as an approach to forecasting in Chapter 10, but the relationships found in building a model will also indicate the effects linked with promotional and other aspects of the marketing mix.

With increasing emphasis being placed on the cost-effectiveness of all operations undertaken by an organisation, promotional budgets will inevitably come under close scrutiny. In common with other areas of a company's activities, analyses will be expected showing effects which can be set against costs. This will always be difficult in the communications area, but the following basic steps will provide some starting information:

(i)   Measure so far as possible the situation before the communications activity begins. This provides a benchmark as well as data for planning purposes.

(ii) Define the communications objectives clearly, and quantify them so far as possible. The objectives should be set in the context of the specific communications activity, as in creating awareness or changing an image for advertising or in creating trial for an in-store promotion. Avoid if possible setting communications objectives directly in terms of sales, which depend on far more factors. Given realism about what the activity is likely to achieve it is far better to state an objective as 'To raise awareness among ABC_1 housewives by 10 per cent', or whatever, rather than merely 'To increase awareness in the market'.

(iii) Measure effects in the appropriate communications dimensions, whether in image terms or responses from the target group, as the activity progresses, and for some time afterwards if necessary. In the final analysis, data systematically collected at the time will carry far more weight than general opinions based only on anecdotal evidence and memory..

Assignments

Does your chosen organisation use advertising, public relations or any form of promotional activity? If so, what are the objectives? What are the target groups? What media are being used? What message is being delivered?

Is there any competitive advertising, PR activity or promotion? If so, select a current campaign and describe the content, the media mix, and what you believe are the target groups. Analyse this information to work back to what you think the objectives and strategy may be. What light does this throw on the suppliers' marketing or corporate strategy?

HOLYPORT VILLAGE FAIR

SATURDAY, 2ND JUNE

ON THE GREEN
HOLYPORT, BERKSHIRE

Hon. Secretary: Maidenhead 20604

A simple message, economical production and judicious siting within a small target area probably make outdoor advertising the most cost-effective medium for local activities or services

Distribution and selling

All the operations of an organisation will grind to a halt unless there are ways of taking the product or service to the customer and making a sale. Care taken with the development of the product, its pricing and its promotion will all be wasted unless the product is brought within reach of the customer and a sale is made. The two operations of distributing the product and selling it are closely linked, and activities in the two areas need careful matching for effective results. The roles and functions of the two activities form the subject of this chapter.

9.1 Role and functions of physical distribution

The whole marketing effort is concerned with optimising the value of a product while trying to minimise the cost of doing that. It attempts to add value to the product through every stage of the exchange process. Value can be added in many ways.

It can be done by changing the form of the item as when raw materials are processed into a finished product. It can be achieved by breaking bulk, for example, when coal is taken from a large stockpile and packed into bags or sacks so that it can be conveniently handled and used by consumers. Value is also added by packaging, for example placing toiletry products into smaller, easily handled and attractive containers that attract the interest of potential customers and are also easy to use or handle. Value may also be added by a change of time, as, for instance, when vegetables are canned or frozen at times of abundance (harvest) so that they will be available at times of scarcity (winter). Or value is added by a change of place; that is, by transporting goods from their place of manufacture or harvesting to the points of sale or purchase. Physical distribution (also referred to as *marketing logistics*), in making products available at the right places at the right times, is said to provide the utilities of place and time. That is, to have value a product must not only be available where it is wanted, but also when it is needed.

(a) Role

Thus the role of physical distribution (PD) is to optimise the value of a product by making it available as described, at the various retail outlets where customers normally expect to be able to avail themselves of it. The activities or responsibilities involved in doing this are summarised in Table 9.1. Note that these do not include the purchasing function. Physical Distribution Management (PDM) may also be called upon to advise on the location of manufacturing units, especially for large operations involving many products sold nationally (for example, mass-

Table 9.1 **Physical distribution – responsibilities**

Depots/warehouses (in-plant and distribution or in-field)
Decisions on size, location, whether owned or leased; facilities and layout; management of; methods of handling goods.

Inventories/inventory control
Decisions on inventory policies; max., min. and reordering stock levels; control procedures, cost of.

Transportation
Decisions on mode to be used (road, rail, water, air); whether transport owned, leased, arranged on annual contract, casual hire, load and journey planning; handling special goods.

Channels of distribution
Decisions on distribution channels to be used (see Figure 9.2).

Delivery patterns
Decisions on delivery times, service levels for customers.

Processing
Drop size/cost analysis; order processing; load building.

Costs
Cost control and allocations; customer account profitability; backhaul waste capacity; labour incentives; refusals and returns; insurance cover as needed.

Administration
Management of PD operations; selection and control of administrative systems and all associated paperwork; correcting errors in dispatch and in order-taking; packing and dispatch, issuing of dispatch notes, shipping documents etc., staffing. Quality check on all items into stores.

(All decisions are taken in consultation with appropriate colleagues from other departments of the Marketing Division, Manufacturing and Finance Divisions and Personnel.)

market consumer goods). The aim is to achieve an efficient system that provides an acceptable level of customer service that does not involve the firm in prohibitive distribution costs.

(b) Functions
The popular or traditional concept of PD is that it is concerned with the efficient movement of the finished item to the customer. However, a totally integrated system takes responsibility for the movement into the factory of all bought-in items, their storage and inventories and movement through the factory in the course of processing them into the finished product. Then PDM is also responsible for the storage of work-in-progress (w-i-p) as it waits the next stage of manufacture and the control and supervision of w-i-p stores. Figure 9.1 illustrates the two concepts, where 'A' represents the conventional and 'B' the total system views.

PD is no longer seen as just another cost centre that can erode profits if it is not properly managed. It is now appreciated as an activity having an important role to play in the marketing mix. Thus increasing emphasis is being given to the evolution of integrated distribution strategies in the context of total marketing systems. Efficiently carried out, PD provides another important, critical and competitive edge to marketing effort.

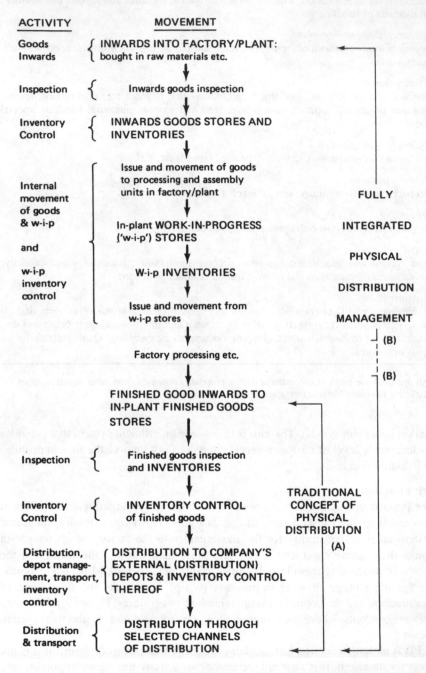

ACTIVITY   MOVEMENT

Goods   { INWARDS INTO FACTORY/PLANT:
Inwards   { bought in raw materials etc.

Inspection   {   Inwards goods inspection

Inventory   {   INWARDS GOODS STORES AND
Control   {   INVENTORIES

Internal   Issue and movement of goods
movement   to processing and assembly
of goods   units in factory/plant
& w-i-p   FULLY

and   In-plant WORK-IN-PROGRESS   INTEGRATED
                        ('w-i-p') STORES

w-i-p   PHYSICAL
inventory   W-i-p INVENTORIES
control   DISTRIBUTION

                        Issue and movement from
                        w-i-p stores   MANAGEMENT

                                                                          (B)
                        Factory processing etc.

                                                                          (B)

                        FINISHED GOOD INWARDS TO
                        IN-PLANT FINISHED GOODS
                        STORES

Inspection   {   Finished goods inspection
                        and INVENTORIES

                                                             TRADITIONAL
Inventory   {   INVENTORY CONTROL   CONCEPT OF
Control   {   of finished goods   PHYSICAL
                                                             DISTRIBUTION
Distribution,   { DISTRIBUTION TO COMPANY'S   (A)
depot manage-   { EXTERNAL (DISTRIBUTION)
ment, transport,   { DEPOTS & INVENTORY CONTROL
inventory   { THEREOF
control

Distribution   {   DISTRIBUTION THROUGH
& transport   {   SELECTED CHANNELS
                   {   OF DISTRIBUTION

Fig. 9.1   Physical distribution – movement of goods

(c) Distribution channels

A channel of distribution (sometimes called a *trade channel*) is the path products take as they move from the producer to the ultimate consumer or industrial customer. The main forms are shown in Figure 9.2, and range from the very simple upwards. In the very simple the producer sells directly to the ultimate industrial user or consumer. This pattern is common in industrial markets where components or machinery may move directly from producer to customer with no intermediaries. It is becoming more common in some consumer markets through the use of *Direct Marketing* which will be discussed later.

Slightly more complex situations arise where there is a single intermediary. In industrial markets a manufacturer may sell to a factor who sells on to the user; or in consumer markets the producer sells to a major retail chain for sale to the consuming public. A similar situation arises with goods moving from producer to consumer via mail-order or direct marketing specialists. Further stages can be involved, as when a manufacturer sells to a factor or wholesaler who sells to a retailer who sells to the public. When goods cross from one country to another, even within the Common Market, factors may be involved who know their home markets, and handle the distribution of imported goods on behalf of 'foreign' manufacturers.

(d) Implications for marketing

In selecting channels, several points have to be considered. First, there is the size and complexity of the producer's operations. Where a substantial number of products are made in large quantities and these are sold on a wide basis nationally, the firm requires a substantial distribution network. In this case, to keep costs down the company would usually prefer to work through wholesalers and retailers. However, some special items may be sold direct to retailers, a franchise holder or to some (large or important) users.

Second, there is the degree of control the firm wishes to exert on the sale and distribution of its products and prices. Going through the 'normal' trade network means that the company can keep some control of the operations. However, the greater the rank or independence of the intermediary, the less control will a manufacturer have over the distribution channel. The company may not be able to dictate the level of stocks to be held or when and how the intermediary promotes or even sells the product.

Third, the firm should consider its financial strength. A financially strong and sound company can finance the right distribution network for its needs. However, direct selling to customers needing large sales, servicing and distribution networks, several depots and substantial total inventories of finished goods, with their resultant high operating costs, becomes impractical for many companies. The use of sales licencees, sole agents and franchisees offered possible solutions. However, care is needed to ensure the right patterns are chosen for the products and work involved. Hasty or incorrect decisions can adversely affect the whole business. The manufacturer may regret the decisions, especially if the terms of the agreement make it difficult or expensive to rectify the mistake speedily.

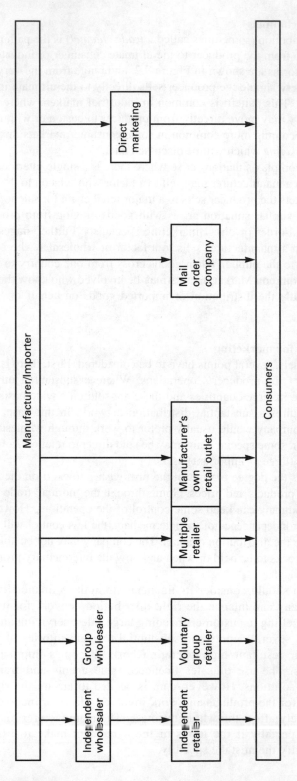

Fig. 9.2   The basic channels of distribution for consumer goods

The fourth point to consider is the nature of the markets. If there are only a few major customers direct distribution may be possible and advisable, especially if they have special needs. If there are many potential customers, widely spread in any geographical area, middlemen (whether wholesalers and/or retailers) will be necessary. Sometimes recourse to direct mail methods can be used but again, as postal and other charges increase, direct mail costs can rise to prohibitive levels. Allied to this is the fifth point, the length of the distribution channel to the ultimate customer and the complexity of it. The help of distribution intermediaries is then unavoidable, since it would be too costly for the firm to become deeply involved in the substantial problems posed in this case.

Finally, the nature of the product has to be considered. For example, perishable foodstuffs need fast-acting marketing and distribution operations using expert wholesalers geared to the fast-moving selling that is essential (as with fish, meat and vegetables, for example). In addition, the completeness of the product line should be taken into account. If a firm is not producing a complete line, selecting a distributor who handles the missing items, even if made by a competitor, should mean that both manufacturers should benefit from the middleman's ability to offer a complete set to customers.

Thus decisions on which channels of distribution to use rest upon how much the manufacturer wishes to be involved in the problems and risks inherent in the work and how well the firm knows its markets and their distribution needs. In theory, the elimination of the intermediaries improves the firm's profitability because it no longer has to pay the necessary trade discounts. However, in practice, the more extensive sales and after-sales services, the larger inventories and greater number of depots required will lead to increased operating costs, the increase often being larger than any savings made on trade discounts. The use of intermediaries also shifts some of the costs and problems off the shoulders of the manufacturer. Further, as the middlemen collectively are in detailed, effective contact with markets and potential customers, market intelligence obtained through them can be more comprehensive than if the firm tried to go it alone. The implications for marketing of choosing the right channels and methods of distribution are considerable.

(e) Impact of marketing on PD

The developments that have taken place in the methods and techniques of marketing have also had an impact on PD. The market-place and its economic, legal, political, social and technological environments are subject to change. Marketing and PD approaches need to change to keep pace with these developments if the basic concept of more efficient and profitable marketing is to be maintained. Therefore it is necessary for executives to re-examine, from time to time, the rationale on which their distribution systems are based. Otherwise they will become out-of-date and inefficient. In current situations the starting point is the need to have a cost-conscious approach to distribution, consistent with providing an acceptable level of service.

(f) Physical distribution systems

In selecting and designing these systems, firms must consider the points mentioned in Sections (d) and (e) above. In practice this means taking note of the markets or market segments to be serviced, the location of manufacturing and distribution systems, the size and nature of the depots required, the availability and location of middlemen and the transportation facilities (roads, railways, sea and waterways, air-freight routes, airports and other termini). The system design will also be influenced by estimates of product flows (total quantities, loads or shipment sizes, size of 'drops'), the personal selling methods used and the delivery times expected by customers. In addition, the distances between pick-up and dropping-off points, whether bulk shipments are required and the perishability of the goods, feature in the system design. Other materials handling aspects to be considered include how the products will be packed (do they need stout packing to prevent damage or deterioration in transit?), whether containers or pallets will be used and the mechanical handling equipment that is available or will be needed. All, in turn, will be constrained by the costs which can be afforded.

In addition the system must possess flexibility so that it can be modified easily when changed circumstances make this necessary. Thus there must be awareness of possible future market developments. Changes in markets, raw materials used, manufacturing locations and distribution and storage technology can demand alterations to the system. For example a major change of recent times has been the greater use of containers and pallets. This led to improvement in the packing and handling of goods with faster transportation times. The development of container ships and ports with the necessary handling equipment speed up distribution to overseas markets while reducing the problems of damage or loss in transit. The choice of system can have significant impact on product design, plant location and design as well as market selection and the communications mix used.

An effective distribution system can be a powerful element in a firm's marketing mix and plays an important part in earning revenue. However, the traditional view of management is that the work is made up of several discrete operations (purchasing, manufacturing, marketing, warehousing, transportation etc.). The management procedures and techniques have, as a result, been devised to ensure that each activity is conducted to maximum levels of efficiency and cost-effectiveness. It was some time before it was accepted that in closely inter-related activities, attempts to maximise the efficiency of any one part, without regard to the system as a whole, only lead to sub-optimisation of the whole.

It is now appreciated that if firms are to minimise total operating costs and optimise revenue, there must be a correct balance between all activity centres. The nature of this balance will vary from industry to industry, even company to company, depending on how firms work best. Distribution is a system comprised of a series of sub-systems. Proposed changes in one sub-system must be checked for their effect on other parts of the system. Indeed the interrelationships and interactions between the different activity centres of the system must be known.

For example offering a peak service involves a complex and substantial distribution system which will be costly. On the other hand, a low-cost system will

Pallets, forklift trucks, and computers to keep track of where each item is located, have revolutionised materials handling, reducing stock-holding and speeding deliveries

necessitate holding limited inventories, using limited transportation and a reduced number of depots. This will result in longer delivery times and give customers a very restricted service. Or using rail instead of air freight will reduce freighting costs, but because of slower transit times capital will be tied up longer since customers' payments will be delayed.

This could affect cash flow adversely. Then delivery delays may force customers to switch their orders to competitors. Or the use of cheap containers may reduce shipping costs but if this leads to more damage and losses in transit, the monetary loss may be greater than the initial saving. If customer goodwill is lost the total losses will be substantial and permanent. Or if a decision is taken to hold lower inventories, to reduce inventory costs, without consideration of the demand pattern and product flows through the system, it will mean more 'stock-out' positions, inability to deliver on time, special production runs and so on. The cost of all this will exceed savings in inventory costs.

9.2   Costs and benefits

(a) Costs
The aim of better PD control is to reduce costs within clearly defined marketing constraints. The marketing-PD interactions mentioned in the preceding sections

need careful consideration. Thus cost control of PD is a complex subject. Yet it is worth doing since good PD represents a marketing value which can be merchandised to customers and so improve the firm's image in their eyes. The important questions that have to be answered are listed in Table 9.2.

(b) Benefits

An efficient and integrated distribution system offers benefits on two levels. First it ensures that customers are served efficiently and within their own acceptable time-scales, so that the firm retains its position as a source of supply without complaints about service or delivery. In delivering to other manufacturing companies where production may be stopped if supplies do not arrive, this is vital. It is equally vital in dealing with other distributors down the line, where failure of the manufacturer's delivery to arrive when expected may be equally detrimental.

The second benefit often has more direct positive effects. An efficient and disciplined distribution system can be geared to provide 'just-in-time' deliveries to customers' premises. This can be most striking in the delivery of components to major assembly lines, as in the car industry. Here there are virtually no inventories of many components, with deliveries arriving just in time to be taken straight to the assembly lines. This not only reduces the customer's inventory costs, but ties his operations more closely to those of the supplier, making the entry of a competitor more difficult. Benefits of an efficient distribution system then accrue to both the supplier and the customer to their mutual benefit.

A publisher's warehouse may contain many hundreds of titles, and picking, packing and despatching anything from a single volume to a shipping order calls for automation of a high order – but still with some human input

Table 9.2   **PD costs – key questions**

COSTS
What are the *transport costs* for:

Firm's own fleet; rail freight; road transport; air freight; sea/water transport; postal charges; forwarding agents fees etc.?

What are the *warehousing costs* for:

Inventories; handling goods received; locating, retrieving and order picking; insurance, heating etc.?

What are the *materials handling costs*?
What are the *packaging* and *packing costs*?
What *other PD costs* are involved?
Are PD costs broken down for home and export markets?

SERVICE REQUIREMENTS
What level of service is expected by customers?
How will this affect inventory levels?
What delivery service is being offered by competitors?
What are the PD and marketing implications of the proposed services?

ORGANISATION
Who is responsible for laying down policies and making decisions on:

forecasts of customer needs; inventory levels; production programmes; number, location and size of depots; selecting modes of transport; order processing procedures; mechanical handling systems; packing and packaging requirements?

Docs the organisation structure permit close co-ordination of PD with marketing and manufacturing operations?
What revision of the structure will improve this coordination and integration?

9.3   Sales and selling

Most organisations need some form of direct communication in marketing their products, either in conjunction with mass methods, or as their main communications activity. The methods used range from traditional face-to-face selling to carefully co-ordinated Direct Marketing campaigns. The mix of techniques, and any links with the mass communications techniques, will vary from one situation to another, but the major methods available will be described in this chapter.

The historic form of direct communication was through the use of salespeople or representatives. This form is still in use but with many modifications from the days when a major fmcg manufacturer might have several hundred salespeople 'on the road'. The growth of the major retail chains has reduced the number of contact or buying points which it is necessary for the manufacturer to service. At the same time the level of skills needed in selling and in negotiation, and the importance of each customer or call, have increased considerably. Costs too have risen, so that in many areas where direct calling may still be useful, telephone selling has taken the place of the travelling salesperson. However personal selling is still a major activity, and a logical point at which to start our discussion of methods.

9.4   Personal selling

Selling involves the personal presentation of tangible products or intangible services and ideas of significance to potential customers (consumer, trade and industry). In its work it receives back-up support from other forms of communication and should form an integral part of the total marketing plan. Personal selling makes a valuable contribution to a nation's economy. Besides providing work for many persons, in and outside the selling function, it is a major creator of demand and thus economic activity. In competitive situations the survival and prosperity of a firm depends on the success of its selling activities.

While selling as part of marketing becomes more effective as a result of the close integration with the other promotional activities, marketing research and product-market planning, it is also enhanced – not belittled – by the adoption of the marketing concept. The aims, objectives and targets for the sales function are more precisely and clearly defined. The sales staff know what has to be done, when, where and by whom. They know what support will be given by promotions, distribution and other integrated, planned marketing activities. Sales prospects are better defined and sales people do not just have to maintain the 'same old slog', knock on doors and request people to buy their products. They know who needs them, what use is made of them, the competitive position and thus who are the better prospects and what sales pitch should be used. In short, they are fully informed on the marketing and sales situations.

Selling and marketing are subject to voluntary and legal controls. In most countries there are many laws controlling or affecting business activities directly and indirectly and new or amended ones reach the statute books in an almost continuous flow. Some executives believe that all firms now need at least one lawyer full time on their staff just to guide them through the legal mazes that confront business people. This belief may be stronger at the present time, following the opening of national frontiers on January 1st 1993. Not only is it necessary to comply with Acts of the UK Parliament but also with EEC Directives and Regulations, and the situation in many industries is subject to change and revision.

(a) Sales objectives and targets
Personal selling covers a very wide range of activities. The range of possibilities is shown in Table 9.3. During any business day numerous sales-persons are explaining the merits of their products or services to executives, consumers (housewives and others), wholesalers, retailers, officials of government and quasi-governmental organisations, doctors, lawyers and so forth. Still more are making various follow-up calls, making deliveries and taking orders for future deliveries, as, for example, confectionery sales staff making routine calls on shops in their territory.

Because of the variety of selling tasks, more than one of which may be needed in any firm, setting sales objectives needs considerable thought. What tasks have

Table 9.3 **Activities of salespersons**

1   *Delivering basic products*: bread, milk, fuels etc. Actual selling is a secondary role but a pleasant manner and good service enhance customer acceptance and should lead to more sales. Only originate new sales occasionally, as a general rule.

2   *Taking orders*: relative routine business (e.g. soaps, cleaning fluids, tinned goods, nuts, bolts, small industrial products) of established items bought for general use; works in the field and contacts buyers in supermarkets, and retail outlets and in industry for items that need little selling; the 'hard sell' is often discouraged. Pleasant personality and good service enhance sales but little creative selling involved.

3   *Inside order-taker*: counter sales staff at retail outlets, travel agents etc. Customers have usually made up their minds and only suggestive selling (e.g. helping consumers decide which holiday to have) is involved besides just serving the customer. Opportunities to do more than this are few.

4   *Technical selling*: putting across the attributes of technical products providing information or advice; really a 'consultant' to 'client' firms. Involves many contacts and conversations to make sale.

5   *Building goodwill*: educating the actual or potential customer as with 'missionary' selling (opening new accounts); sometimes excluded from taking orders and only opening doors for (4) or (2) above.

6   *Creative selling*: of intangible services (e.g. banking, insurance, investment services, tourism/travel, advertising services etc.); more difficult task since intangibles are difficult to demonstrate and consumers have difficulty in gaining good comprehension of them.

7   *Creative selling*: of tangibles such as household appliances, encyclopedias etc.; first makes prospect dissatisfied with present products then sells his/hers.

to be accomplished and what methods have been found to be the best to use? What will be the cost and return? Can the company afford it? These are just some of the questions to ponder. Remember too that besides the choice implied by Table 9.3, cost, limited resources and other reasons may make it necessary for a firm to work through agents (especially overseas), franchise holders (for remote areas) or on a mail-order basis.

The starting point for this work is the corporate objectives in the corporate plan and from these, the marketing objectives as defined in the marketing plan. The marketing targets which set the parameters for sales objectives include the profit to be earned, the sales revenue to be obtained, the annual rates of growth and market shares needed and the markets to be served. Thought must also be given to the need to balance long- and short-term requirements, the relative emphasis to be given to market shares and profit and the degree of customer satisfaction required.

In addition, marketing strategy must be taken into account for this indicates the different emphasis that will be placed on promotional activities. The extent, nature and timing of the latter and their ability to open doors or help to make sales will help to define the size and nature of the selling tasks needed. For example, in mass-market foodstuffs, it is usual to place the emphasis on advertising when the selling activity required is that of the in-field order taker. Sales staff then see that retail stocks are adequate for anticipated demand, the goods have good and effective shelf exposure (or space) and appropriate sales promotions activities are mounted at the right times. The sales strategy then emphasises 'pushing' products into the retail outlets while advertising aims to 'pull' them through to the customer.

With industrial products, personal selling creates interest and seeks orders while advertising paves the way for the sales staff. They do not walk 'cold' into prospective buyers. Advertising here creates awareness while selling creates preference leading to orders. Depending on the services to be sold, the selling–advertising relationship can follow either course. For example with professional services (banking, insurance, etc.) the industrial approach may be best. For travel and holidays, the consumer goods one is usual in that retailers (travel agents) hold stock (an allocation of holidays or facilities) and advertising usually by tour operators generates consumer interest. The marketing and sales strategies will once again be of the 'push–pull' type.

The size of the sales force needed will be determined by the volume of sales and market shares to be obtained and the costs that can be afforded. From this will come decisions on quota (per territory and salesperson) for sales volume or revenue needed and, if possible, the profit to be earned. Thus sales objectives will be quantitative in nature (hard figures specifying sales, profit, market shares etc.) and qualitative (specifying coverage, frequency of contact, degree or level of customer service and satisfaction required) and both will be influenced (or restricted) by the pricing strategy and policy that will apply. In the case of industrial products and capital equipment, the degree of essentiality of these for prospective buyers will also influence the sales objectives that could be set. The more vital an item the greater should be demand and emphasis would be placed on the attributes of the product, especially the benefits they would confer on buyers' own business activities.

To summarise, sales targets are usually derived by taking the company's marketing targets and then breaking them down by territory according to their potential, the degree of competition that would be met and the sales coverage that could be provided with the back-up from promotional activities. Thus if London and the Southeast are believed or known to account for 25 per cent of total demand or has traditionally provided that amount of total company business, then this could be useful starting point. However, trends and developments must be considered. If total demand in the area is known to be increasing how should future sales targets be adjusted? Should they maintain the same market share or, if competition is slacking off, should the company strive for a larger market share? If demand is declining, should effort be switched to other areas leading to lower sales targets for London and higher ones elsewhere? When the quota for a territory has been agreed, the individual ones for the salespersons will be similarly deduced. However, if more salespersons are being added to an area, or some are being withdrawn to the more profitable ones, the final quota will need adjustment.

A more sophisticated method which is not always easy to use involves the projection of demand trends for major individual companies, factories, retail groups and so on. Then the total demand for an area can be compiled, market shares agreed and quota set. The difficulty lies in making these projections. The firm and its marketing staff must have extensive knowledge of the individual units on which these calculations are based. How is their business changing? How will this affect demand for established and new products? What new items will they need? What is their opinion of competitors and ourselves? In practice it is not easy to find the answers to such questions.

(b) Roles of the sales staff

The basic roles and duties of field sales people have been discussed above and summarised in Table 9.3. Two more aspects of *retail selling* need to be mentioned. Sales staff here have two possibilities. First, they can use the technique of *selling* (or *trading*) *up*, which seeks to convince customers that they should buy a more expensive (better quality?) product than they intended originally. Then there is *suggestion selling*, which seeks to broaden the original purchase with related products (e.g. if buying golf clubs why not buy a new golf bag?). Banks and other financial institutions use sales staff for *cross-selling* additional services to existing customers. Thus a customer seeking a mortgage will be offered house and contents insurance as well. Someone seeking a loan for a new car will be offered car insurance. Wealthier customers may be offered stock-broking facilities or financial advice. Such tactics will often be assisted by special promotional campaigns and/or price offers. Now consider the basic roles of some other sales staff.

The *field sales manager* usually controls the operations of a field sales force. This manager must organise the sales force, the disposition of it and the allocation of money assigned to him or her for the sales tasks to be performed. The manager should also motivate the team to achieve, and if possible exceed, agreed targets provided that by exceeding targets problems are not created elsewhere e.g. in production or distribution.

Then there is the construction of clear and concise plans to establish the timing, cost and co-ordination of all the activities of the sales force. This includes the identification and use of precise controls needed, including cost budgeting. Finally, direct responsibility for the appraisal of individual performance and the training and development of salespersons cannot be avoided. In addition the manager makes contributions to the identification of strategies and objectives for the sales force. Other contributors will include the sales force itself and other interested marketing colleagues, including the marketing director or manager.

Where a sales force is widely spread geographically, or the volume of work is heavy or technical and other complexities arise (usually on some regional or industrial basis), field sales managers can be assisted by one or more *sales supervisors*, or *area managers*. They ensure that the points mentioned above are correctly carried out. Because they are in close contact with the salespersons in their area of responsibility, they play a vital role in the motivation of their part of the sales force. They help to overcome the feeling of isolation that field sales staff can feel if they are at a distance from the sales office.

Sales managers are usually responsible to the marketing director (sales director if the selling function is separated from the rest of marketing) for all aspects of the selling task. They also supervise the field sales managers and provide essential back-up when this is necessary. They maintain close liaison with other marketing, manufacturing and financial colleagues in all aspects relevant to the selling role. They also control and manage the sales office and make sure that the procedures (correspondence to customers and field force; invoicing, billing; attention to complaints and enquiries) are followed efficiently. They liaise with colleagues responsible for the distribution side of the business. For those directly responsible to them and for others via field sales managers and supervisors, sales managers are responsible for performance appraisal, training, development, recruitment and remuneration of all the sales staff.

The *sales office* is responsible to the sales manager for keeping all the systems and paperwork operating efficiently and as planned. This is an important role for mistakes in the paperwork (invoicing, billing, stock records etc.) can dislocate, badly, an otherwise good sales operation. Where there is a lot of work involved, a *sales office manager* can be appointed to take direct control of the work. This person is usually responsible to the sales manager but on occasions may report direct to a sales director (if existing) or the marketing manager or marketing director. It depends on the importance of the work but as a rule bypassing the sales manager is not preferred as it can lead to resentment on the part of the latter

Keeping the sales force informed is vital, and although much can be achieved through memo, phone, fax or E-mail, face-to-face meetings are still a powerful way of motivating people as well as informing them of any new developments

and subsequent administrative difficulties. There may also be an *export manager*, who is usually responsible for the export sales of finished products but could also control shipments of components to overseas assembly or manufacturing units. If distribution is not under a separate department, a *distribution manager* would control this work including having responsibility for stock or inventory control.

(c) Organisation

The sales work can be organised in various ways, shown in Figure 9.3. There can be one sales force or separate ones reflecting the general organisational structure. If special technologies or market conditions exist it is usually advisable to have separate sales forces for each important one. Decisions on the organisation and sales forces required will depend on the nature, scope and scale of the selling task. Where products are not homogeneous, or involve different technologies, a more complex organisation and sales methods are needed.

For example, the functional type is common among small and medium-sized firms selling a single product, or a limited range of homogeneous products through similar distribution channels or to similar types of customer. The work is then divided into functional groups or departments. In Figure 9.3(i) the sales manager is responsible for home sales, exporting and international business being handled by some other marketing colleague not shown in the chart. This organisation becomes untenable when the range of products, customers and distribution channels are extended. Dissimilar products requiring different selling and distribution methods for disparate groups of customers involve more work and detail than such a simple organisation can handle efficiently.

The area or regional organisation (Figure 9.3(ii) is one in greatest use by companies with a limited number of relatively homogeneous products in widespread distribution through many outlets. The nature of the product, methods of distribution, the degree of dispersal of the manufacturing units are other factors that must be considered. For example national brewers, bakeries, petrol companies and most major mass-market consumer goods organisations have area-based sales organisations. However, where diversification has tended to make the product range heterogeneous in parts, at least, evolution to a compound structure (Figure 9.3(v)) would be used.

Industrial goods which can be manufactured in several locations, usually with a good geographical spread of users, are also best handled by an area organisation. Again, if there is some disparity between some products (e.g. involving different technologies, or having different applications requiring specialised knowledge) some form of a compound structure will be used. In Figure 9.3(v), 'Product A' is one of these special items, all the rest being, presumably, in general demand.

Most fmcg companies use the area method as do many services (insurance, investment services, travel and tourism). Area sales organisations are able to exploit local brand loyalties, regional differences in preferences and taste and the strengths of, or relationships with, local distribution channels, as well as make maximum use of localised, or nearby, expensive manufacturing facilities. General functional services (marketing research, product and promotional planning etc.) are usually centralised at head office or the main factory for economy.

However, if the regional demands are large enough to justify it, small offshoots of marketing research and promotional departments can be located in the regions.

(i) FUNCTIONAL

Marketing manager or director

Other marketing functions ← → Other marketing functions

Sales manager

Distribution manager | Field sales manager | Sales administration

Area managers, sales supervisors
Field sales force

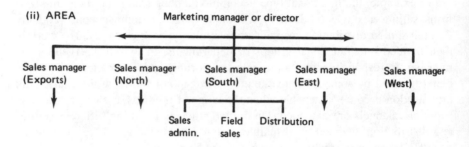

(ii) AREA   Marketing manager or director

Sales manager (Exports) | Sales manager (North) | Sales manager (South) | Sales manager (East) | Sales manager (West)

Sales admin. | Field sales | Distribution

(iii) END USE   Marketing director

Marketing services manager | General sales manager

Sales manager (Oil companies) | Sales manager (Chemical companies) | Sales manager (Metal-working industries)

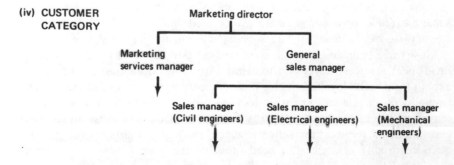

(iv) CUSTOMER CATEGORY   Marketing director

Marketing services manager | General sales manager

Sales manager (Civil engineers) | Sales manager (Electrical engineers) | Sales manager (Mechanical engineers)

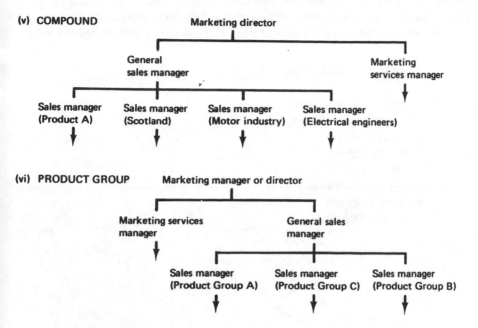

(v) COMPOUND

Marketing director

General
sales manager

Marketing
services manager

Sales manager
(Product A)

Sales manager
(Scotland)

Sales manager
(Motor industry)

Sales manager
(Electrical engineers)

(vi) PRODUCT GROUP

Marketing manager or director

Marketing services
manager

General sales
manager

Sales manager
(Product Group A)

Sales manager
(Product Group C)

Sales manager
(Product Group B)

Fig. 9.3   Types of sales organisation

The end-use and customer group organisations (Figure 9.3(iii) and (iv)) are used when firms sell to different kinds of customers or markets with very specific and differing marketing requirements. The greater or more specialised the technical requirements the greater is the need for specialised sales management and sales forces. Then the end-use approach is used and this is the one favoured by many industrial products manufacturers. The diversity of the products and their service needs are better served in this way and greater customer satisfaction should result.

In the case of mass-market consumer goods sold to different outlets or customer groups there may be need for various selling and promotional techniques. In this case the customer group organisation is preferred. In both cases, the volume of business with the different customer groups or for each product group must be large enough to justify the expense of these methods. Again, the functional services in general use may be located at head office for economy, or in the regions if this is justified and gives more efficient or effective results.

The product group approach (Figure 9.3(vi)) is preferred by many industrial products firms and multi-product consumer goods and durables companies. Here different product groups are sold to different markets or customers through different distribution channels and involve different strategies, pricing and packaging policies, promotional activities, sales forecasting and budgets. With very large firms with considerable turnover in each product group, there may be a separate sales force and manager for each of them. For example a pharmaceutical products firm may split its sales organisation into three, one selling ethical products to doctors, hospitals and dentists, another selling proprietary items to chemists and retail outlets (departmental stores) with chemist counters and a third

Field Sales Areas – UK

1. Charles Greenwood
   Field Sales Manager
2. John Carter
3. David Evans
4. Ian Brown
5. James Macdonald
6. Mary Duggan
7. James Murphy

Sales areas should be set out clearly, and boundaries should be unambiguous. For large areas natural or political boundaries can be used if appropriate as here. For smaller sales territories similar distinguishable boundaries should be set, down to post codes if necessary, tying in location on the ground with effective management information and analysis systems

dealing with sales to veterinary surgeons, animal hospitals and specialist institutions (e.g. RSPCA homes, kennels and catteries). Sometimes, for economy, one sales force may be used for the first two product groups (ethical and proprietary items) but the greater knowledge and expertise required for the first may in fact be wasted on the second.

While increasing competition of all kinds has led to greater diversification of the product range by many firms and thus created the wider use of compound organisations (Figure 9.3(v)), some companies have always needed it. For example a soft drinks firm selling through the usual retail outlets and to homes, door-to-door, would have a manager and sales force for direct sales to the home, usually operating out of local depots and vans. Sales to wholesalers and retailers would be handled by another manager and sales force, with deliveries by the firm's vans out of the various regional depots. If the business is large enough, the trade sales might be organised on a geographical or regional basis. There may be more than one sales force covering the trade in different parts of the country, each with its own field sales manager. This gives better coverage and control and again builds rapport between distributors and the firm. It is able to respond more effectively to local requirements also.

There is no 'one best' organisation. The right one depends on the tasks in hand, the extent, nature or complexity of the selling job and the markets or customers to be served.

(d) The nature of the sales task

The nature or content of the sales task to be performed varies according to the type of points-of-sale used and potential customers' expectations at the different points of the distribution network. First consider the distributors.

When selling to the distributors, the salesperson's task is to persuade the former to hold adequate stocks for the territory and outlets they serve and to mount a continuous sales campaign on retailers and other outlets (supermarkets, departmental stores) to 'push' sales along to the ultimate consumer/customer. Where products are bought by customers direct from wholesalers the firm's sales staff should be prepared to assist wholesalers in this. Associated tasks include helping to deal with complaints of all kinds, servicing the accounts, persuading retailers to take stock from the wholesalers and sometimes working with distributors' salespeople, even helping to train them. The last is important when technical products, capital equipment and household appliances are the items handled.

Thus selling to wholesalers requires not only good knowledge of the products being offered and their uses but high sales skills and knowledge of the typical organisational structure, methods and aims of operation of wholesale enterprises. Apart from the usual economic and financial aspects, the wholesaler is concerned about the reliability of the supplier in respect of assured quality and above all delivery promises. The salesperson must convince the wholesaler on these points and that demand for the product exists. Some firms use missionary salespersons who obtain orders from retailers for placement with specified, prospective wholesaler buyers.

When the ultimate user or consumer buys anything direct from the manufacturer the implication is that the former have already made up their mind on the make, brand, quality and price of the item they want. Usually they are looking for price savings through cutting out the middle-man. However, they may or may not accept the possibility of lower quality of the item (though quality is normally as good as that for the item bought through retailers). Customers will certainly expect the same back-up services as they would obtain from retailers. However, when customers buy direct from wholesalers, it means that while they are expecting some price savings and adequate after-sales service, they have not yet made up their mind about the make or brand to choose. Wholesalers usually carry more than one make or brand. The manufacturer's sales staff in direct selling have to ensure that the contact with customers does end in orders. They are then primarily interested in closing the sale successfully. When customers buy from wholesalers, the manufacturer's people must persuade customers that their products are better than competitors' but must take care not to undermine too forcefully sales of competitive or substitute products. The latter may in fact be of greater importance or profitability to the wholesaler. Company sales staff operating from wholesalers' premises must employ considerable tact. When operating from their own premises (factory, shop etc.) they can employ more 'hard sell' methods and when customers are still doubtful about the item being considered, or are definitely unfavourable to it, then the sales staff must attempt to interest customers in the firm's alternative offerings.

In the case of retailers, most have their own sales force employed in selling their stock. They use various degrees of aggressiveness for this, depending on the importance of the product, the attitudes of potential customers and the competition to be overcome. The firm's staff is then involved in assisting the retail sales force where necessary or requested and in persuading retailers to take and hold sufficient stock from wholesalers or direct from the manufacturer. The latter's people then take their cue from the retailers without sacrificing the objectives and needs of their employers. Where the manufacturer's sales staff are operating from the premises of the retailer (e.g. a 'shop-within-a-shop' in departmental stores), the sales staff will use all the usual ploys to close a successful sale but must not deter potential customers from considering competitive products if they wish.

When selling to retailers, salespersons have to stress patronage motives, in particular the support services provided by the seller. Consequently emphasis must be placed on the more competitive credit terms, delivery charges (if any) and assured prompt delivery that may be on offer. Frequently they may have to spend a good deal of time assisting their retailer customers with window and in-store displays and any full-scale merchandising activity that may be considered necessary and suitable for these outlets.

When selling to industry and commerce, the various points discussed in preceding sections apply. With technical products, the sales staff will have to prepare technical presentations to prospective buyers. A separate presentation may be needed for different end-uses or types of customer. The sales decisions are often based on rational considerations. When involved in executive selling (i.e. selling a wide range of items to more senior executives) considerable creativity is needed with knowledge of all aspects of the items being offered and the uses and technical aspects of interest to the customer.

At exhibitions, the selling task is more one of providing information on the company and its products. Studies have shown that about 40 per cent of enquiries are from unidentified persons seeking a wide range of information. The remainder are serious enquiries from identified individuals or organisations and the information they need is more detailed and precise than from the former group. Usually they have a problem to solve or a new idea and are looking for the means to overcome or carry them through successfully.

In the first instance, salespersons should provide the information with the firm's name and address clearly displayed. They should try to identify the enquirers or at least urge them to contact the firm more formally at a later date. With the second group, identities are known and follow-up visits arranged. With technical products the necessary back-up should be available though very difficult points are normally referred to an appropriate executive at the firm for later follow-up visits after the matter has been investigated or researched.

In all cases at exhibitions or on personal visits, the salesperson forms an essential communication link between the firm and its customers. Salespersons advise the customers on the products or services available and their attributes. They also keep the firm informed of what is happening at the users' end, changing needs, relevant technical developments, what is happening with competition and so on.

9.5 Sales planning and control

Within their chosen markets firms have to keep a balance between satisfying customers' needs and their own financial requirements consistent with the resources and capabilities of the company. The sales and marketing tasks may be redefined as generating a satisfactory income for a sustained period of time, of 'buying' revenues in the markets at lowest possible cost. Many of customers' wants may not be practical (for technical and other reasons), they may be too costly to produce or they may involve the firm in putting too much of its resources into less profitable items at the expense of more profitable ones. They could lead also to producing large volumes of some items, creating problems of stocking and distribution. Much capital may be tied up unproductively, giving problems of liquidity and cash flows.

Salespersons, however, may be interested in selling items which can be sold easily allowing the easy attainment of sales quota. They will also be interested in pushing products which earn the best bonus or commission for themselves, at the expense of other items of equal or greater importance to the firm's total activity. In so doing they may overload the factory and thus there would be insufficient capacity for other items. They also prefer to avoid competition when perhaps facing up to it may be necessary for the long-term survival and growth of the company. The firm itself has to balance customer needs with their own short- and long-term needs. Obtaining the right balance between the last two items is a common problem facing all companies.

As mentioned elsewhere in a different context, the task of the salesperson is not limited to just 'selling'. Potential customers have to be advised or 'counselled' on many points. The more technical or complex the product or service and the buying procedures, the greater will be this counselling. Then the sales force is the additional eyes and ears of the marketing department. If properly briefed and if necessary trained, salespersons can collect a wide range of useful market information which the company needs in its marketing planning and decision-making processes. They help also in the work of merchandising. Then there are the numerous liaisons which the sales force must create between technical and other specialist colleagues and themselves and potential customers. This is particularly important when users complain about any aspect of the product in use. Finally, there is all the help and assistance they must give to wholesalers and retailers as explained earlier. Thus the sales job today is a much more widespread one than before and provides staff with many interesting and challenging opportunities.

(a) Industrial buying–selling models

The planning of sales force activities and of the work of the individual representatives can be helped through deeper understanding of the buying–selling process. Several theories or models have been developed to explain the process, particularly with regard to selling to other organisations. It is useful first to understand that many people may be involved in any buying situation, including:

(i)   *Initiators*, who may start the whole buying process by stating a need for a product or service.

(ii)   *Users*, ranging from production managers to machine operators; may also be initiators.

(iii)   *Influencers* who may be technical people such as architects, scientists, accountants; or lay people concerned with aesthetics or appearance.

(iv)   *Decision-makers* ranging from the managing director for major items, to clerks for routine items.

(v)   *Buyers* who are responsible for placing an order, but who may well have been instrumental in obtaining catalogues or technical data, in drawing up a short list of contenders, and possibly influencing the final decision.

Some or all of these people may be part of the Decision Making Unit (DMU) with whom the sales force has to deal. An ability to sense where the power lies in such a group, irrespective of who may eventually sign the order, is a major asset among sales people and negotiators.

Apart from the people involved on the buying side, there are different types of buying situation, calling for different approaches. Figure 9.4 shows the three main types, and the factors involved on the customer's side. The most simple situation arises in a straight rebuy, involving a repeat order for something bought before. Unless there were problems with the last consignment the procedure will be routine, and in many cases now will be handled by a computer at the customer end linking directly with another at the supplier's end.

A more complex situation arises in a rebuy situation when modifications are needed. The customer's needs will have changed in some way, and some investi-

Buy phases	Buy classes		
	New purchase	Modified rebuy	Straight rebuy
Anticipation or recognition of a problem.	✓	✓	
Determination of character-istics and quantity needed.	✓	✓	✓
Description of character-istics and quantity needed.	✓		
Search for and qualification of potential sources.	✓		
Acquisition and analysis of proposals.	✓	✓	
Evaluation of proposals and selection of supplier.	✓	✓	
Selection of order routine.	✓	✓	✓
Performance feedback and evaluation.	✓	✓	✓

Fisher's model of involvement in purchase decisions

COMMERCIAL UNCERTAINTY	PRODUCT COMPLEXITY	
	High	Low
High	Total involvement	Policy-maker emphasis
Low	Techno-logical emphasis	Buyer emphasis

PRODUCT COMPLEXITY: Standardisation of product; technology; previous purchase history; newness of product; after-sales service; ease of installation and use.
COMMERCIAL UNCERTAINTY: Size of investment; order size; timespan of commitment; potential effect on profit; ease of forecasting effect.

Fig. 9.4   The Buygrid model

gation is needed to find the best new purchase. This can present an opportunity for a new supplier to come in, or at least be considered, and the situation can be dangerous for the established supplier. To counteract this a representative needs to be aware of likely changes among the customers, and be prepared to anticipate the modified rebuy and supply information in advance of a decision being needed.

The most complex situations arise when a new, or perhaps a very infrequent, purchase is planned. These may range from major plant installations downwards, and have wide ramifications through a company, as when buying a new computer network. Here the sales force may be able to do little for years at a time except keep their company and its products known by customer personnel. When a potential purchase situation then arises they should be in a strong position if they have done their homework on what the customer is likely to require, and have established contacts in the right quarters.

(b) Consumer buying–selling models

In many ways these resemble the industrial models, although most routine household purchase will be made by a one-person DMU covering all the roles at once. However children, partners and others may act as initiators, influencers or whatever on occasion. When major buying situations occur, from carpets, holidays, double glazing, or encyclopedias to cars or even a new house or flat, the DMU is expanded and several people may be involved. Door-to-door or telephone salespeople, estate agents and people in similar selling situations become adept in assessing where the ultimate decision rests, and making their pitch accordingly.

For mass-consumer goods various theories of buyer behaviour have been put forward. Briefly these involve the effects of cultural backgrounds, peer groups, individual beliefs and life-styles, family responsibilities and so forth on the one hand, and market factors on the other. Depending on the complexity of the purchase, corresponding largely to the three categories discussed above, more or less time will be spent in making a decision. Many straight rebuys are made without any consideration other than that more supplies are needed. But the situation is not fixed. The balance between people in the DMU is changing. For example, women are exerting far more influence on car-buying than before. Children are having more influence on family eating. And between these consumers and the manufacturers lie the retailers, who can decide whether a product is even available for purchase.

9.6   Recent developments

Sales and marketing thinking and practice change through time as organisations change, technology changes, and expectations change. Two lines of development in particular are affecting the ways in which companies are organising their sales and selling operations. The first is through the recognition of important customers as 'key accounts' and the need for continuous relationships with them, as opposed to simply making a series of sales. This has led to the concept of 'Relationship Marketing'. The second is through the use of more sophisticated methods of handling and storing data about individual households or people, leading to the development of 'Direct Marketing'.

(a) Key accounts and relationship marketing

In many markets manufacturers have found that the number of their immediate customers has been diminishing, despite increasing numbers of final consumers. In engineering for example the numbers of shipyards, plane makers, car manufacturers and so forth have all diminished, and suppliers of components are all tending to deal with fewer immediate customers – despite increased world trade and increased personal travel. In Western consumer markets major retail chains have grown to take the major share of sales in many markets, from food and toiletries to·durable goods and holidays. Here again the suppliers are dealing with fewer immediate customers, each of whom has a significant share of markets which are generally expanding.

In all of these cases, and many more, the importance of these 'key' accounts means that they are not handled by the general salesforce, even where one exists. Each major customer is handled by a 'key account manager', responsible for coordinating all relationships between the manufacturing company and the customer.

Because of the increasing importance of key accounts the concept of relationship marketing is now tending to replace the concept of making a sale in many areas. This applies to both industrial and consumer areas, and for services as well as products.

In industrial markets the concept has long been recognised. A manufacturer of aircraft engines seeks to build a long-term relationship with the major airframe manufacturers so that the engines are offered as part of the completed plane. To this end close relationships will be built up through a team of people, from R&D, from design, procurement, manufacturing, finance and so forth, as well as marketing and general management, linking with appropriate personnel in the airframe organisation. Joint teams from both the airframe and the engine companies may then be involved in developing long-term relations with major airlines. Heading the whole marketing and selling operation will be a 'key account manager', and while the title may vary the post will carry the status appropriate to the business being handled.

On the consumer side key account managers now handle the building of long-term relationships between manufacturers and the major retail chains. The aim, whether for branded goods or Own Label products bearing the retailer's name, is to ensure good relationships which will lead to continuing sales, continuing product development, co-operation over special offers, and other activities appropriate to the particular market. Here the organisation of the interface between supplier and customer is on a basis of co-operation and liaison, rather than along the old lines of each side seeking competitive advantage. Inevitably in either system there may be intensive negotiations over such aspects as prices, of advertising or promotional support and so forth, but within the context of an on-going relationship rather than a quick sale.

Such relationships can lead to much closer co-operation between supplier and buyer, such as just-in-time deliveries to car assembly plants or to branches of retail chains. Development of such close co-operation depends on long-term trust, and once established adds to the problems of competitors in gaining access to the customer. There are benefits to both sides in reduced inventories, possible joint forecasting and planning of deliveries, and so forth, but emphasising that the ultimate aim of the combined distribution system is to get the right products to the right place at the right time, with profit to both sides in the transaction.

(b) Direct marketing

Direct mail advertising, in which letters, brochures, catalogues and so forth are sent to selected individuals, has been used for many years. It is frequently used for industrial goods or services, where there may be only a limited number of potential buyers whose identity can be established from lists of past customers, or trade directories or associations. It has been used to cross-sell products, as with banks offering customers details of insurance or other services; or to sell to past customers, as with holiday companies sending new brochures to past travellers, and so on. It is used by many charities seeking donations from past subscribers or new prospects.

Mail order companies, whether aiming at private customers or industrial buyers, operate in similar ways. Catalogues are mailed directly to likely prospects, but a wide range of products or services is offered as opposed to the more specific offerings made through direct mail.

Recent developments in data handling have expanded the ways in which sellers can contact their prospects, and have revolutionised the selection of prospects. These developments have led to the term 'database marketing', using details of prospects held in a computer to pin-point more closely those likely to buy an offering. Computer analyses of Census data have shown useful methods of segmenting households, and these can be linked to post codes to identify good prospects for swimming pools, double glazing, investment plans and so forth. New routes to specific markets have been opened up, increasing the effectiveness of an established advertising medium.

The mass press and electronic media can be used within direct marketing in either or both of two ways. They can be used to gain a direct response to advertising, through customers writing or phoning to buy the product advertised using a credit card. Originally this facility was available only through the press, usually with a coupon containing coded information about its source, and payment would be by cheque. Now facilities exist for handling heavy and sporadic volumes of telephone enquiries, bringing the electronic media into play, and using credit or charge cards for payment.

In some cases the immediate sale is all that the advertiser is seeking, but in others the names and addresses of enquirers or buyers are fed into a database. Linking the post code to Census data will then establish the type of area in which the contact lives, providing a valuable means of segmentation. There are now several computer-based services on the market linking post codes and Census data, identifying types of housing ranging from run-down inner city tenements to villages with wealthy older commuters. This data is often supplemented with additional information from field studies or other sources. Hence people who have already responded to an offer through the mass media may be more directly targeted by phone or mail with offers to which they have an above-average tendency to respond.

While some organisations have developed their own databases and direct marketing operations tailored specifically to their own needs, this will be too expensive for most companies. To meet their needs Direct Marketing

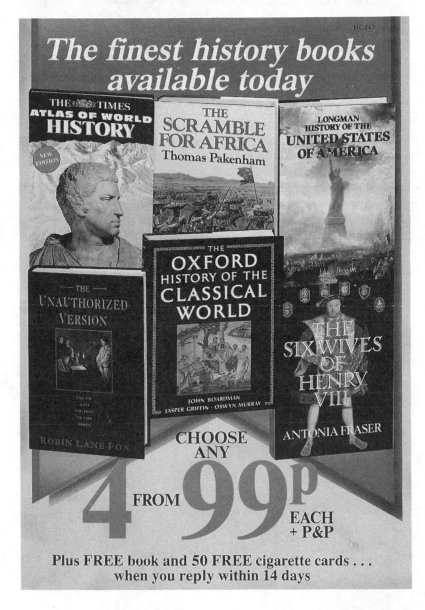

Front page of an insert offering reduced prices and other inducements to gain members for a specialised book club. Such clubs were early users of the advantages of direct response advertising and database marketing

agencies have developed, parallel to advertising or other agencies. Some of these are able to plan, organise and execute all stages of a direct marketing operation on an economic fee basis. Some however specialise in areas such as the supply of address lists for specified market segments, the development, handling and mailing of print or other materials needed or the organisation of phone contacts, and so forth. As with all aspects of marketing, careful analysis of the resources and methods needed to meet an organisation's marketing objectives is needed. However the increasing use of direct marketing, as well as its appearance on many examination syllabuses, indicates that it is filling a need for many organisations.

Assignments

What routes to market are used in your chosen market? Is distribution of the product or service a major problem or cost area? What changes, if any, have taken place in these routes to market during the past five years?

In some markets quick delivery is essential; in others speed may be less important than meeting an agreed date. What qualities are customers seeking in your chosen area? Will they pay a premium for superior service? Are customers lost through poor delivery or distribution?

⬡10 **Forecasting in marketing**

The lot of the forecaster is a hazardous one. Inevitably at some time a forecast will be proved wrong. It will be overtaken by events in ways which were not foreseen. Afterwards memories will remain of the failure when all the more accurate forecasts have been forgotten.

The 'forecaster's dilemma' can also be a problem. In many markets and for many products forecasting sales for next month is quite easy. Sudden fluctuations are rare. Trends continue from year to year. Any seasonal pattern seems to be fixed. Anyone can add 8 per cent to sales in the same month last year and produce a forecast which will be right to within a fraction. It is only when a market becomes less stable, when all other things stop being so equal, that forecasting becomes difficult or sometimes impossible. When forecasts are hardly needed they are easy to produce. When they are most needed they may be almost impossible to produce!

When conditions begin to change, those who have looked more closely at their markets in quieter times begin to benefit. Understanding based on analysis and interpretation of events during more stable periods can provide a platform on which to examine changes when they arrive. Forecasts at such times may be subject to wide margins of error, but at least they are based on analysis, understanding and thoughtful application, rather than hunch or wishful thinking.

10.1 Why forecast?

A good forecasting system should provide three things within an organisation:

(i)   Forecasts of sales etc. based on current plans, monthly, annually or on whatever time spans are useful.
(ii) A deeper understanding, based on statistical analysis, of the ways in which a market works. This could include the impact on sales of company decisions on prices, advertising and offers; the impact of competitive decisions; or external changes in economic or social factors.
(iii) An ability to answer 'what would happen if ...?' questions, or to offer advance warning of opportunities or threats arising in a market.

While routine forecasting in stable conditions may be adequate for the first purpose, it is unlikely to provide much help in the other two areas. But the other two areas are a basic part of Marketing, as defined by the Chartered Institute of Marketing, of anticipating demand. Forecasting is the area in which full use should be made of all available data, information and intelligence within the organisation. Much use will be made of series of sales figures, of advertising expenditures and so forth, but all events surrounding a market need to be considered.

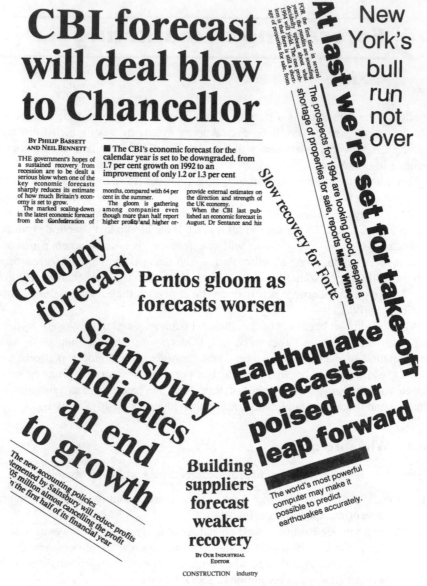

CBI forecast will deal blow to Chancellor

By Philip Bassett
and Neil Bennett

THE government's hopes of a sustained recovery from recession are to be dealt a serious blow when one of the key economic forecasts sharply reduces its estimate of how much Britain's economy is set to grow.

The marked scaling-down in the latest economic forecast from the Confederation of

■ The CBI's economic forecast for the calendar year is set to be downgraded, from 1.7 per cent growth on 1992 to an improvement of only 1.2 or 1.3 per cent

months, compared with 64 per cent in the summer.

The gloom is gathering among companies even though more than half report higher profits and higher or-

provide external estimates on the direction and strength of the UK economy.

When the CBI last published an economic forecast in August, Dr Sentance and his

At last we're set for take-off

FOR the first time in several years, the public are sounding decidedly upbeat about what 1994 will yield. The one problem is that there is still a shortage of properties for sale, from age of properties for sale.

The prospects for 1994 are looking good, despite a shortage of properties for sale, reports **Mary Wilson**

New York's bull run not over

Slow recovery for Forte

Gloomy forecast

Pentos gloom as forecasts worsen

Sainsbury indicates an end to growth

The new accounting policies implemented by Sainsbury will reduce profits £05 million almost cancelling the profit in the first half of its financial year

Earthquake forecasts poised for leap forward

Building suppliers forecast weaker recovery

By Our Industrial Editor

CONSTRUCTION industry

The world's most powerful computer may make it possible to predict earthquakes accurately.

Companies rarely publish their own forecasts, unless they need money. However many trade associations and other organisations release their forecasts, and these can be useful in keeping track of the outside business environment. But you need to get behind the headlines and study the bases for forecasts. Source *The Sunday Times* and *The Times*, © Times Newspapers Ltd 1993/4

Two sets of information then need to be combined in a forecast. One set will be the results of statistical analysis applied to these strings of past data. The other will be the wider knowledge of the market held formally in an Information

System, or less formally by those with experience of the market. The results of the calculations are based on history, and depend in some way on assumptions that the past will be continued into the future. There are times however when events may be foreseen in a market and for which history gives no guidance, and any calculations must be modified in the light of discussion.

It is useful then to distinguish between Projections and Predictions, which are based only on statistical calculation, and a Forecast which is based on both calculation and market knowledge. The following definitions are recommended to avoid confusion about the basis for any figures:

(i)   A *Projection* is the result of using simple averaging techniques to find trends and seasonality in past data, and using these to estimate future movements on the assumption of 'all things being equal'.
(ii)   A *Prediction* is the result of using more powerful statistical analysis to identify factors linked with movements in past sales, and developing estimates making appropriate assumptions about each factor.
(iii) A *Forecast is* the result of merging the statistical projections or predictions with market knowledge, to provide what is agreed to be the best current estimate of future movements.

Market and weather forecasting follow similar processes, using past data to identify any systematic patterns, current data to establish where we are now and calculate predictions, and the skills of experienced people to interpret the figures and develop forecasts

Computers have made the calculation of projections and predictions much easier than before, but however sophisticated the statistical systems may be, some-one should apply marketing knowledge before a forecast is released.

Forecasting in marketing is then part art and part science. The art lies in knowing the market and being able to recognise the significance of changes which may be taking place. The science lies in the application of statistical analysis to provide projections or predictions as starting points for discussion. In this chapter we shall be more concerned with the marketing aspects of forecasting, but some reference will be made to the statistical techniques at the end.

Most departments in an organisation use forecasts, for buying raw material or other supplies, recruiting staff, planning production or distribution, securing finance and so forth. In most cases these forecasts will depend on the expected level of demand for the goods or services being provided. To avoid confusion, or worse, in an organisation, it is vital that all departments start from an agreed central forecast of demand. Each department may then logically 'aim off' to suit its own purposes. In times of shortages of raw materials, the purchasing department may aim at levels above the forecast, to cover itself against lack of stock or price rises. Finance may take a more pessimistic view, and budget on a lower figure to provide a buffer. However if each department first produces its own forecasts and them aims off, there can be chaos. Marketing, with its closer knowledge of outside conditions which may affect demand, and knowledge of its own plans for generating demand, should take a lead.

Uses of forecasts within the organisation are many. For trading organisations a vital figure is of sales revenue, which is likely to be the main source of cash flowing inwards, and have a direct bearing on profitability. For non-trading or not-for-profit organisations there will still be a need to forecast demand as a basis for planning, even without a profit-and-loss account. Forecasts of market demand may be needed to help any organisation in negotiations with bank managers, suppliers, staff and customers on an informed basis.

Forecasts should not be confused with targets, budgets, objectives or other measures of activity. These are all focused on what management would *like* to achieve. They may be based on solid forecasts of expected market performance. But they may be based simply on requirements laid down by a parent company or financial aspects of the corporate plan. Forecasting needs to be independent of such considerations and must be market-related. Then it can perform the useful functions of showing what the outcome of current plans is likely to be, and of giving warning of future threats or opportunities.

If any serious differences appear between forecasts and budgets for a period, the ways in which each set of figures was developed need to be reviewed to resolve any problems. These problems need not be negative. Budgets may need to be revised upwards if the forecast shows more potential growth than planned. However, they may need to be revised downwards if forecasts show that planned sales are unlikely to be achieved.

Every forecast depends on assumptions. For most established products or brands a number of assumptions can be made on the basis of their history, but for many new products no history is available. Hence we need to look separately at ongoing forecasts for existing products and at forecasts for new products. Some special problems connected with new products will be left until the end of this chapter, but there is still a great deal of common ground.

Assumptions used in ongoing forecasts will be based on the experience of managers who have been involved in the market. The most simple assumption, but often the most dangerous, is that market factors will behave in the future as they have in the past. Thus past trends, whether upwards, downwards or flat, are assumed to continue. This is a particularly dangerous assumption in marketing where everyone is trying to change trends to their own advantage. Hence the more that is known about the causes of trends the safer we are likely to be in making assumptions about the future. But assumptions have to be made about other factors as well, such as selling prices, competitive activity, even the weather, which may affect total market sales, and through them the brand sales.

In the end the faith which can be put into any forecast of sales depends on the extent to which we can trust the assumptions. (The same applies in other areas of forecasting, and the reason why different forecasters produce different figures for changes in GNP, unemployment, savings and so forth is that they start from different sets of assumptions. Some assume that government will raise taxes. Some assume improved overseas markets. Some assume lower interest rates and so on. To interpret the differences we need to read the small print behind the forecasts, about the assumptions being made.)

While market forecasts should be developed independently of any objectives, the forecasts themselves may not remain neutral. If all reasonable forecasts indicate that sales of a product will fall rapidly because new improved alternatives are available, the forecast may become 'self-fulfilling'. The forecast will have alerted management to the situation, and rather than wait for the decline to happen they may chop the old product to make way for a new one. The forecast has led to its own conclusion. In a similar way a forecast that, given certain conditions, sales could expand rapidly may become self-fulfilling if management aim to satisfy those conditions, e.g. by cutting prices or whatever.

Some types of self-fulfilling forecast can be highly dangerous and lead companies into a false sense of security. It is not unusual for a forecast to become a sales target, particularly if an acceptable rise over last year is forecast. The sales target may then become the basis for bonus payments to salespeople. The target is hit, everyone is happy, and the trend established is then taken forward as the basis for the next forecast. However if the potential demand was originally underestimated, and the sales force have just eased off after securing the bonus, a gap may develop between potential demand and company supply. Failure to spot this, to provide more useful forecasts, could allow a competitor into the market.

On the other hand a forecast can be 'self-defeating' if management can prevent the assumptions on which it is based from happening. Examples here include cases where forecasts of the effects of price increases have shown severe losses in sales. Faced with such forecasts management try to avoid having to raise prices, by concentrating on reducing costs or other means.

Terms such as top-down or bottom-up forecasts are fairly self-explanatory. In the first, forecasts are made on a total market or a total company basis, and then broken down into brands or sales areas. In the second, forecasts are built up from the individual contributions of brand managers, area managers and so forth. Both methods need to be used with care, but comparisons of the results can be valuable. If a gap develops between the top-down forecasts for a company as a whole and the bottom-up forecasts, this may indicate the extent to which new products will be needed to maintain corporate momentum. Detailed examination of the individual contributions to the bottom-up forecasts will often reveal where the optimists and pessimists are!

10.2   Forecasting and planning

Forecasting and marketing planning are closely linked but separate activities. In some organisations they are separated, with a forecasting department distinct from the marketing department, but however the activities are organised there must be close liaison between the two. The plans made for a brand or an organisation will depend to a large extent on being able to forecast the likely outcomes of alternative strategies or tactics. At the same time the forecasts made for a brand or a product group will normally depend on knowledge of the strategy to be adopted. Forecasters and planners must start from a common set of data, and from common assumptions. There is no point in ignoring forecasts when planning marketing, nor in forecasting while ignoring marketing plans.

The most common need in market planning is for forecasts of sales, either in a market as a whole, for specific segments, or for individual brands. There are three distinct situations which can arise and which often call for different approaches:

(i)   The first and most common situation is concerned with existing products or brands, for which the history has been recorded through internal sales data or external research.

(ii)   The second is concerned with the more difficult situation of a new brand being introduced into an existing market, where some history may be available for the market and existing brands, but not of course for the new entry.

(iii)   The third, which is rare but the most difficult, is concerned with the introduction of an entirely new product creating a new market – but even here there may be some history of products which have previously satisfied the needs of potential customers.

There may also be a need for forecasts with different 'time-horizons'. For example in utility supply industries forecasts of demand may be needed on at least three different time horizons. The immediate need will be for forecasts for only a few hours ahead to help engineers plan plant utilisation during the next shift. Here the day of the week, time of day, hours of darkness, a short-term weather forecast and knowledge of TV programmes may be vital items of input. For medium-term marketing and budget purposes forecasts covering the next year in detail will be needed, and giving a broad picture for the next three or four years. These will depend on a different set of factors, which may include the economic situation affecting industrial demand and the spread of domestic appliances affecting household demand. Prices, taxes or terms of supply, promotional activity, or general energy-saving or conservation policies of government may also be involved. For the long term those responsible for planning and building new plant may need forecasts for the next 50 or 100 years, covering time spent in planning and building the installations and expected plant life. Here long-term trends in manufacturing technology, the geographic spread of industry and so forth may have direct effects. Other trends which may work more indirectly might cover population changes, climatic trends, trends in public opinion and so forth.

In setting up forecasts then we need to start with a set of decisions, about the geographic area and products to be covered, the time-horizons etc. It is also important to consider how far external factors may need to be considered, and what they might be.

A useful starting point is to list the factors which marketing people consider to be important in determining sales levels within the proposed time-horizon. These may often be put into a more dynamic form using a 'burst diagram'. Figure 10.1 shows a burst diagram developed during initial discussions on the medium-term market for a supplier of agricultural machinery, but it can be adapted to most situations.

In parallel with this it may be useful to produce a similar diagram showing who will be using forecasts within the organisation, and for what purposes. Equally most of these people may have vital contributions to make to the forecasting and planning process. They will know about the level of investment the company can afford, the potential limits on production through staff or plant constraints, and difficulties with raw materials or components and so forth.

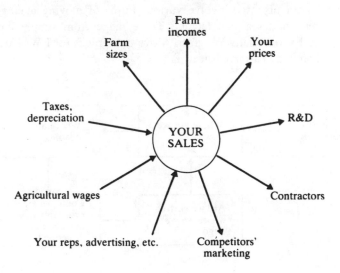

Fig. 10.1   Embryo model – agricultural machinery

10.3   Short-term forecasting

The basic stages in short-term forecasting for existing products, whether for a whole market or a brand, are shown in Figure 10.2. To forecast at all we need to know where we are now, whether in terms of unit sales, market share or whatever dimension we are using. This will form the starting point of the forecasts. However before looking forward we need to look back to see how we have arrived at this point. Hence the need to collect and analyse past data and experience as a base for indicating where we are heading. This involves statistical analysis, but will also involve knowledge of the market in interpreting the results and identifying sources of movements or possible causes of effects.

(a) Simple statistical analysis of past data

A marketing manager does not need to know the technical details of the analytical processes used in forecasting, but it is useful to be aware of some nontechnical factors. A manager should however be able to use a spreadsheet, as an aid to plotting charts as well as making calculations. Seeing the latest figures on a graph is still the best way of appreciating what they might mean.

Initial statistical analysis of back data, say of sales of a product month by month for the past five years, aims to analyse movements into three basic parts:

trends which show any general movements through time;
cyclical or repeated movements, e.g. seasonal patterns;
residual or random movements.

In the most simple, but still valuable, form of analysis the figures are plotted on a chart and then examined by eye. Any trend which is seen can be projected forwards by drawing a good freehand curve through the plot, and any seasonal effects can be seen and drawn in as appropriate. At a more objective level the statistical methods commonly used involve various forms of moving averages to determine any trend and seasonal factors. These range from simple moving annual averages to Exponentially Weighted Moving Averages (or EWMAs), but all can easily be handled in a spreadsheet.

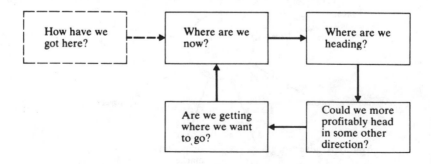

Fig. 10.2   The forecasting/planning cycle

Once firm evidence is obtained of trends and cycles in the data, these can be used to calculate 'projections' of sales at future times. A projection provides estimates of future sales on the assumption that all the trends and cycles involved in the past will continue to act in the same way in the future. This is clearly a major assumption, and it should not be made lightly. However the method provides a useful starting point, and is in common use for short-term projections, particularly where a range of products is involved.

Virtually automatic calculations of projections for a few periods ahead can be made using readily available software in a PC. These projections can be updated as new sales figures become available, and can form the basis for short-term marketing and production planning etc. The programs can produce warnings or exception reports when new sales figures being added for the latest period are significantly out of line with the projections made earlier. Warnings can also be sounded when newly calculated projections differ by more than a stipulated margin from past levels. In these cases the warnings or exception reports ensure that human judgement is called in.

If the trends and seasonal movements obtained from the analysis are plotted against the historic figures, the gaps between the two series will give a broad indication of the 'goodness of fit' expected in projections. If there is a close fit between the actual figures and the calculated figures in the past, then projections into the future should be reliable in the short run. In Figure 10.3 there is a plot of a set of sales figures from a fairly quiet market, with the related projections using moving averages and simple seasonality. The plot shows that on past experience the two sets of Observed and Predicted figures have been close together. Assuming that 'all other things remain equal' the situation may be expected to continue.

Figure 10.4 in contrast shows results for a more erratic market. The main cause of the fluctuations from period to period was the high level of promotional activity for the brand and for competitors. Here the assumption that 'all other things will be equal' clearly does not apply on a period-by-period basis. Projections based on moving averages and seasonality alone would be of little value in period-by-period forecasting, but might still be useful in tracking and monitoring overall trends.

These simple techniques will give a numerical answer to the question 'Where are we heading?', at least on a short-term basis, but it may not always be realistic. The underlying assumption that 'all other things will remain equal' can be very dangerous. We need to know something of the causes of trends or cycles before we are fully justified in making such assumptions. As Alexander Cairncross has so wittily stated:

'A trend is a trend is a trend,
But the question is, will it bend,
Will it alter its course
Through some unforseen force,
And come to a premature end?'

A trend may be due to one or more causes. Causes outside the market may range from slow population changes through to comparatively rapid changes in

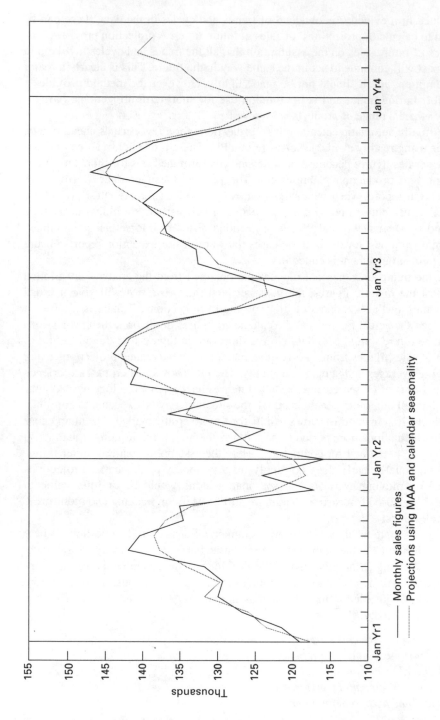

Fig. 10.3   Stable product with little disturbance tracked by simple MAA and seasonality

Monthly sales figures

Projections using MAA and calendar seasonality

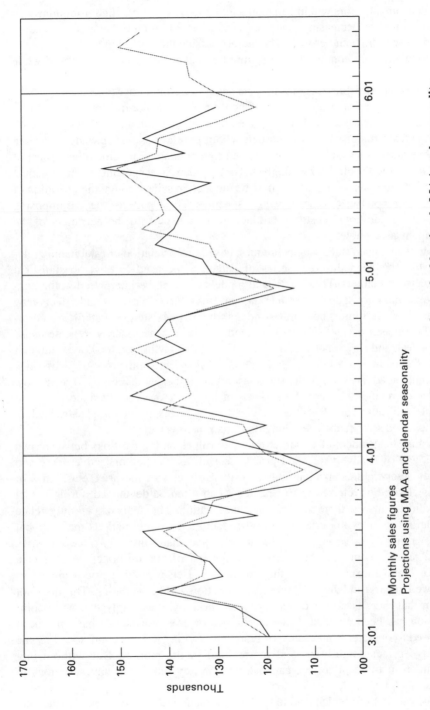

Monthly sales figures
Projections using MAA and calendar seasonality

Fig. 10.4 Product subject to erratic influences poorly tracked by simple MAA and seasonality

the economy. Factors within a market leading to trends may range from improved product quality, decreasing real prices, or increased promotional activity leading to more specific brand growth. The factors outside the control of a company, such as population or economic activity, are often called 'exogenous variables' while those within its control, such as own price or promotional expenditure, are called 'endogenous variables'. Trends may be generated from either type.

Seasonality in sales during a year should not just be accepted as a fact of life. In some markets seasonality may be linked to the calendar, directly as with Christmas cards or indirectly through school holidays as with package tours. In other markets seasonal variation is linked to temperature or some other aspect of weather, as with soft drinks, sunglasses or attendances at sporting events. In some cases spurious seasonal patterns may be induced in sales through the operation of sales force bonuses or other incentive schemes. These patterns may be imposing stresses or additional costs on production or transport, to the detriment of the company as a whole.

More advanced statistical techniques, based on correlation or establishing relationships between different series of data, can be used to develop statistical 'models' of markets. These statistical models can then be interpreted in the light of logic and knowledge of the market, and links between causes and effects may be established. It must be emphasised that the mere existence of statistical correlation between one set of data and another does not necessarily indicate cause and effect, and care is needed in interpreting and applying results. For example, it is not unusual for a company to spend a fairly constant proportion of sales revenue on advertising. A chart of adspend against sales revenue will then show strong correlation between the two sets of figures. However, the underlying and immediate cause-and-effect situation is likely to be one of increased sales leading to increased advertising spending rather than the reverse!

A statistical model of a market may put values on logical links between own sales and own advertising and prices, as well as competitors' advertising and prices, temperature, taxation and so forth. Estimates of the price elasticities or cross-elasticities referred to in Chapter 7 can often be developed during model building. However there is one major reservation. The analysis can only relate variations in sales to variations in other factors. In some markets management believe, rightly or wrongly, that brand sales and shares are very price-sensitive. As a result no-one may be prepared to get out of line on prices. Whenever a major brand moves its price, the rest follow. Hence relative prices are never allowed to vary, and the analysis cannot function without variation. This does not mean that there is no price sensitivity or elasticity, but simply that price competition has been avoided. Price elasticities or cross-elasticities have not been allowed to operate. Brand sales, or brand shares may well be conditioned by the relative prices established and maintained in the market. But without any variation in those prices we cannot establish any links with any variations in sales.

The calculations which lead to the development of the model will also indicate the goodness of fit obtained on the past data, and the reliability which can be expected if the model is used to make 'predictions' of future movements. There is a major problem, however, concerning the assumptions now involved in the predictions. To use the model to provide predictions as a basis for forecasting we need to feed it with expected values of the factors involved for the length of the forecast period. While our own plans for price changes or advertising may be known, we may have to make assumptions about competitive activities, or even about weather conditions. Logical levels for competitive factors will have to be judged from knowledge of the market and the competitive management.

Inputs to the model such as weather can initially be put in on an average or climate basis, but further calculations can be made assuming above- or below-average temperature or whatever. Similarly with other factors, a range of values can be assumed to examine best and worst situations as well as the most likely central one. This procedure not only opens the way to contingency planning, taking account of optimistic and pessimistic situations, but also shows in a practical way how sensitive sales are to such changes in the factors in the model as prices or advertising. This process can become very involved. Suppose that assumptions are needed only on our price, the average price of competitors, and on mean daily temperatures to operate a model. Simply taking a low, medium and high value for each of these three factors will produce a possible 27 predictions, and the amount of calculation calls for sophisticated computer support. The process goes under the name of market simulation.

The use of predictions based on market models depends on more assumptions than is the case with projections, and calls on far more knowledge of the market than simple projection. However, although the development of a market model can take a great deal of effort, it will usually lead to a far greater insight into the functioning of a market, the effects of price changes, or advertising, promotions and so forth, than can be gained from simply looking at the figures. Those who have gained their knowledge of a market through practical experience over a number of years usually have nothing to fear from these analyses. The results normally support experience, but add a quantitative dimension which is valuable in forecasting and planning.

There are three major advantages of having a statistically based model of the market, and of a brand within it. The first is that maximum use is made of historic data to provide insights into how a market works and to guide current thinking. Relationships or elasticities, similar to price elasticities, can often be calculated with respect to internal factors such as advertising expenditure, or to external factors such as average earnings or personal disposable income.

The second advantage is that once the current plans have been fed into the model to assess where we are heading, the likely outcomes of alternative plans can also be assessed. The question can be asked: 'Could we more profitably move in some other direction?' At this point forecasting moves from being merely a routine for planning production or for budgeting, to becoming a more dynamic tool for marketing. With more knowledge of how a market works, and a means for assessing the likely outcomes of alternative actions, comparisons can be made between the expected short-term results of alternative plans, such as between a price cut and an advertising campaign; or the results of attempting to offset a price rise with increased weight of advertising.

The projections from moving averages, or the predictions from models, are only the result of calculations based on past performance in the market. They should not in themselves be taken as forecasts, but only as bases for discussion. In static markets where little is happening the calculated figures may become the accepted forecast without much discussion. In more dynamic markets with active competition the scope for factors to operate which have not appeared before may be far greater. Knowledge that we or a competitor may be about to launch a new range or pack-size, to use a new means of advertising or promotion for the first time, or whatever, may need to be taken into account in developing an agreed forecast. Whatever the situation it is vital that the calculations are reviewed by individuals who know the market, and amended as thought fit in the light of their expectations, before use. The views of other people in the company may need to be brought into the discussions, to check that raw materials, production capacity, transport, finance or whatever will be available to meet the forecast levels of activity, before they can be used for planning purposes.

Whatever methods of forecasting are used, from wet seaweed to market models, some record should be kept of the assumptions made period-by-period and of the agreed forecast. Once actual figures for the forecast period are known, then comparisons should be made, not simply to see how right we were, but to learn more about the market for future use. Even if the forecast was within a reasonable margin of being right, there may still be compensating errors which can yield more insights. If the forecast was way out then the question arises of why. Was it due to faulty methods, whatever they were, or to faulty assumptions about factors? With simple moving average methods any failure of the 'all other things being equal' assumption may cause serious errors in the projections if the causes of disturbance were not appreciated at the discussion stage.

With more complex models the third of the benefits mentioned above comes into play. Once the prices, adspends or whatever are known for a period, comparisons can be made with the assumptions. If there are serious gaps, effort can perhaps be directed towards obtaining better assumptions of factor levels in the future. However there is the question of whether the model itself has remained valid through time. The test for model validity is simply to feed it with the now known factor levels, and to make a 'hindcast'. This is simply done by putting the correct prices, advertising levels or whatever into the model and calculating the expected sales levels. If this hindcast, now fed with the correct assumptions in the model, agrees reasonably with the actual figures, then the model is probably still valid. If it does not, then the model may no longer mirror the market – and something may have changed in the market which is not reflected in the structure of the model. Gaps which suddenly appear between short-term forecasts and actual performance may be the first indication a company has of such changes, and should always be investigated.

Whatever methods of calculation are used the emphasis in developing the final forecast must be on the blending of the numerical results with knowledge of the market itself, and an awareness of developments in the environment surrounding it.

(b) Longer-term forecasting

Boundaries between short-term and longer-term forecasting will vary between industries and between firms in the same industry. For most working purposes we can take the short-term for forecasting as being up to six months ahead, with medium-term forecasts running up to four or five years. Beyond that we are into long-term forecasts.

The longer the forecast term or horizon the less reliance can be placed on the current situation and all the assumptions associated with it. Simple projections using moving average techniques become less useful, although still offer a crude starting point. Short-term cycles such as seasonality become less important, and longer-term cycles of expansion and recession have to be considered. Generally there is a need for a review of factors far beyond those involved in more immediate forecasting.

Some of these other factors will be outside the markets concerned, others within it. Typical external factors which may appear in medium-term models are population, GDP, unemployment, inflation etc., and series of historic figures are available from government and other sources. When developing predictions from models containing such variables, forecasts of future levels will be needed, but these are regularly provided by governments, universities and some specialist bodies. It is not uncommon to find that different sources are producing different forecasts, but the variations stem largely from the differing assumptions used in developing the forecasts. As mentioned above, these assumptions need to be studied when deciding which set of forecasts are to be adopted as a base for a firm's own calculations.

Factors within the market but outside the firm's control must be assessed by these who have the required knowledge as well as through analysis of back data if it is available. Those factors within the firm's control must then be considered in the light of the views of management, the firm's own objectives and strategies, and expected external factors. The results will then be based on a mixture of facts and opinions, of calculation and discussion, with the balance moving rapidly in the direction of opinion and discussion as the time span is increased.

At the further end of longer-term forecasting lies the scenario. A scenario may start from the current situation and current trends but will be concerned with spans of ten years or more. Alternatively a scenario may be written from the future backwards, starting with an independent view of how market demand – say for food, clothing, transport, energy, etc. – might be met in the future, and working back to the implications for intermediate years and the need for present thinking to be modified. Three or more scenarios may be developed, one optimistic, one pessimistic and one central view. The purpose is not so much to indicate what levels of turnover or market size will prevail in the far future, but what general conditions may prevail. From this it may be possible to plan the steps which need to be taken in advance of events to keep a firm in a market or to ensure orderly withdrawal, and so forth.

Areas considered in developing such long-range views should include technological changes of all kinds which may affect the company. These may include the development of new materials or new processes. Some developments, such as new pharmaceutical products or other new complex chemicals, may have long periods of research and testing before being marketed, and may be signalled years ahead. Many likely developments can often be seen within the forecasting horizon, but their precise form, timing and consequences may be open to doubt and speculation. The important point is that the potential impact of foreseeable future events should be considered, so that the organisation is not taken by surprise, can formulate its own plans to defend its position or capitalise on the new development and so forth. Techniques exist for helping to spread the net widely enough to pick up significant factors, but not so widely as to swamp the whole operation.

Such long-term operations may be in the province of general management or even directly under the Chairman or Chief Executive. Marketing, with its views of customers and markets, must be involved in watching for longer-term trends in the existing market as well as looking at potential shifts or complete breaks in the current patterns. For example, developments in CAD–CAM and the use of databases have radically changed the ways in which some production and distribution facilities can be run. Companies which anticipated the potential for rapid changes in design and manufacture, or for more direct contact with selected customers, were able to gain competitive advantage over rivals slow to appreciate change.

Scenario writing is at the extreme range of forecasting, but it is a useful exercise even if only done on an informal basis. It will indicate areas that the organisation should be taking into account in current planning, to ensure that avenues of potential development are not closed off – perhaps by abandoning a research project, selling a site which may be needed for expansion, etc. Equally there should be early warning of developments which may threaten existing markets through social, legal, technological or other changes, either through increasing competition or even extinction. Implications for current research, planning and operations can then be drawn before options are closed off or opportunities missed.

10.4   Into the unknown

The discussion so far has been concerned with existing products and processes in current markets, but a range of forecasting problems can occur where there is little experience to form a basis for calculation or discussion. These may range from needs to forecast the outcome of a type of promotional offer not previously tried in a market, to making initial forecasts of the potential for an innovative new product. In many cases however where we start with a feeling that we are entering new and untried territory, a little research may show that others have been there before and some guidance can be gleaned from their experience.

Figure 10.5 shows one route by which the potential for a new venture, whether large or small, can be developed. While the steps are shown in sequence round a central circle a sequential approach is not necessary, and often the results in one area will be more readily available, and can lead directly to a rapid solution of the problem.

Ideas for new products can come from many sources, from suppliers of raw materials through to customers, not forgetting the whole range of company personnel. Some ideas may be original for new products altogether, some for import substitution, some for products seen locally during trips abroad and so forth. Whoever suggests the idea, or whoever is responsible for initial sifting of ideas, may already have developed some indication of the potential sales, and although this may be an optimistic figure it serves as a useful upper boundary to the discussion.

Even at an early stage it should be possible to make some assessment of the risk profile of the proposal. This should give an indication of the extent to which resources will be needed if the product is to be brought to market. Is the product or service one which could be provided on a small scale, with little capital cost? Or will it involve complex operations which can only hope to become economic on a mass production basis? Such assessment may well be pessimistic as people cover themselves against the inevitable unknown in the system, but they provide an indication of the lowest viable levels. They should also indicate the scale of investment which may be required for the idea, which may be beyond the capacity for the organisation anyway, and mean either abandonment or some form of co-operation with another company. Alternatively, even if the investment would be acceptable, there may be a significant adverse gap between the optimism of the innovator and the assessment of the technical people, and therefore little point in proceeding. However there is a long list of ideas which the innovator hawked around several organisations who turned the idea down, before finding one which

Fig. 10.5   Into the unknown – some possible lines of approach

made a success of it. At the high-tech end of innovation there is the early history of Xerography; at the lower end the Black & Decker Workmate.

Many ideas for new products involve replacing existing products with new, hopefully better, alternatives, but here we are only concerned with radically new products rather than simple developments of current ones. However many radical new products may have their first uses as replacements for something already available. The fax machine for instance was a new entry into part of the telecommunications market previously held by the Teleprinter. Alternatively the use of the new idea may be linked to other products for which there is already an installed base, such as the videotape machine and TV sets. While links like these will not directly provide estimates of likely demand, they may set upper and lower limits to guide early discussion. In many cases however such new products not only replace the old, but lead to expansion of demand. The transistor radio not only replaced older, family-based, valve models but gave a new lease of life to the medium through portability and personal possession. Fax rapidly expanded the market for document transmission, cassettes and the related players expanded the market for recorded music, and later for video.

If the item is already available abroad, what is the sales history there? Can this be related to the domestic market? Are other potential producers likely to come into the market, and on what scale? What lead time or potential does the organisation have, based on its technology, production or marketing strengths? Do these factors indicate fierce competition, or is market dominance possible? Discussion of these factors will help in the development of forecasts of future potential and the related decisions.

Legal or other constraints may need to be considered, including any adverse environmental effects, in making any forecasts. Here it may be necessary to consider forecasts in less tangible directions, such as changes in public attitudes, changes in the law and so forth.

Equally, opinions from experts within the organisation and outside should be sought. This may be done through a 'Delphi' approach, in which opinions are sought from a range of experts who may have something to contribute. They may include experts in materials, production technology, economics, sociology etc., as well as specialists more closely linked to the proposed market. They are asked questions about expected developments in their areas over the next few years, the comments are collated and the general findings sent back to the panel. Members are then asked whether their original answers need revision. After two or three rounds, originally by post, now by fax or electronic mail systems, consensus may be obtained on major issues. The method ensures that a broad view is taken of a proposal through time, and that opportunities are properly investigated, while helping prevent investments in new products in dying technologies and so forth. Very often personnel within a company do not realise the pace or nature of the development of new materials, new processes and so forth, as they may apply to current or future products. The multi-disciplinary approach used in the Delphi technique should help to avoid this form of blinkered thinking. (One major precision manufacturing company invested heavily in mechanical desk calculators, unaware that the electronics industry was about to produce the first desk and pocket calculators.)

This list of points to be considered when venturing into the unknown is by no means exhaustive, and will need modification to meet individual cases. However given some formal approach to the problem, a great deal of information and opinion can be gathered. Some very diverse sources can often help in deciding whether the potential future for a new idea warrants expenditure on further research, or should be rejected before it takes resources better devoted to other ideas.

10.5   A note on statistical models

Most statistical models are based on forms of analysis designed to discover the extent to which variations in one factor, such as the volume of sales, may be linked to variations in other factors. In developing marketing models we normally attempt to link a variable such as our sales to other factors such as our own or competitive prices or levels of promotional activity, the state of the economy or weather conditions, and so forth. Two technical terms are involved:

(i)   *Correlation*, which is a measure of the extent to which variation in one factor such as sales (called the dependent variable) can be related to variations in one or more other factors, called the independent variables.

(ii) *Regression*, which sets out in an equation the nature of the relationships involved.

At the most simple level the relationship between sales and only one other factor, such as price, is measured by a statistic r, called the correlation coefficient. This can vary from +1 where there is a direct and unvarying relationship, through 0 where there is no detectable relationship, to –1 where there is an inverse and unvarying relationship. If sales increase as temperature rises, then there will be some degree of positive correlation and positive values of r. If sales fall with increasing price there will be negative correlation and negative values of r.

In most marketing situations we need to take account of more than one factor which may affect sales, and we move from simple regression or simple correlation to multiple regression and the multiple correlation coefficient denoted by R^2. Since this is a squared number it can only be positive, and ranges from 0 denoting no detectable relationships to +1 in which all variations in the dependent variable can be traced back to variations in the independent variables. A value of R^2 of +1 in a marketing situation almost certainly indicates that there is a flaw in the logic of the calculations.

The correlation coefficients and the regression equations are developed from the raw data through the use of statistical packages or spreadsheets in PCs. The regression equations are expressed in various forms but all reduce to the basic form, which in the case of a sales model would be:

$$\text{Sales} = 1026 - 14.7 \times \text{deflated price} - 3.7 \times \text{OOS} + 12.7 \times \text{TVRs} + 23.7 \times {}^\circ\text{C}\dots$$

Here deflated price is a factor, as is the Out-of-Stock (OOS) situation, the television ratings (TVRs), and temperature (°C). The figures and the factors in the equation will vary from market to market, but the form of the equation remains the same.

The analysis starts with data for the factors which management feel are important, as in Figure 10.1. Various statistical tests are made to determine which of these has a significant effect on sales levels. Provided that the relationships are logical as well, then the factors are brought into the equation, until no other candidates pass scrutiny. The resulting equation should be sound both statistically and logically, but will still need to be tested before being used for any predictive purposes.

Frequently some variant of the original data is needed for full development of the role of a factor in the model. Advertising efforts, for example, may take time to show their full effects, and lagged values of advertising in previous periods are needed. Prices may need to be expressed as ratios or differences against competitors, and so forth. The whole development of a model will depend as much on knowledge of the market as on statistical expertise. Unless marketing people are fully involved in this development, they cannot be expected to have faith in the results and to make full use of the results obtained.

Assignments

Find and plot a string of sales figures for your chosen organisation, or if this is not possible, for a related product or market area using published figures. (Annual reports of public companies or corporations are a useful source. Some other sources are listed in Appendix A5.)

Is there evidence of a trend? What factors do you think might be contributing to any trend, and what figures can you get to test your ideas?

Is there evidence of any seasonal pattern in monthly or quarterly figures? Is this more likely to be calendar related or weather related, or a mixture? What specific factors are likely to be involved?

Draw a diagram similar to Figure 10.1 showing the factors which you think may have an effect on your chosen market, and which would need to be considered when developing a forecast.

What spans of time would be appropriate for (a) short-term and (b) long-term forecasting in your chosen market?

Some other aspects of marketing

In this chapter we shall draw together further ideas on marketing, and look at developments which are taking place.

11.1 Marketing planning and marketing plans

Marketing planning may be done formally or informally, in simple or sophisticated manner. However it is done, planning these days is inevitable when economic and other market conditions pose a choice of alternative courses of action. For example, which factors are important in any analysis of market conditions? Should the marketing be centralised or decentralised for administrative or operational purposes? What should be the firm's marketing goals and social concern or responsibility? Should it be operational- or product-oriented or geographically based? What resources are needed and how can they be obtained? What methods of control and evaluation would be best? How should the various components of the marketing mix be combined and what costs are permitted?

These and other points have made it advisable for there to be formal marketing planning. Whether it is simple or complex in nature depends on the tasks to be done, the problems to be overcome and the sophistication of the staff and how they operate most efficiently. The dynamic nature of markets, their increasing complexity and fierceness of competition have forced executives to give more attention to formal and scientific methods of marketing planning as explained earlier in this book.

The chief marketing executive (marketing director or manager) is responsible for the planning of the goals, product–market offerings, price, organisation and resources in general for the marketing department. These are co-ordinated with the plans of the other divisions (manufacturing, finance, personnel). In fact the planning process starts in each department or sub-department with staff reviewing past performance and identifying the reasons for successes and failure, how the former could be developed and the latter overcome. They can then indicate what performance would be possible in the next planning period, given the *status quo* and given specified additional resources or changes. In co-operative communications with colleagues from other departments, in the marketing division and with appropriate departments of other divisions, agreement is reached on the overall marketing plans that should be implemented in the next operational period.

Communications in the planning work are both vertical (throughout the marketing division) and lateral (between marketing and other divisions). The work is guided by the corporate objectives indicated as desirable by the board and the need to be realistic. Objectives that cannot be evaluated or achieved and strategies and tactics beyond the firm's capabilities have no part to play here. Attempts to incorporate them into the plan can lead only to problems and impede effective action programmes.

Plans are expressed in detail for about the first two years of the planning period and then in progressive outline for later years. Performance is reviewed at the end of every sales period (week, fortnight or month) but plans are not revised until two or three sales periods have passed. This makes sure that response is made only when changes can be judged to be reasonably permanent. That is, no adjustments are made for what may turn out to be just momentary deviations. At the revision stage, a further time period equivalent to the length of the review one is brought into the total plan. Thus the total plan always covers the full number of years for which planning was done in the first instance. This is known as the 'rolling plan' approach. Marketing planning is a continuous process, as shown by Figure 11.1. Note the two-way flow of information as represented by the double arrows.

(a) Marketing objectives
The objectives, or goals, or targets normally used are:

profits (£s)
return on investment (%)
sales (in units) and turnover or revenue (£s)
market shares (%)
profit to sales and other relevant control ratios (%)
annual rates of growth (%) for all the above

They are the means whereby performance can be measured and actions controlled. These goals would be broken down into separate sets of targets where firms operate in more than one technology or industry and where market or customer factors indicate this to be advisable. They become a focus for individual motivation besides being the basis for co-ordination and planning in the marketing division and throughout the enterprise.

The profit target is important since, for any given pricing situation, until it has been established decisions on permitted costs cannot be made. It sets the parameters for the pricing policies to be followed. Further, the profit earned determines how well employees may be remunerated and financiers rewarded for the capital they have placed in trust with the company. The return on investment target judges how well the firm is utilising the assets (capital) invested in it. These two are used by investors to judge if the company is well managed.

The sales and turnover targets indicate what has to be achieved to realise the profit and return goals and what manufacturing, personnel and financial resources are required. Market share targets indicate the competitive abilities of the company and the market positions the firm must achieve to contain or overcome competition. Too small a market share makes the firm vulnerable to larger competitors. Too large a share may invite attacks on its markets by smaller competitors. Annual rates of growth targets offer a reasonable challenge to executives to do better each year and so build the firm's financial and economic strengths for future growth and development.

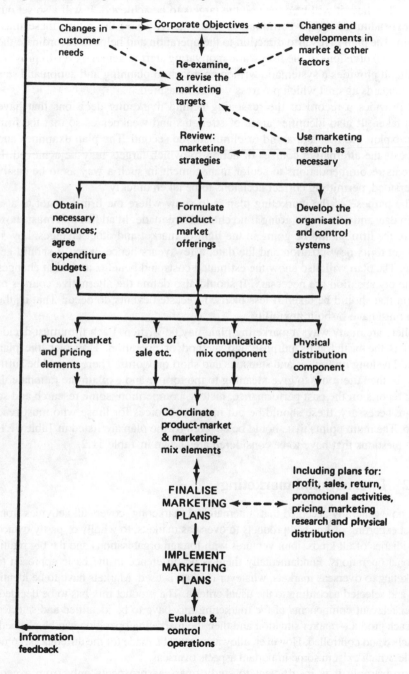

Fig. 11.1   **Marketing planning**

(b) The marketing plan

The marketing plan is the principal operational and control document of the marketing department. It specifies what has to be done, when it is to be done, who does what, how it will be done and the targets to be achieved. It will also set out the expenditure budgets permitted for each activity and the return these must obtain. The plan gives firm direction to the operation and helps to co-ordinate the work of all divisions of the firm while motivating staff to achieve ever-improving results. It provides a systematic written approach to planning and action and sets the standards against which progress will be measured.

It provides a record of the reasoning behind marketing decisions that have been taken. It also identifies areas of strengths and weaknesses so that the firm may exploit the first and avoid or eliminate the second. The plan examines and suggests the alternative courses of action by which targets may be achieved. It presents recommendations to senior management in such a way as to be easily understood, permitting correct decisions to be taken quickly.

The purpose of the marketing plan is to show where the firm has got to at a given date·and where it is going if no changes are made. In addition, it must show where the firm should be going in the light of market and other changes, how it will get to its new position and the date, a few years hence, when it should get there. The plan will also show the estimated costs and benefits and what changes in the organisation are necessary. It should also define the alternative courses of action that should be taken if less likely, forecasted events do occur. That is, the plan must have in-built flexibility.

There are many ways a marketing plan may be written. Each firm must decide what is the best for its purpose and method of operation. However, the plan should be long on figures and statistics and short on words. There should be sufficient of the latter only to give meaning to the former and explain the rationale. If long reports on the past performance, history, competition, some research and so on are necessary, these should be put in as appendices for those who must read them. The main points that should be covered by the plan are listed in Table 11.1. The questions that have to be considered are shown in Table 11.2.

11.2 International marketing

It is now generally accepted that 'international marketing' covers all activities from direct exporting of finished products to overseas markets, to wholly or partly owned subsidiaries of all kinds, joint ventures with foreign organisations and the big multinational operations. Fundamentally there is no difference in the basic approach to marketing to overseas markets, whatever method is used. Markets have to be identified and selected according to the usual criteria. The product mix has to be decided. Other relevant components of the marketing mix have to be identified and selected for each product–market situation and then the marketing operation can be planned, launched and controlled. However, allowance must be made for the differences, some subtle, which exist in some important aspects overseas.

For·example it is insufficient to study overseas prospects only from a geographical viewpoint, that is, according to national boundaries. It is necessary to

Table 11.1   **Contents of a marketing plan**

1   An executive summary. Not everyone needs all the detail
2   Scope and coverage of the plan – products, areas, period etc.
3   Current marketing situation, with appropriate background, with limited history and current trends
4   Opportunities, threats, and other factors to be considered in planning activities
5   Corporate and marketing goals, market shares, volumes, margins etc.
6   Proposed strategy for meeting objectives, under main activity headings
7   Details of activities, by whom, when, and with what facilities or budget
8   The expected results, in financial or other relevant terms
9   Provision for monitoring activities, expenditures and results, together with outline fall-back or contingency planning

Table 11.2   **Marketing planning – key questions**

Markets
What markets do we serve? Why? What market shares do we have? What are the volume trends? What factors are affecting this? Who are our competitors and what are their market shares? How are these changing? What markets should we be in? What arc the ruling prices? How are these likely to change with cost and other changes?

Products
What products are we making? Why? What products are we selling? Why and how? What products are competitors offering? How do they compete? Where and why do they compete with us? What new activities and products are they planning? What product modification, rationalisation and new product development will we need? Over what time-scale? At what cost? How will this affect our prices, profits and return on investment?

Promotion and image
How do customers see our company? How do they see our products? Is there a proper match between the image we would like and the image that customers perceive? How effective is our use of advertising? Are we using the right media? Are we sending the right messages to the right people? Are we using PR effectively?

Price
How important is price in our markets? Do we have adequate information on competitors' prices? Are our prices regarded as low or high relative to our quality? Do we tend to lead or follow price changes? Have we room to increase prices? Do we need to cut prices? Is there pressure from competitors or customers for reduced prices? Could we become involved in a price war? Do our prices give us adequate margins?

Distribution
Which channels and what methods are we using? Why? Which are being used by competitors? Are customers getting the service they need? Any improvements possible? Any cost savings possible? What discounts are offered? Why?

Environment
How are economic, technological, legal, political, social and ethical aspects changing? How will this affect future business? How do population growth and movement affect demand? What is the firm's relationships with customers and society at large? Also with competitors? What other considerations (pollution, consumerism etc.) have to be taken into account?

consider the economic geography of regions (economic development, population, educational standards, income etc.). Ethnic groups have also to be studied and it should be realised that they have the habit of not conforming to national boundaries drawn by politicians. This is particularly so in Africa and the Middle East. Then generally held concepts may not be correct. For example India is (predominantly) Hindu country but it also has the largest Muslim population of any. Language culture, attitudes to change or marketing or business, views about involvements with foreign enterprises, level of wealth, social systems in operation and the marketing and distribution infrastructures existing are other aspects that must be studied and understood. These are listed in Table 11.3 for easy reference, and will be discussed later.

Firms wishing to put their international marketing operations, of whichever kind, on to a sure footing are advised to bring the corporate planning approach to them. Overseas operations must be planned in totality, on a long-term basis and with greater precision than in home markets. The time commitments and risks are greater and more complex. Shunting off the odd order when there is spare capacity at home will not do. Potential customers will turn to other sources if they feel a supplier looks on them as a convenient source of business only when times are hard at home. Overseas customers expect reasonable continuity of supplies, with quality at agreed levels and deliveries honoured to the letter.

International marketing has significance for both the economic development of countries and the profitability of firms. It is important to the economic development of developed *and* developing nations. For developing countries, economic development requires not only markets that link, effectively, urban and rural zones but also the creation of wider marketing activities to generate industrial production and stimulate diversified product-market activities. Marketing is the most important multiplier of developing, growth areas and is thus of importance to developing countries. Besides expanding markets and increasing profits, it helps to accumulate capital, balance international payments, exchange primary produce and raw materials for machinery and equipment, expand production facilities and develop economic expansion and competence. It increases incomes and purchasing power, leads eventually to mass production and distribution and the creation of a middle class whose demands stimulate continuing economic growth. All this is vital to developing countries.

Investigation and analysis of market potential in other countries needs careful planning to ensure adequate coverage of all aspects. Nothing can be taken for granted. Managers in one country generally lack the instinctive feel for another area which only comes from long residence. Much of the background to marketing operations in one's native country comes from knowledge and 'feel' built up simply from living there. This is normally lacking when management is considering operating in other countries, however apparently similar. One basic set of factors to be examined is covered by a *PEST* analysis, covering *P*olitical, *E*conomic, *S*ocial and *T*echnical aspects. The main items are summarised in Table 11.3 but will of course need to be adapted in any specific country/market appraisal.

Table 11.3   **International marketing: PEST analysis**

Political & legal	Government structure Political stability Legal constraints Financial restrictions
Economic	Size of country and population Population structure, age etc. Distribution of income and wealth Wage and cost structures Domestic demand Grants, tax holidays etc.
Social	Language, literacy and culture Urban/rural patterns Social stability Middle/managerial class Dominant life-styles
Technical	Communications facilities Transport and distribution facilities Market infrastructure Technical training and support

(a) Political and legal factors

Apart from the arms industry, there may be little point in considering countries or areas which are politically unstable. Thought must be given to the political framework of the country, the different dogma propounded by the various parties vying for power and the chances of any party obtaining and holding on to power. Often the declared public statements of policy do not always match performance. The latter can be much more severe or liberal than might be deduced from official statements. The real clues are found in what is said in private behind closed doors, the attitude to trade and whether industrial development and contributions by foreigners are seen as helping to meet the nation's objectives.

Further, decisions must be taken on whether the political system is democratic or dictatorial or a mixture of both. Then the permanency of the system must be judged. What is the likelihood of change? What effect would any change have on the economic and business situations? How permanent is any change likely to be? In other words, what is the stability of the system?

Then there is the attitude of host countries to other nations, their governments, political and economic policies. If they favour the firm's home country, prospects should be good. If the host nation detests all that the home country stands for then the firm's prospects should be nil.

The legal framework of foreign countries can be alien to the firm (e.g. for British companies, the intricacies of Napoleonic law as against British case law) and difficult to interpret and understand. Ignorance of the law is not accepted as an excuse for contraventions. So unless a firm takes steps to study the legal systems and procedures of host countries and all associated business and financial regulations and controls, costly mistakes can be made.

An important legal aspect concerns the ownership of business enterprises. Most countries (Britain seems to be the only exception these days) insist, as a minimum, that 51 per cent or more of the equity must be held by local nationals. In some countries essential industries which are capital- and skills-intensive may initially be mainly in foreign hands. However, once established and the necessary skills imparted to local nationals, then the 51 plus per cent rule is applied. Those requiring limited capital and skills which the country has must be almost entirely (about 80 plus per cent) in local ownership. In many countries expatriates are required to train their successors from amongst the ranks of local nationals working for the firm.

As already mentioned, tax laws and regulations must be obeyed. However, restrictions and laws can be imposed or withdrawn at speed and without much prior warning or explanation. It should be remembered too that in new nations politicians, the Civil Service and business people will need time to reach the degree of sophistication, competence and knowledge existing in countries that have been around for many centuries.

(b) Economic factors

Besides attempting to measure the same economic factors as for home markets, particular attention should be given to the *standard of living*. What is the current standard and how successfully is the government living up to its declared aim of improving it? How is the quality of life changing? Is the country poor and interested mainly in staples (foodstuffs, fertilisers, simple agricultural equipment and essential medicines) or is it able to absorb other items, including 'luxuries' and if so, which? Developing countries will give priority to industrial products and equipment they consider necessary for what may be, to them, planned essential industrial development and growth. Consideration should also be given to determining whether the economy is basically sound and stable, what the overall chance of growth would be and the direction that growth might take.

The levels of income and the income structure must also be studied. They indicate the level of prosperity of the country and its ability to consume specific goods. Care must be taken to ensure the firm is comparing like with like. For example some countries pay various grants and allowances to individuals. These may not be included in official statistics on personal incomes. Thus an individuals's discretionary income may be larger than indicated by basic earnings.

The tax structure of the country should also be checked. Tax takes a big bite out of the incomes of consumers in developing countries. However, some countries give employees various tax-free allowances towards rent, cost of living and so on which partly offset the effects of relatively high taxation. Some countries impose punitive tax increases when employees receive increases in their earnings. The 'higher earning levels' can also be quite low by Western standards. In some instances annual salaries over £2,500 (equivalent) can incur tax at 70 per cent or more.

It is also necessary to study the ruling market prices, not only of alternative or substitute products to those the firm has in mind, but also for essential commodities. In some countries essential goods produced indigenously will be less expensive than imported items. In others they can be more expensive. It depends on the availability of the right sort of labour, the right plant and essential raw materials. If the last have to be imported then cost of production may not be much cheaper than imported goods. A study of prices for these items will indicate the probable disposable incomes of consumers and their purchasing power. It will also indicate what sort of manufacturing, marketing and distribution costs will be encountered by the incoming firm. Thus decisions can be taken on whether local manufacture would be advantageous or not.

Finally, it is essential to establish the stability of demand in intended markets and what the prospects are for growth or decline. Obviously firms entering a new overseas market would want several years of economic, market and political stability. Otherwise it would not be possible to build a successful business with a long-term future.

(c) Social factors

These can range from measurable factors such as the urban/rural split in the population to far less identifiable social patterns. The latter are often among the most difficult for an outsider to appreciate, but they can wreck any ill-planned marketing operations.

As for marketing in home countries, the size and distribution of the population must be known. Even if a country has a large population, it will pose marketing problems if this is spread over a large area in small towns and villages, of if it is mainly rural in nature. The size of market segments may be too limited. The population distribution may also be split by geographic features which may form formidable natural barriers to a free flow of trade.

Then the culture and the standards of literacy must be known for reasons stated earlier. Too many dialects hamper promotional and research activities. Methods standard in the home country may be impossible to apply.

Market research among housewives, for example, is not possible in many countries because of overall attitudes to the roles of men and women, and views of what is permissible behaviour. Often the standards accepted as normal in developed countries are not acceptable, or may even be viewed with contempt in other areas. Equally, locally accepted customs and practices, as in the negotiating of agreements, may not be easily accepted by foreigners to the country. In this area, probably more than any other, there is a vital need for good advice from someone who knows the country, preferably from birth, and who knows its customs and business practices.

(d) Technical factors

It is essential for firms to have a sound knowledge of what marketing and distribution facilities exist in target overseas markets. Besides checking on the actual hardware and infrastructure available, its efficiency must be gauged. A country might have an impressive amount of refrigerated rolling stock on their railways. However, if most of it is not in working order, or works for erratic and unpredictable periods because of lack of funds for efficient and regular maintenance, goods needing these facilities would face problems. Further, what road and road transport facilities exist? If roads are poor or non-existent, transport of heavy or delicate equipment would be hazardous. If trucks break down frequently, tyres and other parts fail easily and are difficult to replace, if maintenance is unreliable, or if the right size and type of vehicle are not available and mechanical handling is by man-power only, further distribution difficulties will arise.

Climate and weather must be known. What protection will products need, in use and transit, to minimise corrosion and contamination? Will full tropicalisa tion be necessary? Is there any fine dust or sand in the atmosphere? This can get everywhere and can spoil delicate equipment, leading to frequent breakdown. Does the equipment have to stand in the open under all conditions and how will the climate affect it and its operation? If maintenance facilities are lacking, climatic conditions can cause considerable problems.

The marketing infrastructure of some countries is rudimentary and activities that are standard and usual in the home country may be out of the question. Facilities such as wholesaling, advertising, merchandising, or simply the availability of trained salespeople, may be limited or lacking. Staff in wholesale and retail organisations may lack the knowledge to handle, demonstrate or sell technical or specialised products. Advertising media may be limited and agency support rudimentary. The more common pitfalls are summarised in Table 11.4. On the other hand there may be excellent technical and support facilities in all these areas, which can be utilised and will be effective. Given whatever level of technical facilities exist, can the firm operate with them as they are, or bring its own expertise and staff in to achieve the levels necessary?

Table 11.4   **International marketing: common pitfalls**

1	The home country's products may be too expensive, too sophisticated or wrong in some other aspect of the specifications (e.g. colour, flavour, appearance etc.).
2	Customs, traditions, religion, beliefs and other ethnic factors may not be understood or allowed for sufficiently.
3	Inadequate assessment of product–market possibilities.
4	Political motivations, institutions, objectives may have been misunderstood or misinterpreted.
5	Product–market development plans may have been sequenced incorrectly.
6	Inaccurate interpretation of words or symbols.
7	Incorrect assessment of promotional restrictions, rules and regulations.
8	Ignorance, or the ignoring, of political requirements.
9	Failure to comply with legal requirements.
10	Failure to adhere to ethical, social and religious practices and standards.
11	Initiating company may have failed to develop an indigenous image (as against its own 'foreign' image).
12	Failure to identify with national aims and aspirations, especially economic ones and the desire to improve the quality of life as well as the standard of living.
13	Trade channels may have varied from those of the 'home' market and may not have been fully understood.
14	Attempting operations that are too far in advance of the stage of development reached by the 'host' nation.
15	Failure to develop local nationals to take executive positions in the operation.
16	Mistakes in estimating long-term investment requirements and risks, correct strategies, information flows and controls.

11.3   International marketing: methods

Consideration will now be given, briefly, to the methods available to those wishing to develop overseas business.

(a) Direct exports

This is usually the first stage. It involves selling and shipping abroad products made in the home country. As mentioned, this poses problems when the needs and characteristics of overseas markets differ from those of the home market. Sales potential may be limited unless costly modifications are undertaken. The different usages (and hence values) of the product must also be appreciated.

For example the bicycle in Western Europe is normally used for fun or recreational and sporting purposes. In developing countries it may be an essential mode of transport, and the only one that most people can afford. It is a workhorse too, used to carry an astonishing range of products.

The usual method of entry is through appointed agents. These should have the necessary experience and skills, especially if regular maintenance is needed or if the products are technical ones. Their selection requires careful consideration and

Containers, roll-on, roll-off ferries, and the channel tunnel have all reduced the costs of moving goods out of or into the UK. Marketing must keep abreast of the resulting opportunities and threats

visits, perhaps numerous, to the country to interview and choose them. Their financial strength and integrity should be sufficient for the work they will do and the stocks they should hold. What is helpful here is advice from other firms already operating in the country, the commercial sections of foreign embassies in the home country and commercial attachés of the home country in foreign countries. Reports by major banks, especially commercial or industrial ones, government departments and agencies at home and trade and industry associations all provide useful information and guidance. Regular 'servicing' visits to appointed agents are also important.

(b) Local facilities

As business increases, or because of difficulties in exporting finished goods (host governments may discourage or embargo this), local assembly plants can be set up. In the case of cars and some other equipment, complete kits are shipped out and assembled locally. Sometimes local manufacture of simple components can be used with key components shipped out from home. Or if the business is substantial but not big enough to justify local assembly, the firm may set up a marketing (only) subsidiary or office. This could work independently of the original agents who may still carry on the agency, or, more usually, in conjunction with the original agents. The latter is preferred when host governments are particularly keen on local involvement and investment. Only with highly technical products and where the necessary skills are not available would a firm be permitted to go it alone with a marketing subsidiary.

Then when the conditions (sufficient demand, necessary skills available, economic and political factors and experience) are right, manufacturing and marketing subsidiaries can be set up. These may be wholly owned or be in partnership with local nationals and capital as the laws of the land demand. Joint ventures with relatively sophisticated local firms is another variation in more developed countries.

(c) Multinational operations

For the successful firms, the final stage will be evolution into multinational enterprises. This results when a company has several overseas organisations, now usually a mix of wholly owned subsidiaries, minority shareholdings in local companies and joint ventures, operating in several countries. Trading of components between the different units may go on freely as the enterprise uses the most economical (low-cost) countries for the manufacture of different items.

Multinationals face many marketing and other management problems. The main one centres around the control of the group's activities including policies on the raising and transfer of capital and the remittance of profits to the initiating, or parent, company. Then there is the question of the multinational balancing its policies for profit, sales and return with the economic and other goals of the host countries. Further, because of their size, the total business can be many times greater than the gross national product of the smaller host nations and political pressure can result from this.

Whatever scale or method of operating may be used, decisions have to be reached on the standardisation of pricing, products, distribution and method of selling and promoting the products. The method of operation can range from totally centralised planning by the home, or parent, unit to some generalised statement of intent and financial planning based on a sharing of ideas and values between the different units. In the latter case, the individual companies are left to implement the agreed objectives in their own way, as efficiently as local conditions permit. Thus there would be considerable variations in the detailed activities each would implement.

In some marketing areas, such as advertising or pack design, there may be economies in using common campaigns or designs across the world. However there may still be costs of translation, dubbing, adaptation to local legal or ethical requirements etc. which local conditions may demand. The balance is not always obvious, and there needs to be careful consideration and planning, as well as regular reviews as circumstances and conditions change.

11.4 Marketing of services

Most of the contents of earlier chapters apply generally to both product and service marketing. However it is useful here to bring together some more specific thoughts on the marketing of services.

Service industries span a wide range of activities and form one of the faster growing sectors of the economy of most countries, especially Western developed nations. They range from professional services (accountants, lawyers, doctors, dentists, management consultants, architects etc.) to more general services (post and telecommunications, transport, holiday and travel facilities, tourism, hotels, government departments and agencies such as defence, laundry, education, domestic help, design, research facilities and investment services) and the usual maintenance and repair services. There is also the provision of technical advice and assistance by product manufacturers. They are all required at some time by individual consumers or industrial and commercial enterprises.

The basic marketing approach is similar to that for manufactured goods. The service company must identify profitable market segments from the universe of potential users who have need for its services. It should forecast the size and nature of demand, the ruling market prices and the strength and nature of competition. The needs of the selected potential customers should be analysed to see if the services to be offered really meet their requirements. Forecasts have to be made of market shares, the prices to be used, the estimated profit and return on investment. Decisions have to be made on the resources that would be needed. Then decisions on how the services should be sold and promoted can be finalised. So too can decisions be taken on the organisation needed and the methods of control and supervision which will be used.

Then there are services providing customer benefits which may not be immediately apparent or direct in nature. An example is life insurance which becomes effective when the buyer dies and the benefits are paid to the dependants. Another is the building societies (and banks) who make loans to house purchasers. Customers are free to choose, within specified loan limits, where they live, the type of dwelling they buy, while in times of inflation they will show some long-term

Holes in the wall may be seen both by management and by many customers as highly efficient ways of dispensing cash – but may well lead to a breakdown in the traditional close ties between a bank and its customers

capital gain. The marketing activities of building societies will emphasise these derived benefits rather than the product (house) itself. These and other special characteristics make it difficult to find the true answers to the points mentioned in the third paragraph of this section. In the case of manufactured goods the important factors are obvious and understood and are governed by economic relationships (e.g. costs, life of product, user needs) and technical considerations.

Another difference is the fact that the lack of a physical product reduces the need for distributors or middlemen, though insurance brokers are essential to that industry and fulfil this function. Agency systems have however emerged for various services (travel and tourism, hotels, public transport including airlines, insurance and credit facilities). Then entry is governed by the skills, knowledge and reputation of the vendors rather than by a collection of expensive equipment, buildings and substantial capital. (However, in Britain and some other countries, banks, insurance companies and investment services have to put up substantial funds to satisfy the authorities that they are sufficiently solvent for the business they intend to launch.)

In the case of government services it may not be a case of stimulating demand but rather controlling it and, in hard times, reducing demand. However, in the case of some other government services (public health) they will have to stimulate demand for services such as vaccinations and inoculations as necessities in preventive medicine. Then government departments may have to persuade firms to export more and to convert indifferent groups of consumers to accept other services. They may have to make consumers aware of hitherto unrealised needs. Thus there is a requirement for marketing here also, albeit in greatly modified forms.

For all services, people (staff) are the prime asset, or 'capital' of the firms. Their behaviour, conduct and knowledge are critical factors since customers will rate the firms according to these staff abilities. Apathetic or hostile staff will lose business for a firm, whether restaurant, hotel, travel agent, tour operator, bank or insurance company, to mention a few. A lax lawyer, or unhelpful official in a government agency, will also create customer dissatisfaction. A courier with a tour operator who does not know the country or is not interested in the people in his or her charge will give rise to customer complaints and they may not return the following year to the company. In all these cases the customers will probably transfer their business to a more efficient competitor.

Thus in service industries the 'sales forces', all who deal with customer enquiries and sell the firm's services, are more important than in manufacturing industries. Their role is more substantial even if they do not see themselves as 'salespersons'. So staff management, recruitment and training are very important parts of the planning and design of all service industries.

The pricing of services can also pose problems. The low cost of entry leads to more intensive competition. This, coupled with the inability of customers to evaluate correctly the true worth and relevance of the services they buy, results in prices being low and very slim profit margins. Manufacturing industry's traditional cost-plus pricing methods cannot be followed when staff is the major cost element. Insufficient allowance is made for other cost elements and margins are squeezed further. With some services (travel agents, for example) where their own income and revenue is obtained by a limited discount (10 per cent in the case mentioned) on the total business placed, profit margins are small.

Thus many service industries cannot generate the funds to afford expensive or sophisticated marketing operations. They have to think very carefully about which marketing activities they need and how these can be used efficiently and with minimum costs. Marketing research may have to be done in carefully planned annual packets. With a carefully thought-out programme for several years, a service firm can build a good information bank. Thus service industries possibly need more competent and knowledgeable marketing staff than the average manufacturing company. There is little room for mistakes and unnecessary expenditure.

Greater use has to be made of market and consumer information generated by the company's business. For example people involved in selling should be advised and trained on how to watch for and collate important information. They must also be briefed on the data required. In the travel industry records should be kept of the travel or holiday enquiries placed, the quotations made and the conversion rates to sales. The company's invoices provide information on the country visited, hotel and resort used, duration and timing of the travel and where customers live. They will also show the prices that are being paid. Other needs can also be logged but it will not be possible to gauge their social or job status or their incomes.

However, for tour operators, the courier can help to uncover personal details such as these. In the course of meeting customers, couriers can guide the conversation into areas where the customer will reveal personal details such as job if not income. Also if other remarks are carefully analysed, indications of customers' social status and thus product preference may be indicated. This will add to the work of couriers but it may be worthwhile and is a way out of the difficulties posed by limited funds for research.

With government services, if marketing is not mainly interested in limiting demand, the critical factor is that of choice. Industrialists can refuse to export. Householders can refuse to insulate their homes if they are not convinced it is worth the cost or if they are planning a house move. Mothers can refuse to have their children inoculated. Marketing then has to place the emphasis on persuasion, seeking to influence consumers to reach positive decisions about better health care, better use of educational facilities, energy conservation, relocation of industry or whatever is the government's pressing need of the day.

Another big difference is that users of services have greater personal contact with the staff of service industries. While they cannot, and do not, expect to be able to contact any but the salespersons of a manufacturing enterprise, they do expect to see bank executives, insurance staff, travel agents' and tour operators' executives, investment advisers, lawyers, accountants, garage mechanics and so on, when they have need of their services. Thus staff have to be much more knowledgeable of the services they are offering or at least where to turn up the relevant information quickly and accurately. Failure here will just push the customer down the road to the nearest competitor.

11.5   Marketing in non-profit organisations

It has taken some time for executives to realise that marketing has an important role to play in promoting the activities of non-profit-making organisations, whether publicly or privately organised. It was assumed that as they did not, or could not, make profit, the hard-nose commercial activity known as marketing was neither necessary nor appropriate. Nothing could be further from the truth.

These organisations have to sell their services or ideas to the public. Many organisations (museums, charities, art galleries, orchestras) have to attract sufficient funds to carry on their cultural and social activities. Many educational establishments (colleges and universities) have to raise funds to endow some of their work and to attract customers (students, graduates, post-graduates) to study or do research work at their establishments. Social, sporting and other clubs have to make their existence and facilities known to attract sufficient members to allow the clubs to continue in existence. Even the police need to attract recruits, seek the support of the public they protect and improve their public image. All of these problems are marketing ones.

The approach is similar to that for other services and as set out in the third paragraph of Section 11.4. However, the selection of markets may have to be even more carefully done and the product selection is specialised and limited. Funds are limited so marketing planning and operations have to be considered carefully and carried out with even greater precision. Profligate spending is just not possible.

In some instances, these organisations may also have to limit demand for their services (or in the jargon, be involved in 'demarketing'), because of limited resources, or for other social reasons. For example, medical organisations promote health care or preventive medicine to minimise the incidence of sickness and also relieve pressure on overloaded hospital and other resources. The police seek to educate the public on crime prevention, for example safeguarding the home to prevent burglary, to reduce the incidence of crime. They are also trying to limit the demand on their resources in this area so that they are free to give more attention to serious crime (murder, terrorism and so on). So even here marketing has an important, if not critical part to play.

Many charitable organisations have benefited from the adoption of the marketing philosophy and marketing techniques. Research and analysis have led to a refinement of their target groups, both among donors and beneficiaries. In seeking donors the techniques of direct marketing and computer databases have enabled appeals for funds to be more accurately targeted. Giving donors a 'price list' of what their contributions can 'buy' has proved effective in many cases in lifting the level of donations. Fundraising has become more effective and efficient with the reduction in wasted effort. On the other hand, services have been more effectively aimed at those the charity serves, with deeper research into their needs and into the efficacy of goods or services provided.

Clearly there should be careful selection of the methods used by a charity for raising funds, particularly to avoid giving offence to established supporters. However it would be foolish to ignore the benefits which may be obtained from the proper use of modern techniques and practices. Computers and databases can help with fundraising or the management of beneficial support. Public relations through appropriate media and events can keep supporters and clients in touch, enhance a charity's image, and increase the 'market' for both supporters and beneficiaries.

11.6 After-sales service

For most products and services there is need for some kind of after-sales service (often called 'product services') to customers. After-sales services are needed by both industry and the consumer. They range from expert opinion, advice and assistance on the use or application of the product to maintenance and repair in the case of household appliances, manufacturing plant and other equipment.

After-sales services are required, for example, when household appliances (refrigerators, cookers, washing-machines, vacuum cleaners, other gadgets) require regular maintenance and repairs. They are needed for the same reasons for television sets, radios, tape-recorders, video-tape machines, cars, motor-cycles and lawn-mowers. In industry, maintenance and repairs have to be done on all machinery (drills, lathes, millers, cranes, furnaces and other equipment), trucks (goods and fork-lift) and anything else that is subjected to normal wear and tear.

Then there are the product services required for specialised items. For example, computer users, besides needing normal maintenance and repair services, also require the assistance of experts to help them install and operate the software systems they have bought.

Finally, with bought-in items (metals, plastics, resins, lubricants, fuels and other consumables) users need advice and assistance on their efficient use. This can range from help on how to use expensive fuels and materials economically (vital in times of scarcity and high costs) to highly technical aspects concerning how bought-in goods may be best incorporated into the customer's finished products. For example, paint manufacturers may need advice on which resins to use to improve the corrosion-resistance of their paints. Other manufacturers may need advice on how best to use plastic granules when extrusion or blow-moulding of their products are involved.

However, all these services cost money and costs can be high. While for maintenance and repair services it is normal to charge for the work, in other forms of assistance this cannot always be done (for example, telephone assistance to software users). In such instances the cost is allowed for, to some extent, in the sale prices of the product, but if competition is strong there is a limit to how much can be 'built into' the unit price. Then the service provided must aim at securing greater sales than would be possible without it, to justify the cost of the service.

These after-sales services can play a major role in the way an organisation and its products are seen by people in the market. Good service will encourage further purchase and use of a firm's products. Poor service will drive customers elsewhere. It is then vital that the service is offered promptly and carried through efficiently.

In some markets the services are provided by specialised organisations separated from the original supplier. Garages and home appliance service companies cover most consumer durable goods, but are often franchised or trained by the manufacturers. In other areas the manufacturers themselves supply the service through their own personnel. Whatever method is used it is important that these service personnel are properly trained, and present a good image through their efficiency, dress, transport and so forth. They become, for better or worse, a part of the company's marketing effort. They must clearly appreciate the good they can do in reinforcing customer relations. They should also be aware of the useful feedback they can provide on customers' needs, and on the reasons for faults or failures. They must also appreciate the damage which can be caused to customer relations by poor service generally.

11.7 Warranties and guarantees

The usual form of product warranty assures the purchaser that the item will be replaced, or repaired free of labour costs, or there will be refund of the purchase price should the product prove defective within a specified time. With cars, warranties are normally couched in terms of time (a number of years) and mileage, whichever is the longer. Warranties increase the confidence customers have in the product and its manufacturer and can stimulate demand. The warranty is described as a subsidiary promise or collateral agreement, a breach of which allows the buyer to make certain claims (for damage or restitution of loss etc.) against the vendor. The warranty may be 'express' (deriving from a specific agreement) or 'implied' (deriving from the operation of the law).

A guarantee is an assurance (express or implied) of the quality of the goods supplied (or that the price asked is the lowest on the market etc.). There is usually a promise of a refund in the event of poor performance, or if the goods are not as described. It is used as a sales aid, especially for mail-order or direct mail business. In this case the goods cannot be inspected before purchase and the guarantee is to assure customers of the good standing and reputation of the vendor and the products offered.

The law surrounding warranties and guarantees is now very complex. In the UK both national legislation and EEC Directives may be involved. In overseas markets there will be similar legislation. While the marketing department will be very concerned to utilise warranties or guarantees to show products or services in the best possible light, specialised legal help must be sought in this area. Product descriptions, packs, advertising and all forms of communication must be carefully scrutinised to ensure that statements are not made or inferred, which could lead to heavy commitments later on.

One aspect does deserve increasing consideration from marketing people, in conjunction with technical colleagues. Many modern products show U-shaped failure patterns. Here most failures occur either in the first few hours or weeks of product life, or after several years. If a warranty or guarantee is given covering failure within 6 months of purchase, the whole risk of early failure may already be covered. Extending cover into the period before ageing sets in may then involve very little risk or cost. Extending cover to, say, three years, could be a profitable move if increased sales and profits more than offset the slight added risks.

11.8   Marketing and the environment

Next come the questions of pollution and destruction of the environment or ecology. Both national and international constraints and regulations have increased rapidly over the past decade, ranging from the banning of the ivory trade and of whaling, to the phasing out of PFCs in refrigeration. In the first two examples the improvement is immediate in protecting the threatened species. In the second the changes will take time to bring improvements in the ozone layer which is under threat. With regard to effluent from industry, regulations generally have been strengthened, controls are more stringent and monitoring is increasing (although in many areas it still seems inadequate). The idea that the polluter should pay for remedial work or for preventive action is gaining ground. This will add to costs, and may lead to the withdrawal of some products from the market. It is however providing a powerful stimulus to civil engineering and other organisations with expertise in effluent control, water purification and similar areas. In the public sector similar problems arise with refuse disposal and sewage, as controls are imposed and tightened. Again there are markets here for appropriate expertise, which are being developed.

From a marketing point of view the stance within the company should be in favour of compliance with all possible regulations, to avoid adverse and damaging publicity for itself or its products. Looking outwards, there may well be opportunities arising from the increasing constraints on effluents and other polluting substances. Where a company's processes or products give rise to environmental concern, marketing in conjunction with Research & Development or Technical departments should be seeking cleaner alternatives which will still meet customer needs. Where a company has expertise in the environmental area, either from its own disciplines such as civil or process engineering, or through solving its own pollution problems, there may be opportunities for the marketing of consultancy, control systems or remedial services in the environmental market.

11.9   Marketing, society and consumerism

The traditional concept of business responsibility concerns executives' accountability to customers, investors and employees. With customers, executives are required to provide quality products or services at reasonable prices. With investors, it is a question of securing acceptable return for the funds entrusted to the firm. Finally, with employees it is a question of providing employment at adequate remuneration which is seen to be fair. However, business and marketing's responsibilities are now seen to extend to society at large. It is no longer sufficient to meet only the three points mentioned above. On their own they are not considered socially responsible objectives.

Socially responsible marketing decisions must take into account the eventual long-term consequences of the actions taken. Future generations, as well as existing ones, must be taken into consideration.

There are other aspects of social responsibility. One is the relationship that should exist between this responsibility and the profit motive. In simple theory, it may be justified to strive for optimal levels of profit and to follow appropriate pricing policies. However, if it causes deprivation for the less affluent and poor, is it justified, especially in the long term? Against this, a company can only continue to exist and to provide employment if it can recover its costs and provide a surplus for research and development and future investment. If it is successful it will also be paying taxes, and can argue that the government should be dealing with issues of poverty and deprivation, not the individual company.

(a) Consumerism and consumer protection
Consumerism has developed over the past thirty years, starting in the USA and spreading through most developed countries. It is described as the demand that firms give greater attention to consumer desires, not only with regard to product offerings, but also their standard of life and the long-term effects of the firm's

actions. It is an important part of the drive for greater social responsibility by firms. While again creating short-term problems, it could offer new opportunities and challenges to marketing executives.

For example, the regulations governing the minimum depth of tyre tread permitted on cars, for road-safety considerations, present problems for the consumer who must buy new tyres more frequently. However, if some manufacturers can improve the working life of their tyres to give longer tread wear, they could obtain a bigger share of the market at the expense of those who do nothing about this. Regulations requiring cars to be safer will pose problems for the manufacturers who do not comply quickly enough. Those who can modify their products in a short time would again achieve increases in sales and market shares. However, until consumers are better educated on all related subjects, and thus become more knowledgeable, the claimed benefits of consumerism are not likely to be fully realised.

None the less the present consumer movement seems to be stronger and longer lasting than earlier attempts. Its demands are no longer just about consumption aspects but include assessment of changes in technology, life-styles, public attitudes, affluence and the media. This is due to growing concern about the quality of life as incomes, standards of living and education improve. Another factor is the increased complexity of technology and marketing putting the buyer at an ever-growing disadvantage in relation to the seller. Then there are the stresses and strains developing in the economic and political systems, inflation, pollution, the population explosion, loss of faith in politicians and their institutions. Finally, there is the 'impersonality' due to the increasing size of firms and institutions, aggravated by computerisation and automation. The last two, consumers feel, are causing them to lose identity and just become numbers or cogs in the business and state machines.

On the other hand, not all protests on behalf of consumers are well founded. Many individuals and some organisations are misguided and badly informed. There is the unfortunate but true fact, also, that to the media bad practice is 'news' and good ones generally are not. So the public often gets a distorted view of the real position. Thus care is needed in assessing the true value of any protest both as regards its source and its significance in the total context. Often protests just represent the personal views of the persons making them and are somewhat removed from those of society at large.

There is substantial agreement by business people and consumer organisations that the basic objectives of marketing and consumerism are not in conflict. There has been increasing acceptance of an 'environmental' view by many firms. Marketing is no longer concerned with only profit making (described as 'micro-profit applications') to the exclusion of all else. Company and industry self-regulation is developing, if slowly. Some firms have established consumer affairs departments. They do not deal just with complaints but study the total implications of company policies and actions. Some have produced codes of practice. These changes stress the dynamic nature of the marketing environment. Thus executives must keep themselves alert and informed on these subjects.

In parallel with the rise of the consumer movement there has been an increase in legislation for consumer protection. In the UK there has been legislation in this area since 1893, with the Sale of Goods Act, which consolidated a body of case law which had already developed. This Act has been updated on a number of occasions since. More recently, in 1982, the Supply of Goods and Services Act was passed covering other areas of trade beyond simple purchase. The Acts state that all goods and services must be 'of merchandisable quality' and 'fit for the buyer's purpose'. Other Acts cover terms of consumer credit, hire purchase and similar contracts. The legal situation in these areas is complex, and if doubts arise about the proper course of action, qualified assistance and advice should be sought. Penalties can be heavy.

11.10   Recent developments in marketing

(a) Database marketing and direct marketing

This is an area where both the development and the execution of the methods are heavily reliant on computers. The objectives are to provide very precise target groups for a firm's promotional activity, leading to customers ordering goods or service directly, by mail, phone or fax.

Direct mail advertising has been available for several decades, and specialist companies have been developed to provide mailing lists covering particular target groups. In the past these were generally broad groups, such as dispensing chemists, accountants, traders of various kinds, and so forth. The lists were compiled from various sources, and while efforts were made to avoid duplication and ensure completeness this was difficult using hand methods. By storing the lists on metal plates and other physical devices, batches of envelopes or labels could be produced without too much difficulty.

The development of computers changed the situation. Databases could hold far more data about firms or individuals than could be handled by the old methods. This additional data could be used to extract more specific target groups, which led to far more data being collected and stored. Linked to word processing programs letters can be addressed individually to members of target groups, giving a more personal approach. Alternatively a personalised telephone approach can be used.

There are of course costs of setting up the databases, and of contacting people by post or phone – with fax being increasingly used for business groups. For some companies or products, involved in mass marketing of fmcgs, the methods would not compare with traditional means of mass advertising and field or telephone sales forces. For more specialised markets however, from double glazing and swimming pools to oil futures, the methods are widely used and evidently economic.

Some of the sources of data are the Census and postcodes, as well as field or postal research. Census data on the type of housing in a local area, which is correlated to the life styles of the people living there, can be matched to local postcodes. Linking of geographic and demographic data in this and more complex ways has given rise to the term of 'geo-demographics'. Postcodes can be useful

Databases compiled from a variety of sources can target particular groups of people or households, particularly when linked to records of previous purchases. A prize or a bonus linked to returning the order form can turn a minor impulse into a sale

as a broad method of identification and segmentation, and the Post Office will co-operate with advertisers by delivering material within selected postcode areas. Field and postal research is used to gather information about people's interests, hobbies, recreations etc., and there is only a narrow line between market research and the collection of database material.

There are forms of direct selling not linked to databases. Selling 'off the page' through print media, from the national press to special interest magazines, has long been used, as has the selling of goods via catalogues and home representatives. This form of direct selling has now appeared in the electronic media, where mail, fax or phone response backed by a credit card provides means of placing an order for the goods advertised on radio or TV. One manifestation of the method is the charity appeal on radio or TV, linked to a hotline for donations by credit card.

(b) Internal marketing

In many organisations staff who are neither in marketing nor sales departments come into contact with customers, or at least are seen by them. Any impressions made by these members of staff can affect how customers judge the organisation, for better or worse.

We can consider the efforts made through traditional marketing, through product, price, promotion, place and so on as external marketing. Efforts made inside the organisation to make staff more aware of customers, their needs, their reactions and so forth can be called internal marketing.

Engineers and others engaged in after-sales service are obvious examples of staff involved in customer relations. So are all staff from security guards, gardeners, telephonists and receptionists, who are often the first contacts, through to executives and directors. A scruffy van with a scruffy driver will give a scruffy image. Equally an immaculate van which cuts up a customer on the motorway may damage a hard won reputation for care and courtesy.

Marketing staff should be well aware of the benefits of creating good customer relations at all levels. They now are beginning to take time to ensure that others in their organisations are equally aware of the opportunities for fostering good

Building a database in an esoteric market is often done using direct response coupons. Coding of coupons aids analysis of cost-effectiveness in generating responses and subsequent sales

relationships, and of the damage that can be done by a single unthinking word or act. Spreading awareness of who pays the wages is a start, but a deeper and more positive understanding of customer relations, company policies, and a willingness to help are vital for success.

A spin-off from developing good customer awareness among staff is better feed-back from customers. Staff who are properly trained in customer relations will appreciate more quickly the significance of customers' comments, whether favourable or unfavourable, critical or constructive. This then provides a cheap early warning and response system, which can be of particular value whenever any new or modified products or services are introduced.

The marketing department may be faced with a major problem in developing internal marketing – how it should be presented to staff to ensure their co-operation and not be rejected as just another management gimmick. Like other marketing operations this one needs careful research, planning and execution if it is to succeed.

(c) Relationship marketing

The classical view of market transactions at arms' length, with seller and buyer as antagonists, has never been wholly true. Particularly in industrial markets close co-operation was always needed between component manufacturers and final assemblers. With the development of practices such as just-in-time delivery of components, close co-operation is more important than ever. Continuity and promptness of supply are of prime importance. Hence suppliers need to be properly briefed on forecast demand, modifications to parts, new models or withdrawal of old ones, and so forth.

In fmcg markets the complexities of maintaining stocks on supermarket shelves, with just-in-time delivery which has spread from manufacturing industry, and the fluctuations in trade through the week, again demand co-operation rather than confrontation. To a manufacturer it is far more profitable, given reasonable prices, to retain existing customers than to tout for new ones. To a retailer it is far more satisfactory to have reliable deliveries from established suppliers than to source each new consignment from scratch. Again relationship marketing makes sense, as a leading retail chain has demonstrated over the years.

Relationship marketing does not mean that one partner dictates terms to the other. What it does mean is that deals and terms are negotiated between the parties on a mutually agreeable basis, and with other factors besides price being taken into account. Longer-term stability of supplier–customer relationships can benefit both parties.

Spin-off from relationships of this type can range from customer briefings of suppliers on forecast demand to joint development of new components or products. In engineering such co-operation has long been practised. In consumer markets close liaison between retailers in daily touch with consumers could be valuable to manufacturers. Retailers now obtain indications of changes in buying patterns very quickly through data capture at the point of sale, which can be linked to manufacturers own marketing information and ordering systems. These links then give the retailers more immediate control over deliveries, and thus stock levels. Lags which would previously have led to shortages or surplus stock can be cut, to the benefit of both sides, and ultimately of the consumer. Here the benefits would be fewer frustrating stock-outs, and fresher supplies generally.

(d) Endpiece

None of these three ideas is new. Each however is being revitalised in changing circumstances. The process is common in marketing, which must respond to changing conditions in markets and among customers. Most marketing ideas have been tried by some-one at some time in the past. Where benefits lie is in the foresight to see that the time has come when an old idea can be updated and put to good use. Marketing is nothing if it ceases to be innovative!

Assignments

Does your chosen organisation operate internationally in any way?

What proportion of sales in the domestic market are produced in the country? Where does any balance come from? If there are imports, are there opportunities for import substitution?

Is any form of direct marketing used in your chosen area? To whom is it directed? Is use growing, steady or declining?

What developments in marketing do you think might occur in the next five years? How might these affect marketing and other operations?

Appendices

A.1 Glossary of the more common marketing terms

Above-the-line
: Expenditure on electronic and press advertising, where commission is paid by media to agencies.

After-sales service
: Repair, maintenance or advice service provided by a supplier to a customer. May be under guarantee, contract or on demand.

Appropriation
: The amount available for advertising during a period, or for a specific purpose such as a product launch.

BARB
: The Broadcasters Audience Research Board is an industry-financed operation measuring the audience to broadcast media, and particularly TV.

Below-the-line
: Expenditure on forms of advertising or promotion where no media commission is paid to advertising agencies.

Bias
: Distortion of verbal or numerical information, due to faulty methods of collection, analysis, interpretation or presentation. Not to be confused with Sampling error (see below).

Brand/Brand image
: Originally a brand name such as Oxo or Rover. Extended to cover the whole image of a product as seen by the market, as well as its attributes and uses.

Budget
: Estimate of expenditure over a period, or for a specific purpose or activity.

Circulation
: Numbers of copies sold of newspapers, magazines etc. Normally produced by the Audit Bureau of Circulation, hence 'ABC figures'.

Classification
: Arrangement of data and information by categories – e.g. companies arranged according to the Standard Industrial Classification (SIC), or people according to their age.

Code of Advertising Practice
: The British Code of Advertising Practice is the set of rules governing publication of advertising in most print media. This is a voluntary code, but with some teeth, which seeks to ensure that advertisements are legal, decent, honest and truthful.

Creative brief
: Outline of the content, target groups and overall purpose of an advertising campaign within the overall marketing planning.

Data collection	Any means by which data can be obtained for use within an information system, whether from existing sources such as invoices, or from specific investigations.
Data processing	Often abbreviated to DP. All the processes which take raw data through to being usable information.
Depth interview	Form of unstructured interview allowing deeper probing and discussion of a topic than in a structured, questionnaire-based, interview.
Desk research	Study of secondary data and information not requiring field studies, but often used in preparation for field work.
Direct mail	Literature seeking sales, subscriptions etc. sent to selected individuals or business prospects.
Direct marketing	Marketing operations by which provider of goods/services selects prospects using a carefully compiled database, and approaches them directly by mail or phone.
Direct response	Marketing operations where provider of goods/services seeks to generate sales through direct customer responses from press or TV media advertising.
Forecast	Estimate of future sales or other figures, based on a combination of calculated projections or predictions and knowledge of the market.
Focus group/ Group discussion	Group of people from an appropriate target group brought together in a friendly atmosphere and encouraged to discuss products, attitudes, likes and dislikes etc., to provide insights into consumer or user attitudes and behaviour.
Just-in-time	Processes through which deliveries to customers are precisely timed to meet demand with only the minimum of stockholding. Began with industrial markets, but now being applied in supermarket chains etc.
Key accounts	Major customers responsible for a significant share of sales, and given special consideration. Key account managers have specific responsibility for liaison over terms, deliveries etc.
Keyed advertisement	One where response indicates where the advertisement was seen, through coding of coupons, or different phone numbers or addresses.
Local press	Newspapers circulating mainly within a small area such as a city or a county.
Logo	Company symbol or identifying device.
Margin	The difference, usually as a percentage, between trade buying price and selling price.
Marketing	Defined by the UK Chartered Institute of Marketing as follows – 'Marketing is the management process responsible for identifying, anticipating and satisfying consumers' requirements profitably'.

Marketing mix	The combination of marketing decisions or operations designed to achieve success for a product, company etc. Usually summarised under the four Ps of Product, Price, Promotion and Place, but extended to cover People, Process and Physical aspects, to give seven Ps.
Merchandising	Processes which ensure in-store display of goods, special offers or promotions, to best advantage.
Motivation research	Broad term covering research into reasons why people or organisations buy at all, or prefer one brand to another – or do not buy anyway.
National Press	In the UK, daily and Sunday newspapers with national or very wide circulation, e.g. *The Times* or *Daily Mirror*. Not all countries have national newspapers.
Observation	Techniques of recording events by eye, camera, meter etc. Used for recording TV usage in the home, movements of people, cars, products and so forth.
Open-ended question	One where the respondent may offer a wide range of answers to questions such as 'If you could ask a company to invent something useful to you in your garden what would it be?'
Penetration	The share of a defined market taken by a brand or product. The proportion of the people/organisations in a market who have bought a product in a given time period.
Physical distribution	Means by which goods are moved towards the user. For most consumer goods this is through wholesale or retail warehouses and shops. For industrial products, through factors or direct deliveries.
Pilot survey	Trial run for a survey or other research project to ensure that all aspects such as the sampling scheme, questionnaire and analysis operate as planned.
Point of sale (PoS)	Point where goods and money change hands. Hence importance for display purposes and analysis of sales using electronic data capture. Hence EPOS, EDPOS and other abbreviations.
Postal check	Postal method of checking that interviews have been carried out, by sending short questionnaire to subsample of interviewees. Being replaced by telephone checking.
Postal questionnaire	Schedule of questions sent to informants for self-completion and return.
Prediction	Calculated estimate of future sales or other figures, using models developed from past data. Used as a basis for forecasting.
Press	All newspapers and periodicals accepting advertising matter.

Press relations	Process of keeping press informed about an organisation, aimed at securing maximum publicity for the good aspects, and minimising any bad aspects.
Price	In economics the exchange value of a good or service. In marketing there is normally a series of prices as exchanges take place from the producer or original supplier, through a series of intermediaries, to the final consumer.
Price/demand or Price/volume ratio	Relationship between the price of a product and the demand for it. Price normally is a major determinant of demand, which tends to fall away as price increases. Hence free health services may generate unlimited demand.
Price elasticity	If a price change of 1 per cent leads to a change in sales volume of $-x$ per cent (and vice versa) then x measures the price elasticity. Usually negative as sales fall as price rises.
Price sensitivity	Similar to price elasticity, but seen from the buyer's side. Price sensitivity corresponds to high elasticity; price insensitivity corresponds to low price elasticity.
Pricing strategy	Consistent set of ideas and rules applied to the way an organisation prices its products or brands.
Primary data	Data collected specifically to meet current research objectives, through observation, questioning or experimentation. May be continuous, from panels of stores, consumers, viewers etc., or *ad hoc* from surveys set up for specific purposes.
PRO	Public Relations Officer – person responsible for public relations for an organisation, government department etc.
Product life cycle	Concept describing how brands will rise to a peak of performance in a market, and then decline as competition catches up or tastes change. May last from a few days to decades.
Product screening	Process of examining/testing all aspects of a potential product or idea to ensure that it will fit with corporate and financial objectives, operational needs and the market.
Profit	What is left, if anything, after all earnings have been collected and all debts paid by an organisation. Even not-for-profit organisations have to ensure that this figure is not negative, or a loss, if they are to remain viable.
Projection	Simple extension of historic trends and any seasonal patterns, by eye or by calculation, as a basis for forecasting.
Promotion	All activity aimed at publicising products or services to ensure adequate demand.

Promotions	Specific operations, usually for a limited time, to provide a temporary boost to demand, e.g. through special offers, competitions etc.
Prompted response	Reply to a market research question where respondents are aided by a list of possible answers.
Prospect	Potential purchaser or user.
Provincial press	Newspapers or magazines circulating in a restricted region, outside the capital.
Public relations	Defined by the UK Institute of Public Relations as follows – 'Public relations is the planned and sustained effort to establish and maintain good will and mutual understanding between an organisation and its publics: customers, employees, shareholders, trade bodies, suppliers, government officials, and society in general'.
Publicity	Process of securing attention and imparting a message, usually through editorial or other unpaid channels.
Qualitative research	Research aimed at depth of understanding through intensive discussion with a few individuals. Provides deeper insights into reasons for buying etc., but without ability to quantify their extent. Often results provide a basis for planning wider quantifiable research. Methods may include focus groups, group discussions or individual depth interviews.
Quantitative research	Research based on large samples of people to estimate the proportions with different opinions, beliefs, usage patterns, preferences etc. The numbers needed for reasonably accurate estimates preclude any great depth of questioning with each individual.
Questionnaire	The sequence of questions to be covered in a market research investigation. 'Hard copy' questionnaires are used for mail or face-to-face surveys; electronically stored questionnaires for telephone or E-mail surveys.
Quota sampling	Process of selecting individuals for inclusion in a survey by matching their characteristics against known norms, e.g. selecting 'quotas' of males and females, young, middle-aged and older people etc.
Random sample	Process of selecting individuals for inclusion in a survey by chance alone, irrespective of any characteristics except belonging to the population being surveyed. Most scientific samples, and those where all possible bias in selection must be excluded, are selected using adaptations of the random method.
Rate card	Table of charges for advertising in various media, e.g. costs per page or per column cm for press, or for time slots in electronic media or for cinema or outdoor advertising.

Redemption rate	Rate at which potential 'respondents take up a promotional offer or enter a competition. Needs careful evaluation to avoid runaway costs.
Research	Processes by which new knowledge is obtained either through collecting and analysing primary data from existing situations or from experiments; or through desk research covering the re-appraisal of existing knowledge held inside or outside the organisation.
Respondent	Person from whom information is obtained in a research survey, whether by interview, mail or phone.
Response rate	Rate at which successful interviews or returns are achieved in a research survey.
Sales aid	Any elements of sales promotion (leaflets, slides, samples, showcards, video tapes, media schedules etc.) which back up face-to-face selling activities.
Sales call	Visit to existing or known potential customer for purposes of maintaining good relations and perhaps taking an order; or 'cold calling' on a potential customer to inform of company or its products in hope of a sale sooner or later.
Sampling	In marketing terms, distributing sample packs to attract attention, gain trial and generate future sales. In market research terms, the selection of a representative group of people or organisations for observation, questioning etc.
Sampling error	Strictly not 'error' at all, but the inevitable variation from one sample to another even though drawn from the same base or population. Most common example is the margin of error of about ±3 per cent in the results of electoral opinion polls based on samples of about 1000 respondents.
Secondary data	Data used for research purposes but originally collected for other purposes, e.g. invoice data subsequently used for sales analysis.
Segmentation	Breakdown of a broad and varied market into groups. Successful segmentation results in sub-groups which differ significantly from each other in their requirements, but which are large enough to make it profitable to develop separate marketing or product offerings.
Share	Term used in variety of contexts, but usually involving percentages – e.g. market share, share of advertising expenditure etc.
Structured interview	Interview using a questionnaire in which questions have been carefully worded and sequenced to ensure consistent and comparable data throughout a survey.
Tabulation	Process of analysing research data and turning it into information and knowledge – usually in the form of tables.

Technical press/ Trade press	Publications aimed at people in specific occupations from scientists to store managers. Can be useful media for PR or for advertising aimed at reaching very specific groups. Trade press advertising is a normal part of a new product launch etc.
Test marketing	Final phase of research on new product, when whole marketing mix is brought together in a limited area, to meet acid test of securing distribution and purchases (and repurchases) by consumers. Needs careful planning and control to ensure unbiased results and decisions.
Unique selling proposition (USP)	Any characteristic of a brand which may distinguish it from competitors and which can be used to emphasise its superiority in the market.
Universe	The whole group or population of people or items from which a sample is drawn, and which it should represent.
Unprompted response	Answer to a question given by respondent without any aids to memory, such as lists of names etc.
Unstructured interview	Sometimes known as 'depth interview'. One in which the interviewer will have an agenda to ensure full coverage of topic, but where the method is guided discussion rather than question-and-answer. Often used in initial stages of research to map out the areas of interest, or in industrial research into technical markets.

A.2   Product screen (qualitative)

When screening a new product idea for viability, the following factors are usually evaluated.

Group	Factors
Profit objectives	Size; growth; level of profit; stability.
Market stability	Durability; breadth; captive market; difficulty to copy; stability in recession and wartime.
Growth	Unique character of product/process; export prospects; demand/supply ratio; rate of technical change; improved opportunities.
Marketability	Relationship with existing markets; image; ease of market penetration; competition; user stratification; no seasonal fluctuations.
Production techniques	Ease of development; value added; favoured purchasing position; availability of materials.
R and D	Utilising existing know-how; future development needs; availability of R and D personnel.
Engineering	Reliability of process; utilisation of standard equipment; availability of skills.

Manufacturing	Utilisation of idle equipment, surplus services; upgrading of by-products; availability of resources; absorbs hitherto waste materials; hazardous operations; familiar processes etc.

The usual procedure is to give each factor a 'weight' (ranging from 1 to 5 or more) which reflects the skills, resources, capabilities and methods of the company. These are changed only if some change occurs in the company on these counts. Then each is given a rating according to its importance to the success/ viability of the idea. These can range from –3 to +3; –5 to +5 etc. '0' = not important; (0) = don't know. Weightings and ratings are multiplied and summed. The score resulting is scaled to indicate the idea's chances of success.

A.3   Market screen

With new markets it is advisable to screen them also to check their viability. The approach is similar to that for product ideas but the factors screened are as shown below.

Group	Factors
Market size	e.g. Under £1m. p.a.; £1–3m.; over £3m. etc.
Growth	e.g. Declining, static; growing by –per cent etc. (usually measured in £ and units)
Long-term growth	e.g. Certain decline; static; growth by –per cent etc.
Customer class	e.g. C2, D, E; C2, D; C1, C2; C1; B, C1; A, B; A etc.
Age groups	e.g. All over 60; 45–60; 35–45; 25–35; etc.
And any other relevant groups (e.g. Market share).	

Weightings and ratings are given as for the product screen but in this case the 'weight' applies to the (whole) group. Ratings are given to the various factors according to their importance. However, both the weighting and the rating are fixed and are altered only when the nature of the company (resources, skills etc.) change. Ratings and weightings are multiplied and the resultant scores are summed. In this case the ratings range from '0' (not important) to +5 or more. (Unlike the product screen there are no '(0)' = don't know. While '(0)' signifies the areas in new product ideas which require further study, by the time a market is screened, all the necessary information i.e. factors, are known.)

According to the total score achieved, the viability of the market can be judged. For example over 80 points = immediate exploitation possible; 70–80 points = recheck key factors; 60–70 points = leave for *x* years; under 60 points = abandon. The actual scaling used will vary from market to market, the above being purely indicative for purpose of explanation of the method.

A.4   Product–market screen

Before a decision is finally taken to develop and launch a new product idea or to enter a new market, it is advisable to screen the proposed product–market situation. This screen combines the key factors and groups taken from the product and market screens (Appendices 2 and 3) such as the groups shown below.

Profit   *Market size*
Marketability   *Long-term growth*
Growth   *Customer class*
Manufacturing   *Market shares*
and whatever others are deemed to be critical

The weighting, rating and method of calculating the final score are carried out in the same way as indicated in Appendices 2 and 3. The final total score is measured against the usual scaling scheme and the viability of the final product-market proposition is thus evaluated.

A.5 Select bibliography

Baker, Michael J., *Research for Marketing* (Basingstoke: Macmillan, 1991).

Cowell, Donald W., *The marketing of Services* (Oxford: Heinemann, 1984)

Crimp M., *The marketing research process*, 3rd edn (London: Prentice Hall, 1990).

Cummings J., *Sales Promotion*, 2nd edn (London: Kogan Page, 1992).

Davis, E. J., *Practical sales forecasting* (Maidenhead: McGraw Hill, 1988).

Hannagan, Tim, *Marketing for the Non-Profit Sector* (Basingstoke: Macmillan, 1992).

Harvey, J., *Mastering Economics* (Basingstoke: Macmillan, 1989).

Kotler, Philip and Armstrong, Gary, *Principles of Marketing*, 4th edn (Prentice-Hall International, 1989).

Kotler, Philip, *Marketing Management*, 7th edn (Prentice-Hall International, 1991).

McDonald, Malcolm H. B., *Marketing Plans and how to prepare them* (London: Heinemann, 1984).

Paliwoda, Stanley J., *International marketing*, 2nd edn (Oxford: Heinemann, 1993).

White, Jon, *How to understand and manage public relations* (London: Business Books Ltd, 1991).

White, R., *Advertising, What it is and how to do it*, 2nd edn (Maidenhead: McGraw Hill, 1988).

Winkler, John, *Pricing for results* (Oxford: Heinemann, 1984).

Some other sources of data

The Monthly digest of statistics, HMSO.

The Annual abstract of statistics, HMSO.

The UK Marketing Source Book 1993. A directory of 1200 sources of marketing information. Published for the Advertising Association by NTC Publications, Henley-on-Thames.

The Marketing Pocket Book. Annually. Published for The Advertising Association by NTC Publications, Henley-on-Thames.

Company annual reports.
Chambers of Commerce/Trade
Central Statistical Office – regular and occasional publications.
Business Statistics Office, Newport, Gwent.
Ministries and Embassies
Major market and economic research companies.

Index